T0334417

THE 1999 ANNUAL: Volume 2 Consulting
(The Thirty-Third Annual)

Jossey-Bass
Pfeiffer

THE
1999 ANNUAL:
Volume 2
Consulting
(The Thirty-Third Annual)

Jossey-Bass
Pfeiffer
San Francisco

Published by

Jossey-Bass
Pfeiffer

350 Sansome Street, 5th Floor
San Francisco, California 94104-1342
(415) 433-1740; Fax (415) 433-0499
(800) 274-4434; Fax (800) 569-0443

Visit our website at: http://www.pfeiffer.com

Printing 10   9   8   7   6   5   4   3   2   1

PREFACE

Welcome to Volume 2 of the 1999 *Annual*, which is focused on consulting! As an avid user of the *Annuals* for over twenty years, I have watched them change and grow with the field. They have been a mainstay in my career as an educator, an in-house trainer, an external performance-improvement technologist, and most recently as a consultant and author. I depend on the *Annuals* to challenge my thinking, to increase my knowledge, to enhance my skills, and to provide practical resources for delivery of services to my customers.

Several aspects of the *Annual* series have made it a valuable publication to me and thousands of other readers. Foremost is the desire of the editorial staff to listen to its readers. In 1995 in response to the growing needs of customers, we began to publish two volumes of the *Annual*: Volume 1, Training, and Volume 2, Consulting. The materials in the training volume focus on skill building and knowledge enhancement, as well as on the professional development of trainers. The materials in the consulting volume focus on intervention techniques and organizational systems, as well as on the professional development of consultants. The "performance-improvement technologist," whose role is one of combined trainer and consultant, will find valuable resources in both volumes, which cover some of the same topics, such as "teamwork," from a different perspective. For example, if you are looking for a workshop activity that teaches the advantages of teamwork, turn to Volume 1; if you are looking for an intervention technique to improve the performance of an intact team, turn to Volume 2.

Listening to our readers lead to a practical enhancement for the 1999 *Annuals*. Starting this year, you will find more reader-friendly text. The experiential learning activities, for example, are presented to you in the less formal second person. In addition, we have maintained the personal voice that the authors of the presentation and discussion resources have given their submissions. We hope that this change makes it easier for you to use the *Annuals* and to adapt their contents for your use more quickly. We welcome other suggestions you may have to improve the quality and usefulness of the *Annuals*.

A second aspect that enhances the value of the *Annuals* is our belief that the contents of each volume must be practical and immediately useful to the professionals who read it. The content of this *Annual* has the potential to increase your professional competence and your impact on your clients, colleagues, and the field. In keeping with this, you are allowed to duplicate and modify materials for educational and training purposes, so long as the credit statement found on the copyright page is included on all copies you make. If materials are to be reproduced in publications for sale or are intended for large-scale distribution (more than one hundred copies in twelve months), *prior written permission is required.* Reproduction of material that is copyrighted by another source (as indicated in a footnote) requires written permission from the designated copyright holder.

A third aspect that reinforces the value of the *Annual* is that we solicit materials from professionals, like you, who work in the field as trainers, consultants, facilitators, educators, and performance-improvement technologists. This ensures that the materials have been tried and perfected in real-life settings, with actual participants and clients, to meet real-world needs. To this end, we encourage you to submit materials to be considered for publication in the *Annuals.* At your request we will provide a copy of the guidelines for preparing your material. We are interested in receiving experiential learning activities (group learning activities based on the five stages of the experiential learning cycle: experiencing, publishing, processing, generalizing, and applying); inventories, questionnaires, and surveys (paper-and-pencil inventories, rating scales, and other response tools); and presentation and discussion resources (articles that include theory related to practical application). Contact the Jossey-Bass/Pfeiffer Editorial Department at the address listed on the copyright page for our guidelines for contributors. We welcome your comments, ideas, and contributions.

Thank you to the dedicated people at Jossey-Bass/Pfeiffer who produced the 1999 *Annuals:* Pamela Berkman, Jamie Corcoran, Kathleen Dolan Davies, Matthew Holt, Dawn Kilgore, Arlette Ballew, Carol Nolde, Susan Rachmeler, and Rebecca Taff. Thanks also to Michele Wyman, who assisted with the developmental editing. And, most importantly, thank you to our authors, who represent the rich variety in the fields of training and consulting. In-house practitioners, consultants, and academically based professionals have once again shared the best of their work, ideas, techniques, and materials so that other professionals may benefit. Your generosity is key to the professional development of many of your peers and colleagues.

Elaine Biech
Editor
August 1998

About Jossey-Bass/Pfeiffer

Jossey-Bass/Pfeiffer is actively engaged in publishing insightful human resource development (HRD) materials. The organization has earned an international reputation as the leading source of practical resources that are
immediately useful to today's consultants, trainers, facilitators, and managers in a variety of industries. All materials are designed by practicing professionals who are continually experimenting with new techniques. Thus,
readers and users benefit from the fresh and thoughtful approach that un-
derlies Jossey-Bass/Pfeiffer's experientially based materials, books, work-
books, instruments, and other learning resources and programs. This broad
range of products is designed to help human resource practitioners increase individual, group, and organizational effectiveness and provide a variety of training and intervention technologies, as well as background in the
field.

CONTENTS

---

*See Experiential Learning Activities Categories, p. 7, for an explanation of the numbering system.
**Topic is "cutting edge."

GENERAL INTRODUCTION
TO THE 1999 ANNUAL

The 1999 Annual: Volume 2, Consulting is the thirty-third volume in the *Annual* series, a collection of practical and useful materials for professionals in the broad area described as human resource development (HRD). The materials are written by and for professionals, including trainers, organization-development and organization-effectiveness consultants, performance-improvement technologists, educators, instructional designers, and others.

Each *Annual* has three main sections: *experiential learning activities; inventories, questionnaires, and surveys;* and *presentation and discussion resources.* Each published submission is classified in one of the following categories: Individual Development, Communication, Problem Solving, Groups, Teams, Consulting and Facilitating, Leadership, and Organizations. Within each category, pieces are further classified into logical subcategories, which are identified in the introductions to the three sections.

The last category, Organizations, is making its debut in the 1999 *Annual.* This addition reflects the changing nature of the field, as professionals take on more and more responsibilities in their organizations or as consult-ing professionals to organizations. The more widely accepted role of performance-improvement technologist brings with it more broadly defined responsibilities, often more "organizational" in nature. In addition, after four years of publishing a separate consulting volume, the need to incorporate the broader Organization category in the *Annual* series has become self-evident. We encourage you to broaden your perspective to include this category as you consider submitting material for future *Annuals.*

You will also find a new subcategory in the 1999 *Annual:* "Technology." Much has changed for the HRD professional in recent years, and technology has lead much of that change. Given the important role technology plays, we will continue to publish material that relates technology to the HRD field and how the HRD professional can use technology as a tool.

Another addition to the 1999 *Annual* is the identification of "cutting edge" topics. This designation highlights topics that present information, concepts, tools, or perspectives that may be recent additions to the profession or that have not previously appeared in the *Annual.*

The series continues to provide an opportunity for HRD professionals who wish to share their experiences, their viewpoints, and their processes with their colleagues. To that end, Jossey-Bass/Pfeiffer publishes guidelines for potential authors. These guidelines are available from the Pfeiffer editorial department at Jossey-Bass Inc., Publishers, in San Francisco, California.

Materials are selected for the *Annuals* based on the quality of the ideas, applicability to real-world concerns, relevance to current HRD issues, clarity of presentation, and ability to enhance our readers' professional development. In addition, we choose experiential learning activities that will create a high degree of enthusiasm among the participants and add enjoyment to the learning process. As in the past several years, the contents of each *Annual* span a wide range of subject matter, reflecting the range of interests of our readers.

Our contributor list includes a wide selection of experts in the field: in-house practitioners, consultants, and academically based professionals. A list of contributors to the *Annual* can be found at the end of the volume, including their names, affiliations, addresses, telephone numbers, facsimile numbers, and e-mail addresses. Readers will find this list useful if they wish to locate the authors of specific pieces for feedback, comments, or questions. Further information is presented in a brief biographical sketch of each contributor that appears at the conclusion of each article. We publish this information to encourage "networking," which continues to be a valuable mainstay in the field of human resource development.

We are pleased with the high quality of material that is submitted for publication each year and often regret that we have page limitations. In addition, just as we cannot publish every manuscript we receive, you may find that not all published works are equally useful to you. Therefore, we encourage and invite ideas, materials, and suggestions that will help us to make subsequent *Annuals* as useful as possible to all of our readers.

Introduction
to the Experiential Learning Activities Section

Experiential learning activities ensure that lasting learning occurs and should be selected with a specific learning objective in mind. Although the experiential learning activities presented here all vary in goals, group size, time required and process[1], they all incorporate one important element: questions that facilitate the learning. This final discussion, lead by the facilitator, assists the participants to process the activity, to internalize the learning, and to relate it to their day-to-day situations. It is this element that creates the unique experience and learning opportunity that only an experiential learning activity can bring to the group process.

Readers have used the *Annuals'* experiential learning activities for years to enhance their training and consulting events. Each learning experience is complete and includes all lecturettes, handout content, and other written material necessary to facilitate the activity. In addition each includes variations of the design that the facilitator might find useful. Although the activity as written may not fit perfectly with your objective, within your time frame, or to your group size, we encourage you to use these variations as well as your own variations. Should you wish to look beyond this volume for additional experiential learning activities, we encourage you to peruse the "Experiential Learning Activities Categories" chart that immediately follows this introduction.

The 1999 Annual: Volume 2, Consulting includes twelve activities, in the following categories:

---

[1]It would be redundant to print here a caveat for the use of experiential learning activities, but HRD professionals who are not experienced in the use of this training technology are strongly urged to read the "Introduction" to the *Reference Guide to Handbooks and Annuals* (1997 Edition). This article presents the theory behind the experiential-learning cycle and explains the necessity of adequately completing each phase of the cycle to allow effective learning to occur.

Individual Development: Self-Disclosure

631. Knowledge Is Power: Increasing an Organization's Knowledge Base by Marlene Caroselli

Communication: Building Trust

632. Building Trust in Pairs: An Obstacle Course by Valerie C. Nellen and Susan B. Wilkes

Problem Solving: Information Sharing

633. Systems Redesign: Building and Managing Systems Change by Patricia E. Boverie and Mary Jane Willis

Groups: How Groups Work

634. Crime-Fighting Task Force: Understanding Political Tactics in Groups by R. Bruce McAfee and Robert A. Herring III

Teams: How Groups Work

635. Team Troubles: Preventing and Solving Problems with Self-Directed Groups by Darcy Hitchcock and Marsha Willard

Teams: Roles

636. Risky Business: Assessing Risk by Lorraine L. Ukens

Teams: Conflict and Intergroup Issues

637. Group Sculptures: Analyzing and Resolving Team Problems by Arthur B. VanGundy

Consulting and Facilitating: Consulting: Awareness

638. Press Conference: Improving Communications During Change Initiatives by Gary Schuman and Andy Beaulieu

Consulting and Facilitating: Consulting: Diagnosing/Skills

639. Collecting Diagnostic Data: Which Method To Use? by Homer H. Johnson and Sander J. Smiles

Consulting and Facilitating: Facilitating: Opening

640. A New Twist: Using Symbols To Introduce a Topic by Garland F. Skinner

Leadership: Motivating

641. If You Think You Can: Exploring Corporate Attitudes by Eugene Taurman

Organizations: Communication

642. If We Only Knew: How Organizational Structure Affects Communication Flow by Janet Winchester-Silbaugh

Other activities that address goals in these and other categories can be located by using the "Experiential Learning Activities Categories" chart that follows, or by using our comprehensive *Reference Guide to Handbooks and Annuals*. This book, which is updated regularly, indexes all of the *Annuals* and all of the *Handbooks of Structured Experiences* that we have published to date. With each revision, the *Reference Guide* becomes a complete, up-to-date, and easy-to-use resource for selecting appropriate materials from all of the *Annuals* and *Handbooks*.

EXPERIENTIAL LEARNING ACTIVITIES CATEGORIES

Pins & Straws (162)	V	78	Manager's Dilemma (331)	'83	19	The Good Leader (488)	'92	37
Executive Pie (195)	'77	54	Power Caucus (346)	IX	31	Organizational Structures		
Staff Meeting (207)	VI	39	Management Skills (353)	IX	93	(504)	'93	63
Power Personalities (266)	VII	127	Follow the Leader (369)	'84	38	Today and Tomorrow (604)	'98–1	87
Managerial Characteristics			Management Perspectives			Rope-a-Leader (630)	'99–1	87
(273)	'80	31	(381)	'85	45			
Choosing an Apartment (274)	'80	37	Chipping In (384)	'85	57	**ORGANIZATIONS**		
Power & Affiliation (277)	'80	54	Choose Me (401)	X	85	**Communication**		
Boss Wanted (296)	VIII	15	Quantity Versus Quality (433)	'87	69			
Tangram (313)	VIII	108	Rhetoric and Behavior (478)	'91	51	If We Only Knew (642)	'99–2	121

631. Knowledge Is Power: Increasing an Organization's Knowledge Base

Goals

- To identify the strengths of knowledge management in an organization.

- To identify ways that individuals could increase the shared knowledge of an organization.

Group Size

Any size.

Time Required

Eighty to ninety minutes.

Materials

- A flip chart and felt-tipped markers.

- A transparency or handout of Knowledge Is Power: Exploring Your Contribution.

- A transparency or handout of Knowledge Is Power: Expanding Your Contribution.

- An overhead projector and screen.

Physical Setting

A large room with plenty of space for subgroups to discuss without disturbing one another.

Process

1. Open with the following brief comments about the importance of shared knowledge in organizations.

   "Learning organizations" are mentioned in almost every journal or professional magazine one reads today, even though most people have a difficult time defining them.

   Many employees feel (and research supports their sentiments) that their organizations use less than 50 percent of their intellectual potential. For example, when was the last time someone asked you to identify the greatest contribution you could make to the organization? [Call on a volunteer. Typically, he or she will respond that no one has ever asked that question.] Consequently, we find evidence of Dr. W. Edwards Deming's assertion that the greatest losses are unknown and unknowable. When we fail to make known what we can do for our companies and when others fail to inquire, the loss may be tremendous.

   If we only knew what we know, we could be three times more efficient than we are.

2. Ask participants to find one or two partners. Hand out or show the first sheet, Knowledge Is Power: Exploring Your Contribution, and have the subgroups discuss the questions listed on it:

   - In terms of the work you do, what wastes your time?

   - In terms of the work you do, what would increase productivity and/or profits?

   (Five minutes.)

3. After several minutes, reconvene the total group and ask for several examples of the answers. Discuss their answers briefly, listing themes on the flip chart. (Ten minutes.)

4. Next ask each dyad or triad to join another dyad or triad to form a new subgroup. Distribute flip-chart paper and a marker to each combined group, which will now number four to six participants. Hand out or show the transparency Knowledge Is Power: Expanding Your Contribution. Ask each group to summarize its answers on the flip-chart paper; then allow about ten minutes for subgroup discussion.

   - How is knowledge currently shared in your organization? How should it be shared?

   - How can people be valued or recognized for what they know?

- What causes organizational brainpower not to be utilized fully?
- How can barriers to "brainpower deficit disorder" be removed?
- What analogy best describes how your organization thinks?

(Fifteen minutes.)

5. Ask each group to appoint a spokesperson to give a brief report on ways to manage knowledge better in an organization. (Ten minutes.)

6. Conclude with a large-group discussion, using the following questions:

- What has this activity told you about the knowledge management in your organization?
- What are your organization's strengths?
- What could be done to ensure that individuals make needed contributions?
- What steps can you take personally to increase brainpower in your organization?
- What will you do back on the job as a result of this discussion?

(Fifteen minutes.)

7. Ask participants what proactive steps they will take to manage knowledge more efficiently. (*Note:* One such step might be asking questions such as those on the handouts whenever teams assemble or staffs meet. Encourage participants to move forward with the ideas that they generated during the discussion.)

8. Conclude by noting the truth of the maxim, "Knowledge is power." Say that, in today's fast-paced, technologically expanding work environment, shared knowledge makes the difference between a mediocre organization and a successful one.

9. Ask participants to find partners and trade work phone and fax numbers, or e-mail addresses. Ask them to commit to contacting one another on a specified date to determine the extent to which partners have followed through on any of the ideas they had for expanding organizational knowledge.

Variations

- A volunteer can collect information from all participants, prepare a short report, and distribute it to everyone at the end of a specified period of time.

- The trainer can hold a follow-up session with an intact group to discuss how information sharing is progressing.

Reference

Deming, W.E. (1986). *Out of the crisis*. Cambridge, MA: MIT Press.

Submitted by Marlene Caroselli.

Marlene Caroselli, Ed.D., directs the Center for Professional Development, started in 1984 to assist working adults develop their leadership, management, and communication skills. Her clients include both small and Fortune 100 companies, state and federal government agencies, and educational institutions. She presents seminars and keynote addresses nationally and internationally and is the author of thirty-six books. Additionally, she contributes frequently to the National Business Employment Weekly, The International Customer Service Association Journal, *and Stephen Covey's* Executive Excellence.

Knowledge Is Power:
Exploring Your Contribution

- In terms of the work you do, what wastes your time?

- In terms of the work you do, what would increase productivity and/or profits?

KNOWLEDGE IS POWER: EXPANDING YOUR CONTRIBUTION

■ How is knowledge currently shared in your organization? How should it be shared?

■ How can people be valued/recognized for what they know?

■ What causes organizational brainpower not to be utilized fully?

■ How can barriers to "brainpower deficit disorder" be removed?

■ What analogy best describes how your organization thinks?

632. Building Trust in Pairs: An Obstacle Course

Goals

- To experience the feeling of being in a trusting relationship.
- To identify the factors contributing to trust between individuals.
- To apply a model of trust within the context of the activity, in preparation for future use at work.

Group Size

Five to seven pairs.

Time Required

Approximately one and one-half hours.

Materials

- Blindfolds for half of the participants.
- A length of wood (at least four inches wide and five feet long).
- Several large, empty cardboard boxes (such as those in which food or beverages are commonly delivered) approximately 24 inches long by 12 inches wide by 16 inches deep.
- Several sets of jacks.
- A large sign that says "Travelers' Wall."
- Enough Building Trust Guide Instruction Sheets for half of the participants to have one each.
- Enough Building Trust Traveler Instruction Sheets for the other half of the participants to have one each.

- Enough Building Trust Questions for Guides Sheets for half of the participants.
- Enough Building Trust Questions for Travelers Sheets for the other half of the participants.
- A copy of the Building Trust Lecturette for the facilitator.
- Pens or pencils for all participants.

Physical Setting

Two separate rooms: one that has chairs in a circle or U-shape around a table and another that is empty and out of sight of the participants. The second room should have one wall that has an open door on it and at least five feet of wall space to one side of the door.

Process

1. Prior to the arrival of participants, prepare the two rooms. In one, arrange the chairs in a circle or a U-shape around a table. The participants should not be able to see the second room while sitting in the first room.

   The second room should be empty and large enough to allow at least twelve people to move around freely. Set up the following areas within the second room with as much space between them as possible:

   - Lay the length of wood on the floor, with ample space on either side of it.

   - Place several empty boxes in line with one another, with at least two feet between boxes. Boxes should not be against the wall.

   - Strew the jacks about in a three-foot by three-foot section of the floor.

   - Mark a five-foot section of wall next to an open door by posting the "Travelers' Wall" sign.

   - In one corner of the room, leave an open space with enough room for one person to turn around in a circle with his or her arms spread.

2. Welcome the group in the room furnished with chairs and a table. Introduce the activity with the following remarks:

   During this activity, we will start with an experiential segment and finish with a group discussion and processing session. You will work in pairs and be assigned one of two roles, either "guide" or "traveler."

You will receive written instructions for your role in addition to this explanation.

Each pair will consist of one guide and one traveler. The guide will lead the traveler, who will be blindfolded. Each of you should carefully review the written instructions for your role.

If you are undertaking this activity as pre-existing dyads (for example, manager and employee or experienced and new co-worker), the roles of guide and traveler should be assigned according to your work relationships. For those who are part of a larger group that has been randomly paired, the roles of guide and traveler can be arbitrarily assigned.

You will be given a few minutes to read your instruction sheets and ask any questions. Please take care not to share the contents of your instruction sheets with those who have a different role than you do.

3. Have each pair identify its traveler and its guide. Provide the appropriate instruction sheet to each person. Allow time for the participants to read their instructions. (Five minutes.)

4. Tell the participants that they will have approximately twenty minutes in which to complete the experiential part of the activity. Encourage them to take their time. The goal is not to race through the steps, but to give all guides and travelers a chance to participate fully in the experience.

Say that when the members of a pair have completed the experiential segment, they should return to the first room and remove the travelers' blindfolds, pick up the Building Trust Question Sheets for their respective roles, and take their time answering the questions. Let the pairs know that they can begin the task when they are ready. (Thirty minutes.)

5. While the pairs are completing the activity, place the Building Trust Questions for Guides and Questions for Travelers Sheets in two stacks at one end of the table. As pairs return to the room, direct them to the appropriate sheets and give them pencils or pens. Tell them that they have about ten minutes to answer the questions. (Ten minutes.)

6. When everyone has completed the activity and has had a chance to answer the questions, reconvene the large group and process the experience with the following questions:

■ How did you feel during this activity?

■ The travelers were in vulnerable situations, dependent on their guides. Do you ever feel as though you are in a similar situation at work? Can you provide an example?

- How do you define trust?
- How is trust achieved?
- What did the guides do to encourage trust?
- How could what you have learned during this activity help you as a leader or follower back on the job?

(Fifteen minutes.)

7. If the discussion is not as comprehensive as you would like it to be, deliver the Building Trust Lecturette at this point and then continue asking processing questions, as follows:

- How can trust be built in a setting in which risk and vulnerability exist?
- What can you take back to the workplace from this activity?

(Thirty minutes.)

Variation

- Additional obstacles, based on work-related metaphors, can be added.

Submitted by Valerie C. Nellen and Susan B. Wilkes.

Valerie C. Nellen, M.S., is currently the program coordinator for the Workplace Initiatives Program, where she is a curriculum designer and frequent workshop leader. Ms. Nellen is a counseling psychologist who specializes in organizational consultation and training. Her extensive background in coaching and athletics blend well with her current interests in team performance.

Susan B. Wilkes, Ph.D., manages the Workplace Initiatives Program, a training and consulting unit, in the Department of Psychology at Virginia Commonwealth University. She is an organizational psychologist who is a frequent workshop leader, consultant, and executive coach. Her areas of expertise include career management, management development, organizational change, stress management, conflict resolution, and team performance. Dr. Wilkes is a licensed professional counselor whose background also includes extensive experience in counseling and coaching individual employees for increased job satisfaction and efficacy.

Building Trust Guide Instruction Sheet

Instructions: Welcome to the Blindfolded Obstacle Course! As a "guide," your task is to lead a "traveler" in your care safely through a series of experiences that he or she would not be able to navigate alone. You may complete this task by speaking and/or by physically leading the traveler. It is important, however, that you act as a guide rather than as a proxy. In other words, your role is to facilitate the traveler's navigation of the path and the obstacles, rather than to perform the tasks for him or her.

Above all else, it is your responsibility to protect your traveler. While you are leading the traveler through the obstacles, his or her physical safety supersedes all other concerns.

When your traveler is ready to begin, your first task is to blindfold him or her securely before leaving the room. The traveler should not be able to see through the blindfold at all, but do not make the blindfold restrictive or uncomfortable.

Guide the traveler from the room that you are in now to the room in which an obstacle course has been set up. This should take some time, as your traveler will be adjusting to being blindfolded and will move tentatively.

There are five tasks for you to guide the traveler through. These can be completed in any order and should be navigated with an eye to where other participants are and how you can most easily move from one to the next. Again, please remember that you are *guiding* the traveler and *describing* the tasks, but he or she is responsible for performing each task. The five tasks are as follows:

- Lead the traveler to the section of wall marked "Travelers' Wall." Instruct the traveler that there is a wall in front of him or her, but that a passage can be found through the wall. The traveler's task is to find the door and pass through it.

- Guide the traveler to the section of the room where the floor is strewn with jacks. The traveler's task is to walk across the entire section of floor, from one end to the other, without stepping on anything.

- Bring the traveler to the length of wood. The traveler's task is to step onto the wood and to walk from one end to the other, without falling off.

- Lead the traveler to a corner of the room with nothing in it. Spin the traveler around at least six times. The task is for the traveler to then walk to the center of the room while dizzy.

■ Guide the traveler to the line of boxes. Guide the traveler as he or she walks from one end of the line of boxes to the other, stepping over the boxes as though they are hurdles.

When the traveler has completed all of the tasks, guide him or her back to the first room. There, you can remove the blindfold and then each of you is to fill out the appropriate Building Trust Questions Sheet for your role.

Building Trust Traveler Instruction Sheet

Instructions: As a traveler, your task is to perform a series of five tasks on an obstacle course while blindfolded. Your guide will describe each task to you and will facilitate your performance, as you will not be able to see through your blindfold. Although the guide's role is to be helpful to you, it is important that you actually perform the tasks by yourself.

While performing the tasks, you are free to ask for and to receive help from your guide through either spoken instructions or physical assistance. It is very important that you pay attention to your guide's facilitation of your performance. Note his or her method of instruction and remember things that are helpful or unhelpful to you.

Your physical safety is unquestionably the most important priority during this activity. If at any time you feel that your well-being is in jeopardy (whether due to personal factors or to severely inattentive guidance), you may opt out of finishing the activity, although the obstacles that you will be navigating are not inherently dangerous.

When you are ready to begin the activity, your guide will blindfold you securely. You should not be able to see through the blindfold at all, but the blindfold should not be restrictive or uncomfortable. Your guide will then lead you out of the room and through your five tasks.

When you have completed all of the tasks, your guide will lead you back to this room. There, you can remove the blindfold and each of you can fill out the Building Trust Questions Sheet for your role.

BUILDING TRUST QUESTIONS FOR GUIDES SHEET

What were some of your thoughts and feelings as you read the instructions, prior to putting a blindfold on the traveler?

_____

_____

_____

_____

Did you use spoken instructions or physical assistance or both with your traveler?

_____

_____

_____

_____

Did your method of assistance change with different activities?

_____

_____

_____

_____

What was the easiest part of the experience to guide your traveler through? What made it easy?

_____

_____

_____

What was the most difficult part? What made it difficult?

_____

_____

_____

Which of your actions as a guide did the traveler respond to best?

_____

_____

_____

_____

_____

Which of your actions as a guide were not successful for your traveler?

_____

_____

_____

_____

_____

Did your relationship with your traveler change during the experience?
In what way?

_____

_____

_____

_____

How did trust factor into the activity? What did you do to build trust?

_____

_____

_____

_____

How did the obstacle course metaphorically represent some common
expressions?

_____

_____

_____

BUILDING TRUST QUESTIONS FOR TRAVELERS SHEET

What were some of your thoughts and feelings as you read the instructions, prior to being blindfolded?

_____

_____

_____

What did it feel like to be blindfolded?

_____

_____

_____

What were some feelings that you had about the experience or toward your guide while performing the tasks?

_____

_____

_____

What things did your guide do that were very helpful?

_____

_____

_____

What were some unhelpful things that your guide did?

_____

_____

_____

What do you wish your guide had done that he or she did not do?

_____

_____

_____

Did you ask for help? In what way? Did you receive what you needed from your guide?

_____

_____

_____

Do the feelings that you had during this activity remind you of feelings you have had on the job? In what way are the situations similar?

_____

_____

_____

Did your relationship with your guide change during the experience? In what way?

_____

_____

_____

How did trust factor into the activity? What did your guide do to build trust?

_____

_____

_____

Do any common expressions come to mind to describe the obstacles you faced?

_____

_____

_____

BUILDING TRUST LECTURETTE

What exactly does it mean to trust? In terms of relationships, trust is the extent to which a person is confident in and willing to act on the basis of the words, actions, and decisions of another. Trust includes the very important element of allowing oneself to be vulnerable, based on the assumption that the trusted person will provide protection. Travelers today willingly entered situations that they could not have negotiated alone, trusting that their Guides would see them through safely.

Where does trust come from? Trust has a three-part foundation. The first is *competence*. We are all more likely to trust someone who demonstrates an ability to perform whatever task is at hand. In today's activity, the Travelers were unable to determine whether their Guides were competent or not, as they were blindfolded and could not judge. The Travelers were forced to rely on Guides' competence nonetheless. Travelers recognized that it was the only way to complete the tasks. In general, we as Guides acknowledge someone's competence by delegating important tasks to them and then not checking up to make sure the work is being done properly.

The second piece of the foundation of trust is *consistency*. We are all more inclined to trust someone who demonstrates consistent behavior: telling the truth, demonstrating integrity in word and deed, and honoring commitments. When someone is consistent, we say that we can count on or depend on him or her. We place faith in the statements of consistent people without independently verifying their actions. This level of behavioral predictability is vital to trust. During this activity, Travelers learned to trust Guides who were consistently correct in leading them through the tasks.

The third basis for trust is *care*. When a person demonstrates that he or she cares about our well-being and is willing to put our welfare ahead of his or her concerns, we feel safe. We willingly risk being emotionally, financially, or otherwise vulnerable with a person whom we trust to look out for our needs and keep our secrets. During this activity, the degree of care Guides had was readily apparent to Travelers.

When all three of these components of trust are found in a relationship, we can say that we trust the other person. When one element is missing, we may trust the person in a limited way, but we do not fully give ourselves over to the other person.

The obstacles for this activity were purposely chosen as metaphors of common situations we may encounter. Travelers found themselves "up against a wall," "overcoming hurdles," "negotiating rough ground," "walking on the edge," and "not knowing which way to turn."

633. Systems Redesign:
Building and Managing Systems Change

Goals

- To produce a visual model of an organization's systems.

- To identify system bottlenecks and problem areas.

- To develop solutions for the identified problem areas.

Group Size

Two or more groups of four to six participants from the same organization.

Time Required

Approximately three hours.

Materials

- A bucket of Lego®s or colored blocks for each subgroup.

- Three flip-chart sheets for each subgroup.

- An assortment of supplies for each subgroup that should include markers, pens, paper clips, scissors, masking tape, transparent tape, and several sheets of colored paper.

Physical Setting

One room with a table and chairs for each subgroup. The table must be large enough to hold a sheet of flip-chart paper. The room must be large enough to accommodate subgroups without disturbing one another.

Process

1. Form the subgroups and distribute the flip-chart paper, masking tape, markers, and Lego®s (or blocks).

2. Explain that the goal of this activity is to create a floor plan of the organization's existing facility. Explain as follows:

> With Lego®s (blocks), construct a replica of your plant (office, facility, etc.). Use the colors of the blocks to signify various areas. Lay the flip-chart paper on the table. The layout must fit within the edges of the paper. If the facility has more than one floor, the flip-chart paper must be divided into segments for each floor. You will have thirty minutes to construct the floor plan.

(Five minutes.)

3. Allow the subgroups to continue working until the thirty-minute deadline is met or until they have finished their floor plans, whichever occurs first. (Thirty minutes.)

4. Distribute the transparent tape, scissors, colored paper, markers, pens, and paper clips. Instruct each subgroup to show the work flow of the organization, that is, the manufacturing process flow, the paperwork flow, or whatever they choose. Say:

> Cut the colored paper in strips. Use the strips to show the work process flow. You may also use any of the other materials given to you. You will have twenty minutes to overlay the work process flow onto the floor plan.

(Twenty minutes.)

5. Instruct each subgroup to next show the organization's communication flow. Say:

> Using a different color of paper or markers, show how information flows into, out of, and throughout the organization. Overlay the communication flow over the process flow.

(Twenty minutes.)

6. When each of the subgroups has completed the task, call time. Have each subgroup present its floor plan, process flow, and communication flow to the other subgroups. Have the subgroups critique one another for accuracy. (Ten minutes.)

7. Tell the subgroups to identify and note where work bottlenecks occur, where communication breaks down, where work processes are redun-

dant, or where other problems germane to the organization occur. Allow fifteen minutes. (Fifteen minutes.)

8. In the large group have the subgroups present the problems they have identified. List the problems on a flip chart. Lead a discussion to identify potential solutions for the problems. List the ideas on flip-chart paper. (Twenty-five minutes.)

9. Ask each subgroup to select a different problem to solve. Tell them to decide on a potential solution and to show its implementation on a flip chart by listing the steps required to bring about the desired change. (Twenty minutes.)

10. Lead a concluding discussion based on some of the following questions:

- What visible problems exist?

- Where is redundant work completed?

- Where does work slow down?

- What problems are outside our control?

- Do suppliers and customers create some of the problems?

- Where are the high traffic areas? How is the work process affected?

- Where does communication only go one direction?

- Where is communication likely to break down?

- Where might the rumor mill be started?

- What new problems might be caused by various aspects of the solutions?

- What will you do differently as a result of this activity?

(Fifteen to twenty minutes.)

Variations

- You can save about twenty minutes by having one subgroup show the work flow and the another the information flow.

- If enough Lego®s or blocks are not available, participants can draw the floor plan or use a combination of masking tape and drawing to show the floor plan.

- If there are fewer than eight participants, only one group can be used. Time will be considerably shorter.

- A short lecturette on the process of change could be added at the beginning or before Step 9.

- If organizations are quite large, with multiple sites or huge buildings, the activity can be done for departments rather than whole organizations.

Submitted by Patricia E. Boverie and Mary Jane Willis.

Patricia E. Boverie, Ph.D., *is an associate professor of organizational learning and instructional technologies and psychological foundations at the University of New Mexico. She teaches courses in adult learning theory, consulting, critical thinking, and team/group learning and development. She holds a Ph.D. from the University of Texas at Austin, where she studied organizational, social, and educational psychology. In addition to teaching at the university, Dr. Boverie has had a private consulting practice for ten years.*

Mary Jane Willis is a training consultant for a variety of manufacturing companies. Some of the companies that she has served include General Mills, Martin Marietta, Elastimold, Intel Corporation, Philips Semiconductor and SEMATECH. Ms. Willis also teaches manufacturing skills at Albuquerque's community college. As project director of a National Science Foundation grant, she is working on the implementation of semiconductor manufacturing training programs at community colleges throughout the United States.

634. Crime-Fighting Task Force: Understanding Political Tactics in Groups

Goals

- To familiarize participants with the various political tactics that may be encountered in groups.

- To offer participants an opportunity to observe or experience the effects of hidden agendas and political tactics on group decision making.

Group Size

A minimum of fifteen participants, six of whom serve as role players. All participants who are not role players serve as observers; consequently, the maximum size of the total group is dictated by the number of participants who can sit closely enough to the players to see and hear the role play.

Time Required

Approximately one hour and fifteen minutes.

Materials

- One copy of the Crime-Fighting Task Force Situation Sheet for each participant.

- One copy of the Crime-Fighting Task Force Political Tactics Sheet for each participant.

- One copy of the appropriate Crime-Fighting Task Force Role Sheet for each role player.

- One copy of the Crime-Fighting Task Force Observer Sheet for each observer.

- A clipboard or other portable writing surface for each observer.

- A pencil for each observer.

- Six name tags—one for each role player—filled out as follows:
  - Retired Army Officer
  - Guidance Counselor
  - Farmer
  - Manager in Retail Store
  - Owner of Office-Supply Store
  - Chairperson

Physical Setting

A room with sufficient space and movable chairs to accommodate all participants. The observers must be seated around the role players.

Process

1. Announce the goals of the activity.

2. Give each participant one copy of the Crime-Fighting Task Force Situation Sheet and a copy of the Crime-Fighting Task Force Political Tactics Sheet. Ask the participants to review the material contained in these handouts, then elicit and answer questions. (Ten minutes.)

3. Ask six volunteers to role play the members of the Crime Fighting Task Force. Give each volunteer one of the Crime Fighting Task Force Role Sheets and the appropriate name tag. Ask each role player to put on the name tag and to read and study his or her role for the next few minutes.

4. As the role players are studying their roles, meet with the remaining participants in a different part of the room. Give each a copy of the Crime-Fighting Task Force Observer Sheet, a clipboard or other portable writing surface, and a pencil. Explain that they are to observe the role play, complete their Observer Sheets, and then share the contents of these sheets with the total group. Ask them to read their sheets; then elicit and answer questions. (Ten minutes.)

5. Have the role players sit in a circle with the observers seated around them. Announce that the Crime-Fighting Task Force has twenty minutes to decide how it should spend the $425,000, and ask the role players to begin. (Twenty minutes.)

6. After twenty minutes ask the role players to stop. Review the contents of the Observer Sheet with the total group, asking the observers to report their findings. (Five to ten minutes, depending on the number of observers.)

7. Ask the task-force members to take turns sharing the contents of their role sheets. Point out each role player's hidden agenda. (Five minutes.)

8. Lead a concluding discussion based on the following questions:

   ■ How satisfied were the role players with the way they worked together? How satisfied were they with the results of their work on the task?

   ■ What generalizations can you make about the effects of hidden agendas and political tactics on group decision making?

   ■ When might you have a need to uncover hidden agendas or be aware of political tactics?

   ■ How can you use this information on the job?

   (Fifteen to twenty minutes.)

Variations

■ One or two observers may be assigned to a single role player and report specifically on that player's interactions with the others.

■ The role play may be completed a second time with the role players abandoning their hidden agendas and political tactics. In this case, processing would concentrate on the differences in both process and outcome between the two role plays.

Submitted by R. Bruce McAfee and Robert A. Herring III.

R. Bruce McAfee, Ph.D., is a professor of management at Old Dominion University in Norfolk, Virginia. He has co-written numerous books and articles, including Applications in Personnel/Human Resources Management: Cases, Exercises and Skill Builders *and* Effectively Managing Troublesome Employees. *He teaches courses in employee relations and organizational behavior.*

Robert A. Herring III, Ph.D., is an associate professor of management and assistant director of the Division of Business and Economics at Winston-Salem State University. He teaches courses in the areas of organizational management and busi-

ness strategy and policy. He retired from the U.S. Naval Reserve at the rank of Commander, where he had over twenty years' of active duty and reserve leadership and management experience. His research interests are in the areas of management education, total quality management, and employee assistance programs.

CRIME-FIGHTING TASK FORCE SITUATION SHEET

Six citizens have been appointed by the City Manager to serve on the Crime-Fighting Task Force. This task force has received a $425,000 one-year grant to help solve your city's crime problems. The grant stipulates that "grant funds must be spent in such a manner that crime will be reduced in the least amount of time." The purpose of today's task-force meeting is to determine how the $425,000 should be spent. Five programs are potential recipients of the money:

Program A: Establishing more drug-treatment/counseling centers to treat drug addicts and alcoholics.

Program B: Conducting crime-prevention training for homeowners and business owners. (Individuals would be trained and sent out to homes and businesses to teach crime-prevention techniques.)

Program C: Hiring more police officers.

Program D: Establishing a first-offenders' program. (Counselors would work with first-time criminals with the goal of reducing the number of repeat offenders.)

Program E: Contracting with consultants who would advise the task force on how to spend the money.

The members of the task force may choose one or more of the five, but they must reach a consensus on how to spend the money.

CRIME-FIGHTING TASK FORCE POLITICAL TACTICS SHEET

The following are political tactics that are commonly used in group situations:

Building a Favorable Image: This strategy involves dressing appropriately, drawing attention to one's successes, name dropping, expressing enthusiasm about the organization, adhering to group norms, and exhibiting an air of confidence about one's abilities.

Presenting Information Selectively: This strategy consists of withholding unfavorable information from others, presenting only the information that supports one's own view, and interpreting information in a way that is favorable to oneself or one's position.

Blaming and Attacking: People who use this strategy further their own interests by blaming others for their own failures. They make sure that they will not be blamed when something goes wrong and that they will receive credit when something goes right.

Relying on Outside Experts: As experts outside of a group can be found to support almost any position, some people influence group decisions by quoting experts or inviting them to express their opinions at group meetings.

Forming Coalitions or Alliances: When one or more group members realize that they do not individually have sufficient power to control the decision-making process, they can increase their power by forming a subgroup and imposing their will on other members.

Compromising: This strategy involves giving up part of what one wants in exchange for receiving something of value from others.

Manipulating the Rules: People who use this strategy interpret group rules in such a way as to advance their own personal interests. For example, a manager might refuse one employee's request on the grounds that it is against company policy, but grant an identical request from a favored employee on the grounds that it is a "special circumstance" or that the rule does not apply in this particular case. As most rules can be interpreted in a number of ways, this strategy often succeeds.

Ingratiating Oneself: People try to increase their power by gaining the favor of others. They may, for example, praise others excessively or show excessive support.

Controlling the Meeting's Agenda: One can increase one's power by controlling the agenda of a meeting. One can manipulate the items that appear on the agenda, as well as the order in which they appear.

CRIME-FIGHTING TASK FORCE ROLE SHEET 1

Retired Army Officer

Do not tell anyone the contents of your role sheet until the facilitator asks you to do so.

You are a retired army officer and are running for city council in the elections being held in fourteen months. You are trying desperately to win in what you know will be a tough race. You feel your chance of winning will be the greatest if the task force decides to spend all or almost all of the funds on Program C (hiring additional police to arrest criminals). You realize that the citizens really want the crime problem eliminated now and they want the hoodlums put behind bars. By spending money on more police and having them make arrests, you can claim that "your task force" has solved the city's crime problem. Besides, it will help you to establish a record of being tough on crime, which will certainly help you be elected.

During the role play you must push hard for Program C. You are to use the political tactic of *manipulating the rules*. In presenting your view, keep reminding the task force members that the grant states, that "grant funds must be spent in such a manner that crime will be reduced in the least amount of time." Argue that hiring more police will clearly reduce crime in the least amount of time, as there will be fewer criminals around—at least in the short run.

CRIME-FIGHTING TASK FORCE ROLE SHEET 2

Guidance Counselor

Do not tell anyone the contents of your role sheet until the facilitator asks you to do so.

You are a guidance counselor in one of your city's high schools. You hate your present job and would really like to find a new one. In order to do this, you would like the task force to implement Program A (establishing more drug treatment counseling centers) and spend most of its money on it. As you have had many years of counseling experience, you will be the logical choice to head at least one of these new centers.

During the role play, you are to use the political tactic of *compromising*. Offer to everyone who supports other programs that you will vote for that person's program if he or she will also vote for yours. However, try to have as many new centers established as possible, as that will enhance your chances for finding a new job.

CRIME-FIGHTING TASK FORCE ROLE SHEET 3

Farmer

Do not tell anyone the contents of your role sheet until the facilitator asks you to do so.

You own 1,000 acres and 800 hogs. You really wanted to serve on this task force and lobbied to be appointed. You have a straightforward reason for wanting to serve—you have over ten acres planted in marijuana and don't want to be caught. Your goal in serving on this task force is to persuade the chairperson to like you. If you can convince the chairperson to like you, you will be able to exert influence over him or her in the future, thereby ensuring that your marijuana plants will be safe. Therefore, you are going to use the political tactic of *ingratiating oneself.* During the role play praise the chairperson frequently on techniques used to conduct the meeting or any other behaviors. It is important that you block any efforts to support Program C (hiring more police officers), as it might make your situation more precarious. You would like to hire consultants, conduct numerous pilot studies, or do anything that the chairperson seems to favor (except Program C). Hiring consultants is particularly desirable, as they will slow the process down and allow you more time to exert your influence with the chairperson.

CRIME-FIGHTING TASK FORCE ROLE SHEET 4

Manager in Retail Store

Do not tell anyone the contents of your role sheet until the facilitator asks you to do so.

You are the manager of the clothing department in the city's largest retail store. In addition you have counseled runaway teenagers for five years. You would like the task force to spend most, if not all, of its money on Program D (establishing a first-offenders' program). If all $425,000 were spent, at least eight counselors or social workers would have to be hired, and your favorite cousin, who earned a college degree in social work but has not been able to find a job, would have a good chance of being hired.

During the role play, argue that a first offenders' program is better than any of the other alternatives because it will educate people who are most likely to commit criminal acts—past criminals. In presenting your arguments, use the political tactic of *relying on outside experts*. Thus, you will want to cite experts who agree with you. For example, tell the committee the following:

- Dr. Susan Barnes, a world-wide authority and a professor of criminal justice at UCLA, has stated that 86 percent of the crimes committed in the U.S. are committed by repeat offenders. Based on a review of many studies, she has concluded that first-offender programs are more effective than any other method for crime reduction.

- A report published by the U.S. Attorney General's office entitled, "A Statistical Analysis of Crime in America," concludes that first-offender programs have the best cost/benefit ratio of any crime-fighting technique.

- Bernard Crowley, who is perhaps the leading authority on crime in the Midwest, reported on the TV program *NightLine* that most riots could be prevented if cities were to spend their money on first-offenders' programs.

(*Note:* None of this "expert" information is true, but the task-force members will not know that.)

CRIME-FIGHTING TASK FORCE ROLE SHEET 5

Owner of Office-Supply Store

Do not tell anyone the contents of your role sheet until the facilitator asks you to do so.

You are the owner of an office-supply store in your city. Your goal during this meeting is to impress all of the other task-force members so that they will shop at your store. Also, some of the grant money will have to be spent on office supplies, and you want it to be spent at your store. In order to impress others during the role play, use the political tactic of *building a favorable image*. Therefore, appear very interested in the discussion and nod affirmatively when others make suggestions. State how pleased you are with what the group is trying to accomplish—reducing crime. When opportunities arise, be sure to drop names. Mention that you know the mayor of the city, the city treasurer, and the city chief of police. Mention that, as a store owner, you are an expert on the shoplifting problem. Remember that you really don't care how the grant money is spent; you only care about increasing business.

CRIME-FIGHTING TASK FORCE ROLE SHEET 6

Chairperson

Do not tell anyone the contents of your role sheet until the facilitator asks you to do so.

You are the task-force chairperson. It is your job to assist the task force in arriving at the best possible decision—the one that will be most effective in resolving the city's crime problem. You are to begin by explaining the purpose of the meeting. Be sure to state that there are five alternatives for spending the $425,000 grant, but that the money can be divided among various programs.

You are to conduct an orderly meeting and help the committee arrive at a consensus. Assist the members in defining the problem, developing alternatives, weighing the pros and cons of each alternative, and ultimately making the best decision. Keep in mind that your job is to assist the members, not to dictate to them.

CRIME-FIGHTING TASK FORCE OBSERVER SHEET

Instructions: You are to observe the role play closely and write answers to the following questions:

1. Which political tactics are being used by each of the role players?

■ Retired Army Officer:

_____

_____

_____

■ Guidance Counselor:

_____

_____

_____

■ Farmer:

_____

_____

_____

■ Manager in Retail Store:

_____

_____

_____

■ Owner of Office-Supply Store:

_____

_____

_____

■ Chairperson:

_____

_____

_____

2. When one of the role players uses a political tactic, how do the others respond? (Describe two instances.)

_____

_____

_____

_____

_____

_____

_____

_____

3. What behaviors helped the role players to stay on task? What behaviors lead them off track?

_____

_____

_____

_____

_____

_____

_____

4. How effective are the role players in reaching the goal of achieving consensus about how to spend the money?

_____

_____

_____

_____

_____

_____

_____

635. TEAM TROUBLES: PREVENTING AND SOLVING PROBLEMS WITH SELF-DIRECTED GROUPS

Goals

- To explore the problems organizations encounter when implementing high-performance or self-directed teams.

- To discover ways to prevent these problems.

- To discover ways to overcome such problems when they do occur.

Group Size

Up to twenty participants who have experience with self-directed or high-performance teams in subgroups of four to eight.

Time Required

One and one-half to two hours.

Materials

- One copy of the Team Troubles Handout for each participant.

- One set of Team Troubles Cards for each subgroup copied onto card stock and cut out, with the Team Troubles visual on one side and the situations on the back. (This step may take some time.)

- Paper and pencils for participants.

Physical Setting

Tables with enough space for subgroups to work without disturbing one another.

Process

1. Give everyone a copy of the Team Troubles Handout. Explain the goals of the activity and review the phases that self-directed teams go through, using the handout as a guide. If necessary, describe the responsibilities of a steering committee and a design team. Answer any questions.

2. Ask participants to form subgroups with four to eight members each and to be seated at separate tables.

3. Give each subgroup a set of Team Troubles Cards that have been shuffled and the following instructions:

   ■ Each person, in turn, will select one card from the top of the deck and read the phrase and the situation (S) aloud to the others.

   ■ In your subgroups, discuss what you think should be done to prevent or resolve the problem stated on each card. The person who reads the card is to assume that he or she is a manager or supervisor experiencing the situation. Limit yourselves to one or two minutes of discussion per card.

   ■ After everyone has had a chance to give input on the situation described on the card, read the suggested answer (A) aloud.

   ■ Discuss the answer for about one minute. If the discussion could be lengthy, set the card aside for this time.

   ■ You will not be able to go through all the cards in the time allotted, but do keep moving through the deck to discuss as many situations as possible.

   (Sixty minutes.)

4. Provide a five-minute warning to the subgroups. Debrief the activity by asking the following questions:

   ■ What situations were most like ones that you have encountered?

   ■ What was the most difficult situation to resolve?

   ■ Did you always agree with the answers provided? Why or why not?

   ■ What appear to be some of the obstacles common to each phase?

   ■ What ideas did you decide to implement on the job as a result of your discussions?

   (Ten minutes.)

5. Give out paper and pencils and ask participants to write as many action steps as possible for when they return to their organizations. (Ten minutes.)

6. Ask everyone to find a partner, share and give feedback on one another's action steps, and agree to "check up" on one another at a specified time in the future, probably in three to four weeks. (Fifteen minutes.)

Variations

- This activity can take more or less time, based on your needs. It may not be necessary to go through all the cards. If time is short, you can "stack the deck" in the following ways:

  - Put the most pertinent cards on top.

  - Give each table cards from different phases ("Planning" for one table, "Launching" for the next, etc.) If you do this, be sure that the general discussions cover all phases so groups understand others' situations and possible solutions.

  - Give each table a few representative situations from each of the five phases.

  - If working with an intact work group, hand out only the cards that relate to the phase of implementation the group is currently in or soon to enter.

- Ask the participants to set aside cards that represent problems they think will be particularly troublesome for their organization or team. Then discuss strategies in more detail in the large group.

- Depending on your audience, this activity can be used by organizations implementing self-directed or high-performance work teams in one of these ways:

  - Steering committees can use the cards to forecast obstacles to implementation and discuss how to prevent them.

  - Managers can use the cards to anticipate problems they will experience and to plan appropriate responses.

  - Front-line employees can use the cards to understand what to expect during the implementation.

  - Intact teams can use the cards during a team-building activity.

Submitted by Darcy Hitchcock and Marsha Willard.

Darcy Hitchcock *is president of AXIS Performance Advisors, Inc., a management consulting firm specializing in the implementation of team-based organizations. She has published four business books, including* Why Teams Can Fail and What to Do About It *and* The Work Redesign Team Handbook: A Step-by Step Guide to Creating Self-Directed Teams. *She is on the faculty for the Association for Quality and Participation and sits on the local board for Business for Social Responsibility.*

Marsha Willard, Ph.D., *CEO for AXIS, is co-author of three business books. She holds a Ph.D. from the University of Southern California and teaches graduate-level classes for Oregon State University, the University of Oregon, and Washington State University.*

TEAM TROUBLES HANDOUT

When organizations implement high-performance or self-directed teams, they encounter predictable problems. In a few minutes, you will be given a set of situation cards that are organized around the following phases in the life of a self-directed team:

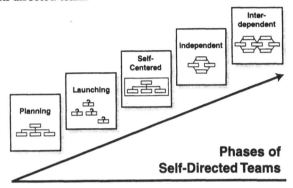

Phases of Self-Directed Teams

Planning

The first phase of team development occurs when the organization is still operating in the old way, but has begun to talk about and plan for the implementation of teams. This causes many to be hopeful and just as many to be anxious about the impending change. People have many misconceptions that contribute to their fears.

Launching

At some point, the organization stops planning and launches a team. This may involve reorganizing people or simply beginning to do work differently. For awhile, performance may dip while people learn new skills and roles.

Self-Centered

Teams often go through a self-centered stage in which they try to serve themselves more than the organization. They may ask for new equipment, four-day work weeks, etc. They aren't yet taking full responsibility for the organization's and customers' needs. During this phase, many people may sit back and let others lead.

Independent

Teams reach a point at which esprit de corps (team spirit) is high. The members are working well together and everyone is carrying a fair share of the load. The down side is that the team may not be integrating well with the rest of the organization. Members may feel competitive toward other teams ("We're the 'A' team") and may fiercely resist changing their membership, even if that is what is best for the organization.

Interdependent

With luck and perseverance, teams eventually reach the point at which they appreciate that their team is really part of a much larger team. They work well across team boundaries, reaching out to pull others in when needed. They take responsibility for the business needs of the organization and are creative about how to meet everyone's needs. In this phase, if organizational systems have not kept pace (compensation, budgeting, hiring, orientation, information management, etc.), these systems will become major barriers.

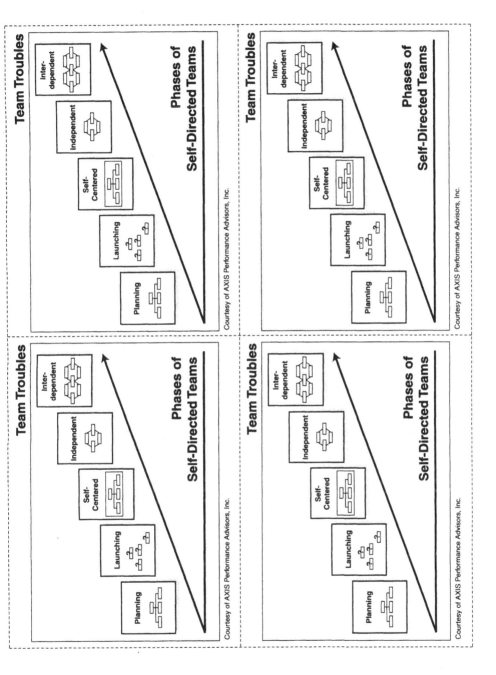

The four panels each contain:

Team Troubles

Phases of Self-Directed Teams

Planning — Launching — Self-Centered — Independent — Inter-dependent

Courtesy of AXIS Performance Advisors, Inc.

PLANNING

S. Employees have heard about the possibility of going to self-directed teams through the grapevine. They assume the reason management wants to do this is to eliminate jobs.

A. Your answer may be similar to:
The Steering Group should prepare a carefully crafted and honest written explanation about the reason for moving to teams and communicate this to all employees, providing opportunities for two-way discussion.

PLANNING

S. Employees see what's in it for the organization to use a team structure, but do not believe that they will be better off.

A. Your answer may be similar to:
Employees will be skeptical of listening to people who have a vested interest in implementing teams (management, consultants). Provide opportunities for them to hear from employees in other organizations via site visits, conferences, etc.

PLANNING

S. Employees see no real need for change.

A. Your answer may be similar to:
Sell the problem, not the solution. Give employees the information you have about your organization's performance, competitive pressures, etc. Educate front-line employees by taking them on site visits, sending them to workshops, etc.

PLANNING

S. Employees are jaded by past "management programs" that came and went. They are biding their time because they assume this will blow over too.

A. Your answer may be similar to:
Avoid giving this effort the same trappings as previous "programs," such as slogans, big kick-offs, or major communication efforts. Focus on the end result of quality and customer satisfaction instead of teams as a means to that end.

PLANNING

S. Some employees are downright militant about this change to self-directed teams. They say what made America great was competition, that teams are just another form of communism, and so on.

A. Your answer may be similar to:
Let them vent. Often other team members will argue with them. If not, give them as much information as you can about the proven effectiveness of teams and give them opportunities to talk to effective teams in other organizations. Explain that work is too complex for us to succeed without cooperating, that we need to focus on our real competitors. Using a sports analogy might help. This emotional argument may not be overcome until the individual experiences the difference himself or herself.

PLANNING

S. Employees complain that management is pushing self-direction on them and that if management were truly interested in participation, they would not push this change.

A. Your answer may be similar to:
Assuming that self-direction is a critical strategy for survival, stress the urgency to move ahead and again sell the problem instead of the means to a solution. Increasing employee involvement on the Steering Group and improving communication may also help.

PLANNING

S. Everyone seems excited about the upcoming change to self-direction; even the supervisors seem to be looking forward to it. However, you suspect that each person is interpreting what self-direction is differently.

A. Your answer may be similar to:
The Steering Group must define specifically what the long-term and short-term responsibilities of the teams will be. These must be communicated to all employees. A cross-section of employees should set acceptable standards of performance.

PLANNING

S. Employees want to know if they will be paid more because they will need to do more. They grumble that this is just another way to get people to do more work for the same pay.

A. Your answer may be similar to:
Ideally, you should have plans to incorporate a group compensation plan into the implementation so that you can respond that all employees will share in the improvements in productivity. Stress also that giving them the power to make their own decisions will make them happier. Elicit an example of something that drives them crazy now that they will be able to resolve on their own. Contact with teams in other organizations can also help.

S. Employees seem to have a great deal of misinformation about what self-directed teams are and what this change will involve.

A. Your answer may be similar to:
Communicate and educate. Provide communication and a training overview to all employees soon after the decision to implement or consider self-directed teams becomes public. Explain what you know, what you don't know, how they can participate in the decision-making process, and how you will keep them informed.

S. Supervisors *say* they support this change, but conversations in the hall would indicate otherwise. They fear for their jobs and loss of status. Secretly, they are certain employees won't be able to perform the new functions and fully expect this effort to fail. Their strategy is to wait it out.

A. Your answer may be similar to:
Define and communicate an employment security policy to resolve the fear. Describe this process as one of moving everyone up a layer in the organization. Explain that after supervisors have given up most of their traditional tasks, they can take on even more challenging work. Let supervisors define their own roles and provide substantial and ongoing support. Let them talk to ex-supervisors in other self-directed organizations.

S. Because of poor management/employee relations, employees are distrustful of management's motives for this change. They don't believe that management is serious about wanting to improve employee satisfaction.

A. Your answer may be similar to:
Make an important symbolic gesture to demonstrate your willingness to change. This gesture should not be something that will be perceived as superficial. Examples include eliminating assigned management parking spaces, eliminating time clocks, providing information that was never shared with employees before, involving employees in key decisions, etc.

S. The design teams are going through the motions of creating a reorganization plan, but they seem to lack an understanding of what they are doing and why. Their communication to the groups they represent has suffered as a result, lacking confidence and commitment.

A. Your answer may be similar to:
Break the design process into small steps and develop a structured way for them to receive feedback from their work groups after each step. Provide the design team criteria for their re-design and coach them through the decision-making process. Use small groups to encourage open discussion. Make sure they have clear goals and outcomes.

LAUNCHING

S. Instead of assigning people to teams, the Steering Group decided to let people sign up independently. The deadline for signing up is in three days, and so far no one has put his or her name on the sign-up sheets.

A. Your answer may be similar to:
Encourage team members to put together their own coalitions and to sign up together. If possible, explain that team members can request reassignment after a three-month test period.

LAUNCHING

S. Today is the first day of the reorganization. People seem to be walking on eggs. You suspect you may only be in the eye of the storm.

A. Your answer may be similar to:
Do lots of "management by walking around." Encourage people and explain your willingness to resolve any problems that inevitably will come up. Conduct rumor-control meetings on a regular basis (once per week) to provide an official forum to discuss progress, issues, and misconceptions.

LAUNCHING

S. You have announced the new reorganization. The design teams seem tentative about their new designs, fearing attacks from the naysayers.

A. Your answer may be similar to:
The design should be completed only with significant input along the way, eliminating most of the potential for attack. In addition, you can present the redesign as part of a three-month test phase, after which the redesign will be re-evaluated. You may also want to teach the design team presentation skills, including verbal techniques to diffuse hostility.

LAUNCHING

S. A valued employee who has always performed well but is somewhat of a loner comes to you and says he or she wants to be removed from the team.

A. Your answer may be similar to:
Ask questions to determine why the individual is dissatisfied. If possible, coach the team to resolve the issues. Ask for a commitment to try to work out the differences within a specified time. If the individual is a prima donna, emphasize his or her excellent past performance and explain the importance of sharing information. Discuss how being a team member will change his or her role and how you plan to reward changed behavior. If you have exhausted all options, help the individual find a position in a traditional portion of the organization.

LAUNCHING

S. The design teams believed they had thought of everything, but inevitably there is confusion. Other departments, customers, and even supervisors seem unsure who to contact to perform specific tasks.

A. Your answer may be similar to:
Plan an end-of-the-day short meeting each day for the first week to discuss what went well and what problems were encountered. Write this information on a board or flip chart. Emphasize what is going right. Use coaching skills to keep people calm and to help them consider problems rationally. Provide teams with a simple problem-solving process and help them use it so they can begin to solve their own problems. Be available to help.

SELF-CENTERED

S. In the midst of the implementation, the team leaders became frustrated. The only way to get things done seemed to be to do it themselves. Consequently, they are now acting like traditional supervisors.

A. Your answer may be similar to:
Provide training and coaching on participative skills. Sit in on meetings and observe; give feedback. Help the leader identify one or two things to work on at a time. Encourage people to set aside time at the end of each meeting to process the meeting or use meeting effectiveness surveys.

LAUNCHING

S. It is one week into the reorganization, and the confusion is taking a toll. People are grousing that things worked better before. You've had some customer complaints and quality problems as well. Productivity is down and emotions are up.

A. Your answer may be similar to:
Remind teams that you expected things to grow worse before they got better, that learning new skills and methods always creates problems. Emphasize what is going right. Use coaching skills to keep people calm and to help them consider problems rationally. Provide teams with a simple problem-solving process and help them use it so they can begin to solve their own problems. Be available to help.

SELF-CENTERED

S. Teams were permitted to select their own team leaders. Several teams seem to have made poor choices, selecting individuals who enjoy being in charge and griping. The team spirit is suffering, but the team members seem unsure what to do.

A. Your answer may be similar to:
Help the teams establish procedures for selecting and changing team leaders. For instance, they may decide to rotate team leaders every two months until everyone who wanted a chance could demonstrate his or her abilities. After that initial period, they may decide to vote in a leader for six months at a time. Helping the team establish and conform to ground rules may also help.

SELF-CENTERED

S. Because the team leaders were selected by management, the teams are suspicious of everything they do.

A. Your answer may be similar to:
Except in rare cases, teams should have the ability to select their own leaders. Anyone appointed by management should be viewed as a temporary, transitional leader. Encourage that person to involve other team members as soon as possible, behaving more like a mentor than a leader.

SELF-CENTERED

S. Several team leaders are having trouble managing their meetings. The meetings have become either one-way exchanges or forums for complaining.

A. Your answer may be similar to:
Provide training and assessment methods for team meetings. Make your own observations known without embarrassing anyone. Help the team establish group ground rules. Make sure the teams have clear reasons for meeting and have clear goals.

SELF-CENTERED

S. Lacking good role models, several team leaders are behaving like traditional supervisors. They don't seem to know how to encourage participation.

A. Your answer may be similar to:
Provide training and coaching on participative skills. Help the teams develop specific meeting roles, such as a time keeper, recorder, leader, process observer, etc. Sit in on meetings and give feedback. Help the leaders identify one or two things to work on at a time. Encourage them to set aside time at the end of each meeting to process the meeting or use meeting effectiveness surveys.

SELF-CENTERED

S. Team leaders are paid more, and consequently the team members think the leaders should be responsible for extra hand-off responsibilities.

A. Your answer may be similar to:
Divide the role of supervisor into logical clusters of responsibilities and assign different people to take on those roles. For instance, special roles might include training, safety, quality, customer contact, meeting management, etc.

SELF-CENTERED

S. Team members are becoming fed up with their team leaders acting like traditional supervisors. There have been some ugly exchanges, and several team leaders have been deposed. Now the leaders are turning against this movement toward teams. They don't think being a team leader is worth the grief, as they are not paid more.

A. Your answer may be similar to:
Prevention is the best medicine here. You should have avoided this through coaching team leaders, establishing rotation policies, and the like. As it is too late now to prevent this, increase your coaching of and involvement with the team to help them establish ground rules and use effective communication techniques. Emphasize that everyone is struggling to change.

INDEPENDENT

S. Team members are finally taking on significant responsibility, and leadership is being shared among all team members. Performance is better, and the teams feel really proud of their accomplishments. However, this sense of team spirit is inhibiting cross-team cooperation and learning.

A. Your answer may be similar to:
Create opportunities for teams to share information in a low-key environment. This might include providing training to people from various teams, having people with similar responsibilities (quality coordinators) meet regularly to discuss shared issues, etc.

INDEPENDENT

S. One team member is not carrying a fair share of the work. The other team members complain to you, but seem unwilling to confront this person.

A. Your answer may be similar to:
Encourage individuals to confront the nonperformer privately and, if that does not succeed, to deal with it in a meeting. Help individuals role play the situation. Institute regular team feedback meetings and teach all team members how to give nonthreatening feedback. Help the team members create a process that they can use whenever a team problem arises.

INDEPENDENT

S. Several teams perform the same function, but on different shifts or for different customers. You notice that Team A's performance is significantly better than the others and you want the other teams to learn from Team A. You suggest that Team A brief the other teams on their methods. Team A seems reluctant to do so, but because of your insistence does share its approach. The other teams have not improved, and cross-team relations are worse than ever.

A. You answer may be similar to:
Avoid placing teams in competition with one another, as was done here. Create opportunities for teams to share information in a low-key environment. Now that there is competition, change the reward systems so that teams succeed only if they cooperate and share information, or find something that each team is doing particularly well and ask them each to prepare a presentation or newsletter article on that topic.

INDEPENDENT

S. One team member is not carrying a fair share of the work. The other team members want to have a team meeting to confront this person. You feel they will need help to pull this off.

A. Your answer may be similar to:
Institute regular team feedback meetings and teach all team members to give nonthreatening feedback. Help the team members structure a process that they can use whenever a team problem arises.

INDEPENDENT

S. Success has been addictive. The teams now want to take on some of the long-term hand-offs (such as deciding compensation) before finishing all the short-term hand-offs.

A. Your answer may be similar to:
The Steering Group should have identified short-term and long-term responsibilities. If this is the case, remind the teams of the hierarchy of responsibilities and explain the rationale for it. If this is not the case, ask why teams want each responsibility, why they think they are ready, and what is the worst thing that might happen if they take it on. Make sure their reasoning is appropriate. If the teams have thought through the issues, you may want to give them the responsibility in clearly defined stages with specific guidelines or criteria (quality and customer satisfaction cannot be hurt, adequate documentation must be provided, etc.). Inform the teams of any legal or regulatory requirements and provide them any necessary training or coaching.

INDEPENDENT

S. One team has come to you with a recommendation for changing to a four-day work week, a decision that rests with management. You are afraid that this change would cause scheduling problems and hurt productivity and customer service. However, because this is the first suggestion the team has brought to you, you do not want to have to turn it down.

A. Your answer may be similar to:
List your concerns and any criteria you may have for the decision (quality and customer satisfaction cannot be hurt, adequate phone coverage must be provided, etc.). Then let the team develop solutions to the issues. If the team is able to overcome your objections, implement their idea on a trial basis and agree to verify that the criteria you set are met. Be careful to raise all your relevant objections and criteria at the beginning. It is not fair to add to the list after they resolve the issues you gave them.

INDEPENDENT

S. One of your teams is about to make a decision that you think is unwise. Because they are now responsible for this decision, you cannot overrule it.

A. Your answer may be similar to:
Coach and question. Ask what they think might be possible positive and negative outcomes. Help them identify alternatives. If necessary, raise your concerns while reaffirming their responsibility to make the decision. Verify consensus in the group if not all members seem to be participating.

INDEPENDENT

S. After the chaos of launching the teams, this stage seems great. Productivity is up, and teams are working well together. They seem to have become complaisant at this stage and to have lost the urgency to continue the change.

A. Your answer may be similar to:
Institute meaningful measures for the team to track for themselves and continue providing important business and competitive information to them. Begin linking them to customers and suppliers. Benchmark their performance against competitors, and focus on continuous improvement.

INTERDEPENDENT

S. Teams are now fully self-directed and the organization has reaped handsome rewards. Most employees are much more satisfied with the team approach, but they are beginning to question why the organization has all the financial benefits. There have been discussions about implementing a gain-sharing compensation program; realistically, implementation is over a year away.

A. Your answer may be similar to:
Obtain employee involvement in developing a new group-based compensation system. Use small or nonmonetary recognition awards to keep teams motivated.

INDEPENDENT

S. During cross-training, several employees have made some expensive mistakes. You want to reassure the teams that they should continue cross-training, but at the same time prevent such major mistakes.

A. Your answer may be similar to:
Help the teams analyze what the causes and costs of the mistakes were. Stay future-oriented by asking them to decide what could be done to prevent these types of mistakes in the future. Reiterate that good-faith mistakes and reasonable risk taking will not be punished.

INTERDEPENDENT

S. In the first two years of this change effort, all the easy gains were made. Now, productivity improvements and skill development have both slowed, significantly decreasing the growth in employee income.

A. Your answer may be similar to:
Enter a phase of renewal. Analyze the needs of your internal and external environment and make appropriate changes. Encourage those in the self-directed portion of your organization to become leaders or consultants in other portions of the organization. You may even want to provide entrepreneurial opportunities within the organization, such as offering employee ownership or spinning off independent business units.

INTERDEPENDENT

S. Several of your external customers have resented dealing with team members instead of management. You thought their attitudes would change, but customers continue to call you personally.

A. Your answer may be similar to:
Set up joint meetings in which you can help facilitate the relationship between the customers and the team members. Invite the customers to visit your site and educate them on self-direction.

INTERDEPENDENT

S. The teams have begun to think of themselves as invincible, incapable of making mistakes. They have become isolated from outside information. You fear they are going to make some drastic mistakes.

A. Your answer may be similar to:
Educate them on the dangers of "group think." Expose them to outside information and make sure that the group process contributes to open discussion of all points of view. Re-examine existing measures and their data. Focus on continuous improvement.

INTERDEPENDENT

S. The teams have become satisfied with the improvements so far and are not pushing for continuous improvement.

A. Your answer may be similar to:
Benchmark their performance to other organizations and publish this information. Gather customer feedback data to discover how the teams' services could be improved.

INTERDEPENDENT

S. Because there was so much initial effort put into the organizational design to create self-directed teams, there seems to be significant resistance to redesigning again. People remember how much effort went into the change and how uncomfortable the change process was, and they feel as if they have built the "perfect" organization. Because the environment has changed significantly, they do not see the need to change again.

A. Your answer may be similar to:
When you introduce self-direction and work redesign, you should position it as a never-ending process. Sell the problem again; educate all employees on the changes in the environment that are causing a need to change. Streamline the analytical process, as many are already familiar with the concepts and procedures.

636. Risky Business: Assessing Risk

Goals

- To explore the conditions for and implications of taking risks.

- To learn to assess the level of risk and its impact on decision making.

- To provide an opportunity for groups to identify the risk level of current problems or decisions that require resolution.

Group Size

Twenty to forty participants, preferably from intact work groups, in subgroups of five to ten.

Time Required

Approximately two hours.

Materials

- A copy of the Risky Business Quotations Sheet for each participant.
- A transparency made from the Risky Business Quotation Tally Sheet.
- A copy of the Risky Business Work Sheet for each participant.
- A pencil for each participant.
- A transparency projector and screen and washable transparency markers for the facilitator.
- A flip chart and felt-tipped markers.
- Five prepared flip-chart sheets, each with one of the following headings: "Reward," "Support," "Resources," "Expectations," and "Experience."
- Another flip-chart sheet with the following prepared headings, dividing the page into four parts: (1) Level of Risk Involved; (2) Likelihood of Making a

Mistake; (3) Probable Consequences for Project, Team, or Organization; and (4) Benefits vs. Risk.

- A roll of masking tape.

Physical Setting

A room large enough so that participants can work in groups without disturbing one another.

Process

1. Explain that this session will focus on a team's ability to take risks. Summarize by giving the following background information before continuing.

   People hesitate to take risks to different degrees. Every decision that one makes contains some element of risk, perceived differently by different people. Obviously, some risks are worthwhile; others should be avoided.

   Work teams must also weigh the benefits against the risks when they make decisions. An important factor that must be considered with teams is how well individual members of the team are in alignment in their risk orientation. The organizational environment also plays a large part in a team's willingness to take risks. It follows that organizations that expect individuals and teams to "go the limit" must create an environment that supports and fosters risk taking and that individuals must strive to identify, understand, and accept the level of risk associated with the decisions they must make.

   (Five minutes.)

2. Ask the participants to divide into subgroups of five to ten each, preferably as members of a natural work group.

3. Distribute a pencil and one copy of the Risky Business Quotations Sheet to each participant. Ask participants to select the one quote from the list that best describes their individual philosophy about taking risks and mark it with a "I." Next, ask participants to select the quote that they think best represents the current risk-taking practices of their team as a whole and mark it with a "T." Finally, ask participants to select a quote that best represents what they perceive to be their organization's approach to risk taking and mark it with an "O." Tell them to discuss their choices for a few minutes in the subgroups. (Fifteen minutes.)

4. Record the number of participant responses, by a show of hands, for each quotation, for the Individual, Team, and Organization. Record responses on the Risky Business Quotation Tally Transparency. (Five minutes.)

5. Lead a discussion with the total group by asking the following questions:

   ■ What reasons did you have for choosing particular quotes?

   ■ In general, do the quotes people chose reflect a willingness to take risks or avoid them?

   ■ Can you give some examples of past team or organizational actions or decisions that reflect this view?

   ■ How well do the quotes you chose as individuals mesh with those chosen for your team?

   ■ How well do the quotes you chose for your team reflect the ones chosen for your organization?

   ■ How do you think that this affects how your team approaches risk?

   (Fifteen to twenty minutes.)

6. After the discussion, distribute one copy of the Risky Business Work Sheet to each participant. Announce that the subgroups will have approximately fifteen minutes to discuss the questions on the work sheet and to take notes. (Fifteen minutes.)

7. After the fifteen minutes, call time, reconvene the total group, and discuss each question. Record responses on the appropriate prepared flip-chart sheet as the discussion proceeds, then post the sheet before moving on to the next topic. (Twenty minutes.)

8. Ask the participants to again form into their subgroups and to identify two specific examples of current problems or decisions they are facing that involve some risk. Give them a few minutes, then turn to the final flip chart you prepared. Ask each subgroup to use the chart to identify the following for each example: (1) Level of risk involved; (2) Likelihood of making a mistake; (3) Probable consequences (project, team, organization); (4) Benefits vs. risk. (Thirty minutes.)

9. Reconvene the large group. Ask each subgroup, in turn, to present one of its examples and to share a summary of its discussion. Close the session by asking the following questions:

   ■ What have you learned about your own orientation toward risk?

   ■ What have you learned about the affect that risk can have on teams?

- How can teams learn to take appropriate risks?
- What does your team need to do more of or less of in the future in regard to taking risks?

(Twenty minutes.)

Submitted by Lorraine L. Ukens.

Lorraine L. Ukens, M.S., *is the owner of Team–ing with Success, a consulting and training company specializing in team building and leadership development. She is an adjunct faculty member in the HRD graduate program at Towson University and the author of several training books and games, including* Getting Together: Icebreakers and Group Energizers *(Jossey-Bass/Pfeiffer) and* Working Together: 55 Team Games *(Jossey-Bass/Pfeiffer). She is currently president-elect of the Maryland chapter of ASTD and will serve her term during 1999.*

RISKY BUSINESS QUOTATIONS SHEET

"Just do it."

"Seize the moment."

"Look before you leap."

"Opportunity knocks but once."

"Strike while the iron is hot."

"Nothing ventured, nothing gained."

"Better to be safe than sorry."

"Slow and steady wins the race."

"When in Rome, do as the Romans do."

Risky Business Quotation Tally Sheet

Quotation	Individual	Team	Organization
Just do it.			
Seize the moment.			
Look before you leap.			
Opportunity knocks but once.			
Strike while the iron is hot.			
Nothing ventured, nothing gained.			
Better to be safe than sorry.			
Slow and steady wins the race.			
When in Rome, do as the Romans do.			

The 1999 Annual: Volume 2, Consulting/© 1999 Jossey-Bass/Pfeiffer

RISKY BUSINESS WORK SHEET

REWARD
What is the payoff for taking a risk?

SUPPORT
What backing will the team receive for taking a risk?

RESOURCES
What are the resources required to make taking a risk successful?

EXPECTATIONS
Does the organization assume that this team will take risks?

EXPERIENCE
How has the organization responded to risk taking in the past?

637. GROUP SCULPTURES: ANALYZING AND RESOLVING TEAM PROBLEMS

Goals

- To increase awareness of the advantages and disadvantages of working in teams.
- To identify specific team strengths and weaknesses.
- To generate ideas for improving team performance.

Group Size

Two to six intact work teams. Teams larger than seven members should be divided into subgroups of four to six members each.

Time Required

Approximately two hours.

Materials

- Ten to twenty small novelty items for each team (e.g., corks, play money, pipe cleaners, clay, small rubber animals, balloons, novelty erasers, dice, balls, string, lollipops, crayons, rubber bands, paper clips, small rubber people, small Post-it® Notes).
- One flip chart and felt-tipped markers for each team.
- A copy of the Group Sculptures Lecturette for the facilitator.
- Masking tape for posting the flip-chart paper.

Physical Setting

A room large enough to accommodate all the teams. Each team should have its own table and chairs.

Process

1. Introduce the activity by asking the participants: "From your experience, what would you say are some of the major *advantages* of working in teams?" If necessary offer one or more of the following as examples:

   ■ The ability to pool knowledge.

   ■ The opportunity to consider different perspectives.

   ■ The ability to generate ideas based on others' ideas.

   ■ Increased acceptance of team decisions.

   ■ Increased motivation to implement team decisions.

   ■ Higher quality decisions.

   Write the participants' responses on a flip chart and avoid any detailed discussion. (Ten minutes.)

2. Ask the participants: "Based on your experience, what are some of the major *disadvantages* of working in teams?" If necessary, offer one or more of the following as examples:

   ■ Group decision making consumes more time than individual decision making.

   ■ Perceived status differences can reduce participation.

   ■ Conflict can reduce contributions and satisfaction with the team.

   ■ Pressure can be used to push for conformity.

   ■ Fear of or disinterest in team communication can reduce participation.

   ■ Consensus is difficult to achieve.

   Write the participants' responses on a flip chart and avoid any detailed discussion. (Ten minutes.)

3. Ask the participants to divide into natural work teams. Teams of eight or more should be subdivided into smaller teams of four to six. (Five minutes.)

4. Ask the teams to generate examples of how the different advantages and disadvantages listed earlier might apply to their teams. Ask each team to select a member to record the results of the discussion. Ask the teams to review the results of their discussion and select one example each of the most significant advantage and most significant disadvantage that applies to their team. (Ten minutes.)

5. Ask each team to report to the large group the most significant advantage and disadvantage affecting their team and why they chose it. For example, a team might note that the diverse personalities on their team provide unique perspectives, but that, on the other hand, pressure to conform prevents the team from generating as many creative ideas as they would like. (Five minutes.)

6. Summarize with the Group Sculptures Lecturette. (Five minutes.)

7. Ask each team to brainstorm—while deferring judgment—potential areas of concern or weaknesses within the team. That is, ask them to identify what specific behaviors or processes could be improved (e.g., communication, leadership, decision making, problem solving, team climate). Ask that items listed be as specific as possible. For instance:

■ "Some people are afraid to speak up during group discussions."

■ "Some people don't pull their own weight."

■ "Some team members have misunderstandings when interacting."

Ask each team to select a recorder to list brainstormed items on the flip chart. Ask each team to generate at least five items. Caution team members to avoid evaluating suggested items or criticizing any team member by name. (Ten minutes.)

8. Ask each team to examine the novelty items placed in the center of each table. Explain that their task is to use the items to create a sculpture that represents at least three areas of concern listed on their flip chart. For instance, a team might:

■ Place a cork in a mouth made of clay. ("Some team members are reluctant to speak up.")

■ Use string to tie erasers to some figures and place lollipops next to others. ("Some people don't pull their own weight"—the erasers—"while others do most of the work"—the "suckers," as represented by the lollipops.)

■ Tie a small, inflated balloon to one or more figures. ("Some team members have misunderstandings when interacting" to illustrate how communication can get "blown" out of proportion.)

(Ten minutes.)

9. Ask a representative from each team to describe his or her team's sculpture to the other teams (who are invited to gather around the sculpture being described). (Ten minutes.)

10. Instruct each team to brainstorm silly, exaggerated ways to address the concerns described previously. For instance:

- To increase participation, "Shoot people who don't participate."
- To get people to pull their own weight, "Bribe them."
- To prevent misunderstandings between team members, "Tattoo results of discussions on one another's bodies."

Ask each team to select a recorder to list brainstormed items on the flip chart. (Ten minutes.)

11. Ask each team to try to generate at least one practical idea from each silly or exaggerated idea. A team might transform the above ideas into more practical solutions such as:

- Set participation quotas for each team member (e.g., each member must contribute at least three ideas or comments during each one-hour meeting).

- At various points during a project, team members do a check to evaluate whether contributions seem balanced.

- Prevent misunderstandings by having each team member verbalize his or her understanding of the team's decisions or comments.

(Ten minutes.)

12. Ask representatives from the team to describe their practical ideas to the large group. Ask for any additional suggestions. (Ten minutes.)

13. Conclude the session by asking the following questions:

- What have you learned from this activity?
- What areas does your team expect to improve?
- What steps can you take to ensure that you improve team performance?

(Twenty minutes.)

Variations

- Shorten the activity by deleting Steps 1 through 5, the advantages and disadvantages.

- Use the novelty items as a small team warm-up activity. Instruct the teams (regardless of team membership) to create sculptures describing the organization in general. Each team then (1) describes its sculpture to the large group; (2) creates new sculptures that improve any weaknesses identified; and (3) reports to the large group.

Submitted by Arthur B. VanGundy.

Arthur B. VanGundy, Ph.D., is professor of communication at the University of Oklahoma and president of VanGundy & Associates, a creativity consulting firm. He has over twenty years' experience training teams in creative problem solving and designing and facilitating brainstorming retreats in new product development, marketing, and technical problem resolution. Dr. VanGundy's clients include Hershey Foods Corporation, S.C. Johnson, Monsanto, and the Singapore Civil Service College. He has written ten books, including Brain Boosters for Business Advantage *(Jossey-Bass/Pfeiffer) and* 101 Great Games & Activities *(Jossey-Bass/Pfeiffer).*

Group Sculptures Lecturette

As is true of individuals, teams have strengths and weaknesses. Some teams have more awareness of their strengths and weaknesses than do others. It is especially difficult for team members to be aware of these because they are so close to the situation.

Sometimes, team-development activities such as team-generated sculptures can increase the team members' awareness. Symbolic structures and relationships can help teams identify their weaknesses in a nonthreatening way. Once weaknesses have been identified, the door is open for ideas and actions to improve team effectiveness.

The sculpture activity we will do here is designed to help your team evaluate its performance and consider ways to make improvements. Before starting, here are a few key terms you might want to consider when evaluating your own team. In general, effective teams excel at the following:

- *Problem Solving:* Analyzing problems and overcoming obstacles to achieving goals.

- *Decision Making:* Generating and selecting decision criteria and applying these criteria to multiple alternatives.

- *Communication:* Sending and receiving verbal and nonverbal messages, assigning and interpreting meaning effectively, and using timely and appropriate feedback.

- *Listening:* Selecting, noticing, understanding, and evaluating messages.

- *Conflict Management:* Clarifying misunderstandings, uncovering conflicting goals, achieving creative management, or resolving conflicts.

- *Goal Setting:* Establishing clearly defined goals supported by all team members.

- *Planning:* Developing plans to achieve goals and putting them into action.

638. Press Conference: Improving Communications During Change Initiatives

Goals

- To improve communication and buy-in during times of organizational change.

- To provide leaders with an opportunity to deepen alignment during a change effort.

Group Size

Any size intact work group from an organization undergoing change with its leader, who is your "client" for this process. (Also can be conducted via teleconference.)

Time Required

One and one-half to two hours.

Materials

- A copy of the Press Conference Facilitator's Role Sheet for the facilitator.

- A copy of the Press Conference Ground Rules Sheet for the leader or client.

- Audiovisual equipment for the initial presentation, if needed.

- 3" x 5" index cards, at least ten per participant.

- Paper and one pen or pencil per participant.

- A flip chart and felt-tipped markers.

Physical Setting

Any.

Process

1. Prior to the session, read the Press Conference Facilitator's Role Sheet carefully and decide what you will do if any of the situations come up. Try to anticipate questions, given the organization in question.

2. In advance of the session, agree on or modify with the group's leader the Press Conference Ground Rules Sheet. Also agree on the amount of time to be devoted to the questioning process.

3. After the leader understands and has agreed with the ground rules, privately coach him or her on how to introduce the approach and ground rules to the participants. To the degree possible, the leader should describe the format to the participants and should introduce the facilitator, signaling that he or she will willingly engage in the process and has retained the facilitator for support and advice.

4. Help the leader to prepare a personal statement such as, "I am hoping you will take full advantage of this opportunity because I really do want everyone to clearly understand the situation we are facing together." (Ten minutes.)

5. The leader's presentation should be brief, usually 10 to 12 minutes. If there are questions from participants, explain that the questions and answers during the press conference will help them to fill in any gaps. (Ten to fifteen minutes.)

6. After the leader presents his or her personal statement, have him or her review the next steps, asking for full participation and reassuring employees that they can raise any issues that might be puzzling or troubling them.

7. Hand out ten 3" x 5" index cards and a pencil or pen to each participant. Ask the leader to leave the room while the group prepares questions. This signals that participants are free to discuss any ideas with one another and that there are no restrictions on what questions can be asked.

8. Divide the participants into subgroups of four to six members each. Tell the subgroups that they may discuss what they would like to know for awhile and then generate questions collectively or simply generate questions individually and then compare questions, discarding those that are redundant. Remind participants that they may pose any questions they wish for their leader. Tell them they will have thirty minutes to generate questions, and ask each subgroup to elect a spokesperson to read the questions generated by that subgroup.

9. At the end of twenty-five minutes, ask each group to prioritize its questions. (This is helpful if time runs out.) (Thirty minutes.)

10. When the groups are ready, invite the leader back into the room.

11. Review the role that you will be playing during the process. Answer any questions or concerns people may have.

12. Have spokespeople ask questions using a round-robin approach, in which each subgroup in turn asks one question. Tell participants to listen closely to all questions and responses. Continue the round-robin questioning until the previously announced time limit has been reached or the group appears satisfied. This may happen before all questions have been answered. If this is so, ask each group to identify one final question. (Thirty to fifty minutes.)

13. After the last question from each group has been answered, ask the following questions:

   ■ What was most surprising to you during this process?

   ■ What affect will this press conference have on your organization?

   ■ How will the information you have heard affect your future actions?

   (Ten minutes.)

14. Ask the leader to make a few concluding remarks and thank everyone for their candor and openness in addressing issues. (Five minutes.)

Variations

■ Questions may be given to the facilitator to be read anonymously.

■ You may wish to conduct several of these activities for follow-up:

   ■ Meet with the leader to probe his or her satisfaction with the session.

   ■ Explore employee feelings with the leader.

   ■ Help the leader find ways to reply to any questions left unanswered.

   ■ Meet with employees to understand their reactions to the session.

   ■ Present the leader with feedback about his or her delivery and answers.

   ■ Conduct a formal evaluation to determine whether the session had the desired impact.

   ■ Identify other interventions to help this group with the change confronting them.

- Modify the press conference format for future use with the same group.

- Plan another press conference periodically.

- For especially broad or important topics, the press conference may be hosted by a panel of the organization's leaders. Typically only one would deliver the presentation, but then all would contribute to answering the participants' questions.

- The press conference format can be used whenever an organizational change warrants it. Possible situations include technological change, competitor threats, strategic change, restructuring, downsizing, reengineering, cultural change, acquisitions, or organizational crises. The format can also be applied during the normal course of business to address the ongoing issues, concerns, questions, and information needs of employees at all levels directly.

- In order to create a sense of accomplishment, the facilitator may want to experiment with some type of tracking system that shows the progress being made on issues that are brought out. For example, a flip chart or wall surface can be used to post the index cards that have been addressed, as a way of visually depicting progress. As a variation, the flip chart can be divided into two columns, one for questions addressed satisfactorily and the other for questions requiring follow-up.

Submitted by Gary Schuman and Andy Beaulieu.

Gary Schuman, Ph.D., is a consulting psychologist and president of CDL Consulting, Inc., a human resource consulting and training firm with offices in Baltimore, Maryland, and Washington, D.C. Dr. Schuman helps organizations create practical, hands-on strategies for designing and implementing large-scale change efforts and developing and empowering the workforce. His particular expertise is in coaching and employee development, change management, senior-level team building, and customer service. Dr. Schuman has worked extensively in organizations as diverse as Aetna Insurance, Apple Computer, Fidelity Investments, The Gap, Hallmark Cards, Lockheed-Martin, and MTV. Dr. Schuman received a Ph.D. in counseling psychology from Florida State University.

Andy Beaulieu is founder and president of Results for a Change, a Washington, D.C.-based consulting firm that specializes in using rapid-cycle improvement projects to change culture and systems, build client confidence, develop key skills, and produce concrete gains. Mr. Beaulieu also facilitates process improvement, develops teams, and provides other OD consultation. He has consulted to organizations such as Fidelity Investments, Showtime Networks, World Bank, Volvo of North America, USF&G Insurance, American Airlines, Veteran's Administration hospitals, NAS-DAQ, and British Petroleum.

Press Conference Facilitator's Role Sheet

Your role, both before and during the press conference, is to help the organization achieve greater trust through open, honest, complete communication between leader and followers.

Coaching the Leader

Because many leaders are unaccustomed to the rigor of group questioning, work with the leader in advance of the session to determine desired outcomes, ground rules, and format for the session; to anticipate the kinds of questions that may be generated by various factions; and to consider alternative responses that truly address the issues. The leader's success is essential to a good outcome for the session.

Contracting with the Leader

As with any other OD intervention, you as the facilitator must understand the objectives, style, and limitations of the leader. Your "contracting" with the leader will affect the way in which the activity is positioned, designed, and implemented.

Facilitating the Question-and-Answer Period

Your role during the question-and-answer phase is key. Listen closely to the questions and answers, being on the lookout for the following dynamics:

- The leader skirts the issue.
- The leader inadvertently answers a different question from the one asked.
- The leader's answer is misinterpreted.
- The participants debate or challenge the leader's reply.
- The leader becomes defensive.
- The answer has implications that should be probed further.
- The audience is no longer interested in a particular question or line of questioning, but the leader is still talking about it.

If any of these occur, intervene to keep the process on track and productive. Intervention can take the form of helping to redirect or clarify an answer or probing for other implications or answers.

In addition, you may want to "take the pulse" of the audience, using queries such as, "Is this working well for everyone?," "Should we pick up the pace?," or "Are you receiving the type of information you are seeking?"

PRESS CONFERENCE GROUND RULES SHEET

- Any question is legitimate.

- If the leader is asked a question that he or she is not sure how to answer or that involves on-the-spot policy making, the leader has the option to say, "Great question, but let me think about it!" It is then the leader's obligation to keep track of the issue and get back to the group in a timely manner.

- The leader should attempt to answer each question succinctly and directly. If the issue remains open, the leader can describe the key alternatives that are still under consideration.

- During the questioning, the facilitator may interject to push for greater clarity. The leader should view this behavior not as challenging, but as helpful toward achieving greater understanding.

- If the group is asking only "soft" questions, the facilitator (and/or leader) may confront the group to go beyond the superficial and "safe" topics to the more challenging issues that are probably on everyone's minds.

639. COLLECTING DIAGNOSTIC DATA: WHICH METHOD TO USE?

Goals

- To familiarize the participants with various approaches to collecting diagnostic data.

- To allow the participants to practice selecting the appropriate data-collection method.

Group Size

One to five subgroups of three to six members each.

Time Required

One and one-half to two and one-half hours, depending on the size of the group.

Materials

- One copy of the Collecting Diagnostic Data Collection Methods Sheet for each participant.

- One copy of the Collecting Diagnostic Data Questions Sheet for each participant.

- One copy of the Collecting Diagnostic Data Cases Sheet for each participant.

- One copy of the Collecting Diagnostic Data Answer Sheet for each participant.

- A flip chart and felt-tipped markers in assorted colors for each subgroup.

Physical Setting

A room large enough that participants can meet together and separate into subgroups without disturbing one another.

Process

1. Explain the role of data collection in the consulting process.

2. Distribute the Collecting Diagnostic Data Collection Methods Sheet as a reference and briefly review each method. (Ten minutes.)

3. Divide the total group into subgroups of three to five members each.

4. Tell the subgroups the purpose of the activity. Distribute and review the Collecting Diagnostic Data Questions Sheet with the group. Explain that the subgroups will use the questions to resolve several cases.

5. Distribute the Collecting Diagnostic Data Cases Sheet to the subgroups. Assign each subgroup one or two different cases and ask them to answer the case questions. Tell the subgroups that they will have thirty minutes in which to answer the questions for each case. Ask each subgroup to post its answers on a flip-chart sheet. Monitor the time and check to see if any subgroups need help. If you have assigned two cases, provide a signal at the half-time point. (Thirty to sixty minutes.)

6. Reconvene the large group and have each subgroup present a summary of each case and the subgroup's responses to the questions. (Thirty to fifty minutes.)

7. Lead a concluding discussion, reviewing the types of data-collection methods identified. Ask the groups:

   - Why was each data-gathering method chosen?
   - Do all of you agree that it was the best choice? Why or why not?
   - What are the pros and cons of the chosen data-collection method?
   - What is the most important thing you have learned about data collection today?

   (Twenty minutes.)

8. *Optional:* Distribute the Collecting Diagnostic Data Answer Sheet if you wish. (Ten to fifteen minutes.)

Variations

- The participants can be asked to provide cases from their own experiences.
- All subgroups can be given the same case or same set of cases. Each subgroup then presents its approach to gathering the data and the subgroups debate the best approach.
- The subgroups can be permitted to choose the case(s) they wish to work on.

Submitted by Homer H. Johnson and Sander J. Smiles.

Homer H. Johnson, Ph.D., is a professor in the Center for Organization Development at Loyola University in Chicago, where he teaches and consults in the areas of continuous improvement, strategic planning, change management, and consulting skills. He is the co-author (with Sander Smiles) of the forthcoming Consulting Skills Fieldbook.

Sander J. Smiles, M.S.O.D., is a senior consultant in the organizational effectiveness practice area of Baxter Institute, an internal consulting group for Baxter Health Care, where he consults in the areas of strategic planning, organizational design, innovation management, and Kaizen methods.

COLLECTING DIAGNOSTIC DATA COLLECTION METHODS SHEET

The one caveat for any data-collection method is that "one point does not make a straight line or trend." Using more than one data-collection technique will enable both consultant and client to be much more confident about the conclusions that are reached.

The following are the most typical methods of collecting data.

Interviews (Individual or Group)

One of the best tools for gathering data is simply to talk to people. Interviews take time, but are one of the consultant's best sources of information. Talking to people allows a consultant to solicit information about how people feel about their work, their organization, and the barriers and opportunities they perceive. Interviews are crucial when the consultant's goal is to help individuals or groups learn more about themselves and how effectively they are working. The interview is also the best data-collection method when some of the questions may require clarification, when some of the answers (responses) may have to be explained, when the consultant does not know all of the issues (so cannot design a data-collection instrument around them), and when the consultant may want to pursue topics further as they come up.

No matter what the type of interview (face to face, focus group, or telephone), determining whom to interview is a critical step. If you cannot interview all of a target population, it is important to interview a representative cross-section of that population.

The interview should be free of interruption. The person(s) being interviewed should be put at ease so that more information (and more honest information) will be offered. The procedure and norms should be explained, and permission should be obtained if the interview is to be recorded. The interviewer should ask neutral, open-ended questions as much as possible to avoid "leading the witness" and to allow the respondent to explain the answers. Less complicated and less threatening questions should be asked first. The interviewer must be careful to remain objective and consistent from one interview to the next. Scheduling many interviews back-to-back can be tiring and confusing and can diminish the interviewer's objectivity. Using prepared scripts can help to ensure standardization of multiple interviews.

Taking notes, in the respondents' own words, on standardized forms can help to ensure accuracy of the data. The interviewer also should watch for nonverbal cues that may need to be followed up. Active listening also can help to elicit more information.

After the interviews, the collected data is tabulated and reported in some way to the respondents. If it is group data, it is generally discussed with the group, which often is given an opportunity to decide whether or not the data make sense.

Surveys, Questionnaires, and Rating Scales

When a consultant needs information about a large population or widely dispersed group, and when the specific issues or topics to be explored are known, instruments such as surveys, questionnaires, or rating scales can be very useful. They are the least expensive forms of information gathering.

Developing questionnaires that will obtain accurate and consistent answers is a science. The consultant must be sure that the questions asked will yield the information being sought. Survey questions should not be ambiguous or confusing. They should not be presented in a biased way. The items or questions also should be written in a way that does not indicate "social desirability," so that the respondents will answer honestly, not the way that they think they "should." No item should present more than one actual thing to be rated or ask more than one actual question. Closed-ended questions limit the responses; if the respondent must select from multiple categories, include an "other" category and ask for specifics. Finally, the items or questions must be constructed in such a way that the responses are able to be tabulated and assessed in order to yield useful data.

Testing a draft questionnaire or pilot survey with several people prior to using it with the target population is important. The test-run responses can be analyzed, and unclear items, inconsistencies, perceived bias, and other defects can be corrected before the instrument is presented to the target audience.

Direct Observation

Observing people while they actually work can be very revealing. If the consultant has been asked to analyze specific jobs or to monitor how different groups interact, direct observation can be useful. Observations can be made in the work setting or in a laboratory setting (simulation). The consultant must remain objective and consistent in documenting the observations. The consultant also must remember that the act of observation can influence the behavior of the people being observed.

Documents or Records

Reviewing formal publications, press releases, correspondence, and reports often can reveal how a company or department is working or what its values are. If the consultant has a lot of time or needs information that is only accessible from the past, this method may be helpful, but because this method takes so much time, the consultant must be clear about what information is being sought. Without a clear objective, the search can be overwhelming.

Information-System Reports or Statistics

Computers increase the amount of data and statistics available in organizations. As performance indicators, metrics are a key aspect of today's management climate. The consultant may even be able to design performance metrics from already existing data. The information can be graphically represented, and trends or specific issues can be highlighted. A consultant may be asked to determine why performance is declining; metrics are a key aspect of that analysis. The consultant must be careful to understand what the data actually represent and to verify reliability and accuracy. Knowing how the data originally were collected can be crucial.

Process Mapping

The technique of visually representing a system with different types of symbols is called process mapping. Consultants often use this technique when they want to understand a complex system and how the different parts of the system interact. The consultant must be careful to have a good understanding of the system or be working with someone who does if a process map is to be accurate. A process map is just a one-dimensional picture of a system, so the consultant must keep in mind the people, structure, and relationships that lie behind the map.

Simulations

Simulations are forms of observation in an artificial setting or set of circumstances. The consultant may be testing a new process or assessing how potential candidates handle different aspects of a particular job. Simulations must truly reflect the conditions they represent or the data obtained will be meaningless. Observer objectivity must be maintained in simulations. Observers must be trained so that they are consistent and have agreed-on standards and definitions of what is being observed.

Personal Diaries

Individuals can be asked to keep personal logs of the events they are experiencing and the meanings they attach to those events. In the hands of a trained observer, this information can reveal patterns of behavior or trends in a group that are not detectable by other methods. This information is subjective and time-consuming to produce and read. The consultant's training in this area is critical to the use of this technique.

Critical-Incident Technique

Critical incidents are reports or descriptions of things that people in a group report having done or having been observed doing by others. Often, groups and/or individuals are unable to specify accurately why something is not working. Critical-incident reports have been found to be quite useful in enabling people to reconstruct specific events or to describe certain processes. If a consultant is asked to identify high-performance behavior or optimum ways of doing specific tasks, this technique is very useful. The key to its success is to identify the right people to be interviewed and to recognize that these incidents are facts or specific reports of observed behavior from qualified sources, not opinions.

COLLECTING DIAGNOSTIC DATA QUESTIONS SHEET

1. What is the purpose of the proposed assessment/study? What problem are we trying to solve? What is the desired outcome of the study?

_____

_____

_____

_____

_____

_____

_____

2. What information do we need to solve this problem? What do we want to know?

_____

_____

_____

_____

_____

_____

_____

3. How will we collect the data? What data-gathering method will be used?

_____

_____

_____

_____

_____

_____

COLLECTING DIAGNOSTIC DATA CASES SHEET

Instructions: Answer the questions from your Collecting Diagnostic Data Questions Sheet for each of the cases below that was assigned to your subgroup. In particular, decide what methods of data collection would be best in each case and the pros and cons involved. You will have thirty minutes for each assigned case. Post your answers on the flip chart.

1. There have been numerous complaints from customers of Company A that their orders are not being delivered on the date promised, that it takes too long to receive orders, and that frequently there are errors in the order. Reportedly, the Customer Service Department has kept a record of the complaints received.

2. Several employees at Company B have complained to the Human Resources Manager that their boss is a tyrant who is insensitive to the ideas of others, frequently "puts down" employees, and occasionally swears at employees.

3. Company C recently acquired Company X. The two companies have very different cultures. Company C wants a smooth transition into one company, but is concerned about a possible "culture clash." The president of Company C wants you to help with the transition, but wants you to understand and be sensitive to the different cultures.

4. Company D has experienced explosive growth. It now has 3,000 employees in fourteen locations and wants to be an "employee friendly" organization. Executives want to know how employees feel about the company and to answer the question: "Is this a good place to work?"

5. There have been numerous complaints about the alleged unfairness of the pay scale at Company E. People with similar responsibilities are being paid different rates. The pay scale seems to be somewhat arbitrary and depends on how much clout your boss has with those higher up in the organization.

6. The New-Product Development Group at Company F wants assistance in determining what types of new products and services should be given priority.

7. Company G, a distribution company, sells a large variety of products to a large variety of retailers. Overall sales have been declining, and the company marketing department executives question whether it should be more selective in targeting its products or customers.

8. Company H, a manufacturing company, has been plagued with the overfilling of aerosol cans for one of its products. The pounds per square inch of the filled cans occasionally are at a dangerously high level, and the production department supervisor fears that an accident might result.

COLLECTING DIAGNOSTIC DATA ANSWER SHEET

1. First, the consultant to Company A would want to collect details regarding the nature and frequency of the complaints. The case indicates that the complaints are well documented by the Customer Service Department. A good starting point would be to look at their records and identify the major problems. Next, the consultant would take one or two of the major complaints, determine the cause, and then take steps to eliminate the problem.

2. The consultant to Company B would want to start with individual interviews with the employees in the unit with problems to determine (and document) more specifically the nature of the boss's behavior, the frequency of each occurrence, and the number of employees who have been targets of his or her inappropriate behavior. This process would document the problem and provide information on which recommendations for corrective action could be based.

3. The consultant to Company C has several possible courses of action. Some consultants might conduct a survey of a sample of employees of both companies, using a cultural questionnaire. Another approach would be to conduct focus groups with the employees in each company to find out what it is like to work in each company, as well as to find out what policies or behaviors are important to the employees. The consultant also could observe behavior, for example, how people dress, how meetings are conducted, how formal people are in their interactions, etc. The exact method selected should be based on what the consultant wants to find out about the two cultures.

4. Company D seems to present an ideal case for a survey. There are a large number of employees in several locations, and the consultant wants to solicit their perceptions about the company. Several excellent job-satisfaction questionnaires are available. The human resources manager at each location could supervise the administration of such a questionnaire.

5. Company E's problem probably requires two approaches. The consultant can use interviews or focus groups to identify more specifically the nature of the perceived unfairness in the pay scale. Depending on the information gathered by these methods, it would be important to examine company records to determine if, in fact, there is an actual basis for the allegations.

6. Two common techniques for answering Company F's questions are interviews and focus groups with present customers, potential customers, and salespeople. The consultant can probe in depth what customers like about the company's current products, how the products might be improved, what customer problems require a solution, and what new products would be of interest to the customers.

7. The consultant should look at Company G's sales records to determine which products are doing well and which products are doing poorly. Also of interest are which types of customers show strong buying habits and which are no longer buying products. The consultant might also look at the future market potential of various products sold by the company.

8. A good approach would be to diagram Company H's can-filling process and determine (with a cause-and-effect diagram) where and what the likely causes of the problem are. Then the consultant and client could test each possible cause to see which is the actual cause.

640. A New Twist: Using Symbols To Introduce a Topic

Goals

- To introduce the topic of a training session and to stimulate thought about that topic.

- To allow participants to create tangible symbols of their perspectives of the topic.

- To encourage dialogue and participation.

Group Size

Six to twenty participants. However, a larger group may be accommodated by adding extra time for more participants to describe their creations.

This activity is most effective as an introduction to a training session on a new topic.

Time Required

Thirty-five to forty-five minutes.

Materials

- Three different-colored, 10-inch pipe cleaners for each participant.

- A flip-chart page displaying a question or statement concerning the session topic (see Process, Step 1).

- A flip chart and markers or an overhead projector with blank transparencies and markers.

- Masking tape for posting.

Physical Setting

A room large enough to allow participants to see one another's creations and hear them described. Moveable chairs should be provided.

Process

1. Prior to the activity, draft the topical question or statement that the participants will be asked to symbolize with their pipe cleaners and ultimately describe to the rest of the group. Make sure that the question or statement links closely to the learning objectives for the session. Write the final question or statement on flip-chart paper so that it can be posted during the activity. For example, a group that is examining the mission of an organization for the purpose of improving product quality and customer satisfaction might be given this statement: "Use your pipe cleaners to create a symbol of your company's major product and the various internal forces that contribute to the successful manufacturing and/or marketing of this product." This statement requires the participants to begin thinking about what it takes to create a product that sells.

   Another example might be more applicable to a training session. Here the training topic (say Total Quality Leadership) might be the object of the statement. In this event, the participants might be asked to "Create a symbol of what you understand Total Quality Leadership to be." Again, you will receive a variety of perspectives that will open discussion and be valuable to understand how each person perceives the topic.

2. Just prior to the participants' arrival, place a set of three pipe cleaners at each person's seat.

3. Introduce the posted statement and explain the task. Elicit and answer questions. Let the participants know that you will be asking for volunteers to share their completed creations with the rest of the group, but that no one will be compelled to share. Tell the participants that they have ten minutes to complete their creations and then ask them to begin. Note that the statement should remain posted throughout the activity. Give the group five to seven minutes to think and create individually. Some will be pretty quick; others will need incubation time. (Ten minutes.)

4. After ten minutes tell the participants to stop working. Ask for volunteers to show and describe their creations as well as the rationales for those creations. Choose several participants and encourage them to keep their comments to two minutes. After each presentation clarify remarks, entertain questions, and provide positive reinforcement. Do not discourage people from continuing to create as others are sharing. (Fifteen to twenty minutes—three or four minutes per presentation.)

5. Using the following questions, encourage the participants to comment on their experience of the activity.

- How did you react to the task?
- What were your thoughts and feelings as you worked?
- What themes came out in the creations?
- What were the similarities?
- What were the differences?
- What can you conclude about the session topic after completing your own creation and viewing other people's creations?
- How does your own creation illustrate what you hope will happen during the session?
- What might this activity forecast for the rest of the session?

Capture major points and themes on the flip chart. Leave these posted throughout the session and draw from them to help participants connect to the topic and goals of the training session. (Ten to fifteen minutes.)

Variations

- Participants may be encouraged to refine their creations or to make new ones during the course of the session as learning occurs or viewpoints evolve. A periodic check with a participant who demonstrates such actions might lead to a worthwhile discussion.

- The original or altered creations may be used at the end of the session to review what the participants have learned.

- If you are working with an intact team or group, tell the leader about the activity prior to the session. When you are establishing the objectives, agenda, participant/facilitator roles, and other necessary agreements, the leader should be given an understanding of the activity. The leader's response to this activity in the group setting is critical to the success of the activity. If the leader is quick to pick up the pipe cleaners and go to work, others will usually follow.

Submitted by Garland F. Skinner.

Garland F. Skinner, a career naval officer and former CEO of a major industrial organization, is a trainer and consultant on leadership issues. He specializes in strategic planning and customized interventions with top managers. For six years he conducted the Senior Leaders Seminar for the Department of the Navy, addressing the leadership aspects of total quality. In that capacity he advised over 3,000 top naval officers and federal employees. As a private consultant and trainer, he has worked with a variety of organizations in both the private and public sectors. He is a former member of the board of directors for the United States Senate Productivity and Quality Award for Virginia and a member of ASQ.

641. IF YOU THINK YOU CAN: EXPLORING CORPORATE ATTITUDES

Goals

- To increase understanding of how managers,' supervisors,' or leaders' actions affect employee attitudes.

- To increase awareness of ways in which actions taken or not taken impact employees and company culture.

- To illustrate that the same actions can have different effects on different people.

- To inspire participants to change behaviors that may cause negative attitudes in the workplace.

Group Size

Twenty to twenty-eight participants from supervisory positions in five to seven subgroups of three to four each.

Time Required

Approximately one and one-half hours.

Materials

- An overhead transparency of the If You Think You Can Quote.
- A copy of the If You Think You Can Lecturette for the facilitator.
- A copy of one of the If You Think You Can Situation Sheets for each subgroup.
- A copy of the If You Think You Can Discussion Starters Sheet for the facilitator.

- Paper and a pencil for each participant.
- An overhead projector.

Physical Setting

A room large enough so that all subgroups can work at tables without disturbing one another.

Process

1. Show the If You Think You Can Quote while you deliver the If You Think You Can Lecturette. (Five minutes.)

2. Assign participants to subgroups of three to four members each. Give each subgroup a copy of one of the If You Think You Can Situation Sheets.

3. Tell the participants to read the situation sheets carefully and determine how their potential responses could impact the employee's attitude in each case. (Twenty-five minutes.)

4. Reconvene the entire group. Ask each group in turn to share its situation and potential impact briefly. (Twenty-five minutes.)

5. Wrap up the discussion with the following questions:

   - How similar were these situations and responses to your own workplace experience?

   - What do you think impacts workplace attitude the most?

   - How does employee attitude create organizational culture?

   - What have you learned from this activity?

   - What will you do differently at work as a result of this experience?

   (Twenty-five minutes.)

6. Display the If You Think You Can Quote transparency again and ask, "How does this quote relate to our discussion?"

7. Summarize by saying, "Attitudes and beliefs about what is important to an organization are caused by what management does and does not act on. Employees learn what is important to their own well being by watching what their managers do. Company culture is the sum total of individual attitudes."

Variations

- Each subgroup can be assigned more than one situation if time permits.
- The activity can be tailored to the needs of any group by selecting fewer situations or adding your own.
- The group can be asked to identify actual situations and discuss their impact on their workplace.

Submitted by Eugene Taurman.

Eugene Taurman is an organization development consultant helping companies that want to adopt a continuous improvement culture. His emphasis is on driving high levels of improvement and employee engagement through continuous improvement. Mr. Taurman studied the new wave of management concepts in Japan, then applied that knowledge in a U.S. technical manufacturing company and has been helping others for ten years.

IF YOU THINK YOU CAN QUOTE*

"Attitude is more important than the past,
than education, than money, than circumstances, than what other people think or
say or do. It is more important than appearance, giftedness, or skill. It will make
or break a company, a church or a home."

—*Charles Swindoll*

---

*Charles Swindoll. *Strengthening Your Grip.* (1990). World Book Publishing.

IF YOU THINK YOU CAN LECTURETTE

A trucking company billboard states, "Attitude is everything!" That seems right. After all, Henry Ford said, "If you think you can, you're probably right. If you think you can't, you're probably right."

Given that attitude is so important, it should be at the top of every manager's list to mold appropriate employee attitudes. Managers often complain about their employees' poor attitudes, but do not know what to do. They may say, "If only employees had a better attitude!," "If only they were motivated!," or "The problem around here is attitude!" They talk as if they have nothing to do with those negative employee attitudes. After all, isn't attitude developed through people's life experiences?

But attitude is not just something that employees develop on their own. Many times, bad or inappropriate attitudes on the job can be attributed directly to company policy or to managers' actions or lack of them. Although genetics, past experiences, and one's home life may play a part, experiences on the job contribute the most to workplace attitudes. Managers have an opportunity to influence employees forty hours a week. It follows that if indeed "attitude is everything," managers at all levels should accept some of the responsibility for creating the "right" attitude in the organization. It also follows that they must learn how their own actions and those of their predecessors have created the prevailing attitudes that they may wish to change.

What types of work experiences influence employee attitudes? The answer is *all* of them. Everything that happens to an employee at work affects his or her attitude in some way. Any negative incident will have a small impact, but if there is widespread negativity, it can cause a company-wide "bad" attitude.

Company culture is the sum of all employees' attitudes and the actions or responses of employees to each situation as it comes up. Workforce attitudes and beliefs about what is important to an organization and about what is required for personal success within the organization are heavily influenced by managers,' supervisors,' and other leaders' actions or lack of them.

The activity we will do next will help you see some possible ways you as a supervisor influence employee attitudes and perhaps unintentionally contribute to a negative company culture.

IF YOU THINK YOU CAN SITUATION SHEET 1

Instructions: Read the situation described below and the potential responses the manager could make. Then determine how each response could impact employee attitudes.

Helpful Sue

Sue gave her boss an idea she had come up with for solving a chronic and frustrating problem.

Potential Responses

- "I'm too busy now, tell me later."
- "That won't work."
- "We tried that before."
- Took the idea to his boss and did not give Sue credit.
- Listened, but did not act.
- "Good idea, let's see if we can make it work."
- "Let's discuss it at our next department meeting."
- "We tried something like that and got (these) results. Do you have a new angle? Are things different now?"

Impact on employee attitude:

IF YOU THINK YOU CAN SITUATION SHEET 2

Instructions: Read the situation described below and the potential responses the manager could make. Then determine how each response could impact employee attitudes.

Troubled John

John found a bad part. He took the part and some ideas about how to solve the problem to his boss.

Potential Responses

- "You dummy! You ought to be fired for that!"
- "Gee, thanks! Now let's get rid of it."
- No response.
- "Let's see if we can find the causes so we won't make any more bad parts."
- "Do you have any ideas about how to solve the problem?"

Impact on employee attitude:

IF YOU THINK YOU CAN SITUATION SHEET 3

Instructions: Read the situation described below and the potential responses the manager could make. Then determine how each response could impact employee attitudes.

Chatty Cathy

Chatty Cathy lacks focus, cannot seem to stay on task, and asks the same questions again and again. She takes longer than others to do her tasks and yet is always ready to clock out early. She seems overly familiar with her boss and co-workers. Cathy is often late and has countless excuses for her poor performance and short hours.

Potential Responses

- The boss ignores the situation.
- The boss has a discussion with Cathy about expectations and then ignores the next problem that comes up.
- The boss makes changes in assignments to accommodate Cathy.
- Cathy is dismissed.

Impact on other employees' attitudes:

IF YOU THINK YOU CAN SITUATION SHEET 4

Instructions: Read the situation described below and the potential responses the manager could make. Then determine how each response could impact employee attitudes.

Pedro Tried

Pedro was assigned a job he did not know how to do. He told the boss, who said, "Go ahead and try anyway." He tried valiantly but without success.

Potential Responses

- "Let's get you some help so you can learn how to do this."
- "What are you doing? Don't you know better than that?"
- No response. Boss ignores the problem and allows Pedro to struggle.

Impact on employee attitude:

If You Think You Can Situation Sheet 5

Instructions: Read the situation described below and the potential responses the manager could make. Then determine how each response could impact employee attitudes.

Watchful Wanda

Wanda, a new employee, watches a senior employee chat on the phone with a friend while a customer is kept waiting.

Potential Responses

- The boss steps in and waits on the customer.
- Wanda's boss sharply reprimands the senior employee in front of the customer.
- Wanda's boss calls the senior employee aside to remind her of her responsibilities to customers.
- None. The senior employee's behavior is allowed to continue.

Impact on employee attitude:

IF YOU THINK YOU CAN SITUATION SHEET 6

Instructions: Read the situation described below and the potential responses the manager could make. Then determine how each response could impact employee attitudes.

Joe Antidote

Joe responds by working feverishly to resolve a problem with some bad parts that was caused by a mistake he made. He reworks the parts to meet the customer's delivery date, often working overtime. He receives regular visits from his boss and provides reports on his progress to the boss.

Potential Responses

■ The boss discusses the situation with Joe in private and clarifies what Joe has learned.

■ The boss pats Joe on the back and allows him to work overtime to make up for any mistakes he makes in the future. This is observed by others who rarely have problems, rarely work overtime, and complete their work on time.

■ The boss openly discusses the problem Joe had as a learning experience for all.

Impact on employee attitude:

IF YOU THINK YOU CAN SITUATION SHEET 7

Instructions: Read the situation described below and the potential responses the manager could make. Then determine how each response could impact employee attitudes.

Sue Ling Worries

Sue Ling, a supervisor, regularly has to work on inappropriate jobs that have been accepted by the company sales department, that is, jobs that cannot be completed efficiently with the equipment available. Sue Ling tells her boss about the situation.

Potential Responses

- No change occurs.
- "You're right, I'll talk to the sales force right away." (But no action is forthcoming.)
- "We have to get more efficient around here."
- "Let's all get together and see whether there is a way we could handle this type of job in the future."

Impact on employee attitude:

If You Think You Can Discussion Starters Sheet

Helpful Sue

When a supervisor's response to an employee's idea is perceived as lack of interest or a put down, the worker may feel inadequate. An idea is part of a person. If a manager has no time to listen or discuss, then the message is that the person is not worth much.

If a boss takes credit for an employee's idea, mistrust results. Submitting an idea is an important step for a worker. It engages the person's mind and heart. Working together with a manager promotes more ideas and helps the worker grow in the job, feel appreciated, and feel good about himself or herself and the company.

Troubled John

If the supervisor shows anger, John may start hiding bad parts. However, the second, more casual response or ignoring the problem could signal to John that bad parts are okay with his supervisor. Searching for causes tells John that the company is concerned with quality and that he should strive to make good parts. The last possible response shows John that his opinions matter to his manager and may help him feel better about the company.

Chatty Cathy

In this case, the manager's reactions to Cathy's behavior on the job send a signal not only to Cathy but to other workers as well, defining acceptable behavior on the job. Workers will make assumptions about the company's values and about what they can do themselves.

If the boss ignores the situation, it sends the signal that poor behavior will be tolerated. Good workers may feel demoralized and others will take advantage of the lax rules. Cathy's co-workers who are picking up the slack for her will feel overworked, frustrated, and less likely to cooperate with her or their supervisor.

If, however, Cathy is dismissed, other workers are likely to have more respect for their manager and feel better about doing their best for the company.

Pedro Tried

A worker's response to new challenges in the future depends on how his or her supervisor handles initial failure. People who are ignored by their supervisors when they are having problems are unlikely to try new tasks in the future. Workers who are criticized for failure when trying something new (or who observe that others are) may feel insecure and be overly cautious in the future. The person who was criticized may feel resentful and sabotage his or her supervisor and the company. Supervisors determine whether failure is seen as something to learn from or something to be avoided at all cost.

Watchful Wanda

If the supervisor takes no action and allows bad behavior to continue, Wanda (and others) will tend to do the same themselves, even if they do not necessarily approve. They may eventually repeat the behavior, only to be reprimanded or fired themselves. Other employees learn whether the customer is important to the company and whether embarrassing an employee is okay by observing the supervisor's actions.

Joe Antidote

In this situation, Joe may learn that the only way to receive attention from his boss is to work overtime and use a "fire-fighting" mode. The boss may be inadvertently implying that to be noticed Joe has to find problems and fix them. The company culture may promote working overtime to fix problems, rather than not allowing problems to happen in the first place.

If a boss rewards fire-fighting—whether advertent or not—there will be other fires to fight. If the boss rewards finding quick antidotes, there will be a need for more antidotes. If the boss rewards smooth operations, then people will try to make things run smoothly.

Sue Ling Worries

If speaking to her boss about a problem brings no solution, Sue Ling learns that the company is not interested in her problems. Sue Ling learns that the company is probably wasting money bringing in jobs that are not appropriate for its current process, and Sue Ling may believe that the company is not concerned about wasting money or delaying other customers' work.

Sue Ling and others who work on the jobs in question may grow to resent the sales department more and more and become less cooperative, even when doing "normal" jobs, and morale will suffer. Worse yet, employees may believe that the supervisor is not knowledgeable or cannot be trusted or is afraid to talk to sales! This can be demoralizing to all who report to this supervisor.

If the boss meets with the sales department and is successful in implementing a new procedure to deal with the job, he or she will be seen as a "hero" and will gain employee loyalty.

642. If We Only Knew: How Organizational Structure Affects Communication Flow

Goals

- To observe the impact of organizational structure on communication.

- To demonstrate that any organizational structure helps communication in some situations and blocks communication in others.

Group Size

Ten to twenty people.

Time Required

Approximately one hour and forty-five minutes.

Materials

- If We Only Knew Situations Sheet, pre-cut.
- One name tag per participant.
- Flip chart and felt-tipped markers.
- Paper and pens for participants.

Physical Setting

A room with enough space for all participants to rearrange chairs easily.

Process

1. Tell the participants that this activity will give them an opportunity to observe how organizational structure can impact organizational communication. (Five minutes.)

2. Have participants form subgroups of eight to ten people. Give everyone paper and pencils. Then have the subgroups develop organizational structures for a hypothetical organization based on the following instructions:

> You are members of a company that gives financial advice to its customers. Like most companies, you will need an organizational structure, a way of knowing who does what.
>
> Your customers range from small companies to large. They expect fast, accurate answers to their questions and good research to back up your recommendations. In your business, it is important to keep generating new customers, especially the large ones. Because your business is giving financial advice, it is very important that you have a *research function* that keeps up-to-date on the latest trends. It is also a business that is heavily regulated. You must file *regular reports* to government and agency regulators. It is critical that these reports be correct. Having good *internal controls* and *smooth operations* is also important. Because your company is often in the news, it is important to *protect your organization's reputation.*
>
> Plan how you will organize yourselves to suit the needs of your business. You will have about fifteen minutes to decide what type of organizational structure you will need.

(Twenty minutes.)

3. After the groups have planned their structures, hand out name tags and ask the participants to arrange themselves *physically* into the organizational structures they have designed. Give the following instructions:

> Arrange your chairs to show the organizational structure you have developed in your group. Decide who will sit in each position. Think of your structure in terms of an organizational chart or in terms of who will need to have offices close together. Write your designated "position" in the organization on your name tag and attach it to the front of your clothing.

(Five minutes.)

4. Check to be sure each group is ready, then say:

> I will now distribute descriptions of several different situations that have come up to people in your organization. I will give them to the person whose job title seems to indicate that he or she might normally hear about these situations first in a real organization. If you receive a piece of paper, either keep it (which indicates that you will handle the situation) or hand it to the person you think should deal with it. If you will handle part of the situation and then pass it to someone else to finish the job, write your position on the strip before

handing it on. If you do not think that the person in your position would take action on the situation, pass the paper along to the right person without writing your position on the strip. If you must share the information with more than one person, write all positions you think should be included on the piece of paper and then hand it on to the position nearest to you. Each person must pass the paper to everyone on the list. During the activity you may not leave your chair, but you may talk to one another.

(Twenty-five minutes.)

5. Hand the strips of paper out as best you can, based on positions participants have assigned themselves. Allow fifteen minutes for the groups to deal with the ten situations.

6. After all the situations have been distributed to the appropriate job functions, ask participants to report on which job functions were given situations to handle. Help the participants process the experience with the following questions:

■ Were you able to assign responsibility for handling all situations to the appropriate position?

■ Which positions were given the most situations to handle? Do any positions have nothing to handle?

■ How evenly spread are the situations? Why?

■ How many "middlemen" surfaced (those whose job was to hand situations to someone else without taking action)?

■ How many hand-offs occurred?

■ How often did communication go up or down the chain of command?

■ Did the group share information with everyone who needed to know?

■ Did all people receive information?

■ Was information ever passed over or around another person who was "in the way"?

■ Did the group adjust its communication flow to fit the situation, or did it always use the same structure?

■ How could you apply what you have learned to your own organization or department?

(Thirty minutes.)

Variations

- Introduce half of the situations, process the group's observations, and allow the groups to rearrange themselves, if desired, before introducing the second half of the situations.

- Use actual situations from the workplace that the participants are facing.

- Assign several participants the role of observers to take notes on the process as the groups are working. Ask the observers to report on their observations after the groups offer their own assessments.

- Allow groups to redesign their organizations and see how a second set of "situations" you write would be handled, given their previous experience.

Submitted by Janet Winchester-Silbaugh.

Janet Winchester-Silbaugh, M.B.A., CEBS, CCP, is a consultant affiliated with The Synergy Group Limited, an organization development consulting firm in Albuquerque, New Mexico. She works with organizations adjusting to changes in their environments, doing strategic planning and providing the tools for organizations to understand the system dynamics that are barriers to change.

IF WE ONLY KNEW SITUATIONS SHEET

A customer calls with a routine request for financial advice.

Your mail room must buy new equipment.

A large potential customer calls to ask what your company can do for him or her.

A government regulatory agency calls asking questions about the accuracy of information on a report you have just sent to them.

An angry customer calls.

One of your research analysts finds that your competitor's new product is taking away some of your customers.

An employee in the Sales Department makes an exception for a customer, which is against company policy.

An article in the newspaper is highly critical of your company.

Your organization agrees to create and implement a new product for a major customer.

Your CEO hears that your competitor has tried to hire your entire research team.

---

ntroduction
to the Inventories, Questionnaires, and Surveys Section

Inventories, questionnaires, and surveys are important tools to the HRD professional. It may be difficult for participants and clients to look at themselves objectively. These feedback tools help respondents take stock of themselves and their organizations and understand how a particular theory applies to them or to their situations.

These instruments—inventories, questionnaires, and surveys—are useful in a number of training and consulting situations: privately for self-diagnosis; one-on-one to plan individual development; in a small group to open discussion; in a work team to help the team to focus on its highest priorities; or in an organization to gather data to achieve progress.

You will find that the use of inventories, questionnaires, and surveys enriches, personalizes, and deepens training, development, and intervention designs. Many can be combined with other experiential learning activities or articles in this or other *Annuals* to design an exciting, involving, practical, and well-rounded intervention.

Each instrument includes the background necessary for understanding, presenting, and using it. Interpretive information, scales, and scoring sheets are also provided. In addition, we include the reliability and validity data contributed by the authors. If you wish additional information on any of these instruments, contact the authors directly. You will find their addresses and telephone numbers in the "Contributors" listing near the end of this volume.

Other assessment tools that address a wider variety of topics can be found by using our comprehensive *Reference Guide to Handbooks and Annuals*. This guide indexes all the instruments that we have published to date in the *Annuals*. You will find this complete, up-to-date, and easy-to-use resource valuable for locating other instruments, as well as for locating experiential learning activities and articles.

The 1999 Annual: Volume 2, Consulting includes three assessment tools in the following categories:

Groups and Teams

The Organizational I-Boundary Inventory: A Model for Decision Making by H. B. Karp

Consulting and Facilitating

A Strategic Human Resources Audit by Sophie Oberstein

Quality Principles Measure by Joe Willmore

THE ORGANIZATIONAL I-BOUNDARY INVENTORY: A MODEL FOR DECISION MAKING

H. B. Karp

Abstract: Organizations are becoming more complex as they continue to restructure. With this increasing complexity comes a growing concern about how to maintain effectiveness in an ever-changing system. This article presents a model for determining one's personal values and the organization's values, at a given point in time, thus establishing parameters for making decisions in the organizational setting. It is based on two established theories. The first, the Political Savvy Theory, concerns functioning in and as a group. The second theory, the Gestalt Theory, provides a process for increasing self-awareness, with the view toward discovering how one may be stopping oneself from being as effective as possible.

The Organizational I-Boundary Inventory is a sixteen-item instrument that allows the respondents to assess their own values and those of the organization and then compare the two sets of values. The Inventory may serve as a self-assessment instrument; as a foundation for coaching individuals; and as a basis for intra-group analysis and team building.

O rganizations are moving toward increasing complexity, as they continue to merge and restructure themselves. Not only are organizational systems becoming larger, but they are becoming more diverse as well, and the guidelines for appropriate effective behavior are becoming less clear as each new change occurs. The dilemma is that the old and established organizational paradigms no longer point to "one best way" to address the problems being faced.

Rod McLuhan's (1964) famous statement that "The medium is the message" may indicate a way to perceive organizations and communications within them. That is, just as systems are in a state of merging and becoming more complex, so must be the theories and applications being developed to understand and cope with them. The Political Savvy Theory and the Gestalt Theory, for example, can be combined and used effectively in determining how best to function in an organization. Applying these practical theories results in a range of appropriate choices that an individual can make in an organizational situation.

POLITICAL SAVVY THEORY

"Political savvy" is a term coined by Billie Lee (1992) to describe what it takes to be effective in today's organizations. Lee's work is based on the initial work of Jinx Melia, whose classic book *Why Jenny Can't Lead* (1986) focused on how women were disempowering themselves in male-dominant systems and what they had to do to become individually more impactful as a political force. Lee took these concepts well beyond the parameters of feminist issues and applied them to effective functioning in large organizations in general. Building on Melia's work, Lee developed the polar concepts of "Bear Fighters" and "Cave Dwellers." Lee stated that, although both concepts are important in organizational functioning, effectiveness in meeting team and organizational objectives now requires a greater emphasis on the attributes that were necessary to be an effective bear fighter in pre-historic times.

From strictly a historical perspective, Bear Fighting characteristics are stereotypically male and aggressive, whereas Cave Dweller characteristics are stereotypically female and nurturing. Bear Fighters, as a group, conform to a totally different set of characteristics and demands than do Cave Dwellers. The function of "bear fighting" is to achieve an objective that cannot be met by a single individual—to function as a team in order to accomplish what is essential for the survival (or success) of everyone in the community (or organization). "Objective" in this sense means a goal that is too large or too complex for any one individual to accomplish successfully, such as fighting and killing a bear. The function of "cave dwelling," on the other hand, is to provide a safe and supportive environment for all community members. The major characteristics of the two types are listed in Figure 1.

The underlying premise of the Political Savvy Theory is that the majority of organizations today operate mostly from a "Cave Dwelling" set of assumptions that have risen from the human relations movement in the 1960s and 1970s, typified by the assumption that good work is a direct result of good working relationships. Lee's assertion is that today's organizations must now incorporate the "Bear Fighter's" assumptions if they are going to survive and prosper. This assumption certainly seems accurate in view of such trends as the global economy, quickly and easily achieved product parity, and the growing emphasis on providing excellent service as the only viable way to compete. Both sets of skills are of equal value, the important thing being

---

Bear Fighters:

1. Put the task before the individual.

2. Operate in an uncontrolled environment, adapting to and using change.

3. Seek accomplishment, minimize risk, and use results as a guide.

4. Compete to get on the team and are admitted based on the team's needs.

5. Form unlimited alliances to accomplish tasks.

Cave Dwellers:

1. Put the individual before the task.

2. Operate in a controlled environment, adhering to the rules.

3. Seek safety, avoid risks, and use personal comfort as a guide.

4. Are admitted to the community based on shared values and acceptance.

5. Form a limited number of interpersonal relations within the cave.

Figure 1. Characteristics of Bear Fighters and Cave Dwellers

that people learn when and how to meet each separate set of needs. As Lee suggests, competent people develop both bear fighting and cave dwelling skills; savvy people know when to use each.

GESTALT THEORY

The word "Gestalt" is German in origin and can be defined as "a clear, emerging figure." Gestalt therapy was developed by Fritz Perls in the clinical setting and has been described by many as "therapy for normal people." It emphasizes the health and development of the entire self. Along with being an approach for strengthening individuals by helping them make better choices, it has also become an approach for increasing individual effectiveness and making changes in organizations.

In the Gestalt view, all human characteristics and capacities operate in polarities, such as hostile/supportive, kind/cruel, or good/evil.

Figure 2 illustrates the entire range for human experience on the aggressive/passive polarity. A "+ 7", at the extreme left, is as aggressive as it is humanly possible to be. Likewise, a "+ 7" at the extreme right is as passive as it is humanly possible to be. Each individual capacity, or sub-boundary, crosses two polarities at two points indicated by the "I."

This example shows the results of the author's Organizational I-Boundary Inventory. The two interior marks represent his sub-boundary on the Aggressive/Passive continuum. That is, a range from 4.7 to 2.8. What this says, in terms of behaviors, is that the author is aggressive enough to go after what he wants that is "unclaimed" by others, at one extreme, but no more aggressive than that, and passive enough to keep a low profile in the face of a direct threat, but no more passive than that. The significance is that these two points describe the extent of his capacity on this continuum and identifies him uniquely.. The points define when a "Yes" becomes a "No." When the sub-boundary is added to the hundreds of others that make a person up, the result is that person's "I-Boundary," that distinctive configuration of charac-

Figure 2. The Aggressive/Passive Continuum

teristics and capacities that makes each person absolutely unique and recognizable. Figure 3 displays a sample configuration that includes all eight of the polarities.

Several assumptions are implicit in the concept of I-Boundary:

1. Because these are capacities only, rather than behaviors, there is no bad way to be or bad capacity to have.

2. The prevailing situation and a person's capacities determine what actions are appropriate or inappropriate, effective or ineffective.

3. Each individual's I-Boundary is so unique that effectiveness lies in being aware of who one is, valuing that uniqueness, and clearly demonstrating that uniqueness to others.

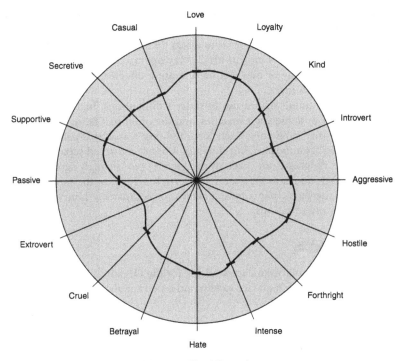

Figure 3. The I-Boundary

INTEGRATION OF THE THEORIES

"Political Savvy Theory" and "Gestalt Theory" provide us with a means for becoming more aware of our political and interpersonal effectiveness in the work setting. By changing the designation of "I-Boundary" to "Organizational I-Boundary," and by setting up the poles of the continuum in terms of Bear Fighter/Cave Dweller capacities, we have a means for conducting a "thumb-nail" analysis of what the organization's values are, what the person's values are, and how well the two sets of values are matched.

The Instrument

The Organizational I-Boundary Inventory is a tool for (1) assessing a respondent's awareness of his or her organization's political environment and (2) measuring the respondent's effectiveness in that environment. The instrument is based on the Political-Savvy Theory and the Gestalt Theory and provides a means for the respondents to assess their own values and the values of the organizational systems in which they operate, and a basis for determining how they may or may not be operating effectively within their systems' political structures.

The instrument makes use of sixteen dimensions, half of which are "bear fighting" or achieving capacities, and the other half being "cave dwelling" or supportive capacities. Each "bear fighting" capacity is paired with its "cave dwelling" counterpart, but the questions are answered separately on a 7-point scale, ranging from "strongly disagree" (1) to "strongly agree" (7). By answering each question for themselves as well as for how they see their organizations, the participants have a means for comparing their values with those of their organizations.

Validity and Reliability

No validity or reliability data are available for the Organizational I-Boundary Inventory. It does have high face validity and is well based in established theory.

Uses for the Instrument

The Inventory has several applications:

- The instrument and the model may be used in training on the topic of organizational politics.

- The instrument may be taken and scored by an individual for self-analysis purposes.

- The instrument and model may be used with the members of an ongoing work group, team, or department. In this case the facilitator would briefly explain the concept, have all group members complete and score the instrument, and then facilitate a discussion looking at how similar and different the members perceive the political values of their organization.

References

Karp, H.B. (1996). *Personal power: An unorthodox guide to success*. Lake Worth, FL: Gardner Press.

Lee, B. (1992). *Savvy: Thirty days to a different perspective*. Colorado Springs, CO: Billie Lee & Co.

McLuhan, M. (1964). *Understanding media*. New York: McGraw-Hill.

Melia, J., & Lyttle, P. (1986). *Why Jenny can't lead: Understanding the male dominant system*. Sauguache, CO: Operational Politics Inc.

H.B. Karp, Ph.D., is presently on the faculty of management of Christopher Newport University in Newport News, Virginia. He also is the owner of Personal Growth Systems, a management-consulting firm in Chesapeake, Virginia. He consults with a variety of Fortune 500 and governmental organizations in the areas of leadership development, team building, conflict management, and executive coaching. He specializes in applying Gestalt theory to issues of individual growth and organizational effectiveness. He is the author of Personal Power: An Unorthodox Guide to Success *and* The Change Leader: Using a Gestalt Approach with Work Groups.

ORGANIZATIONAL I-BOUNDARY INVENTORY[1]

H. B. Karp

Instructions: The following sixteen statements describe attitudes about organizational life. Respond to each statement below *twice.* First circle the number that best represents your personal view. Then, put an "X" through the number that, in your opinion, represents your organization's view.

1 = Strongly Disagree 2 = Disagree 3 = Mildly Disagree 4 = Neutral 5 = Mildly Agree 6 = Agree 7 = Strongly Agree

1. In effective organizations, task accomplishment takes precedence over individual well-being.   1   2   3   4   5   6   7

2. It is alright to disregard organizational rules and policies when they get in the way of task accomplishment.   1   2   3   4   5   6   7

3. A manager's primary obligation is the growth and development of his or her people.   1   2   3   4   5   6   7

4. Employees who do not follow and respect organizational guidelines are not good team players.   1   2   3   4   5   6   7

5. Providing an opportunity to achieve is the organization's primary obligation to its staff.   1   2   3   4   5   6   7

6. The most important thing for team members to share is their objectives.   1   2   3   4   5   6   7

7. Providing a safe and secure environment is the organization's primary obligation to its staff.   1   2   3   4   5   6   7

8. The closer the interpersonal relationships of team members, the better.   1   2   3   4   5   6   7

[1]I would like to thank Diane LaMountain, whose assistance was critical in developing this work.

9. In effective teams, agreements are
openly made and are honored among
team members.   1   2   3   4   5   6   7

10. Each team member should take care
of himself or herself before providing
support to other members.   1   2   3   4   5   6   7

11. Good team members do not ask for,
or expect, "payment" for favors done
other team members.   1   2   3   4   5   6   7

12. In terms of providing support, it is
important that each team member
take care of his or her teammates first.   1   2   3   4   5   6   7

13. Team members are obligated to state
clearly and directly what they want or
need from the group or its members.   1   2   3   4   5   6   7

14. An effective team must be able to work
in unclear and ambiguous situations.   1   2   3   4   5   6   7

15. Good team members should be able
to anticipate and respond to the wants
and needs of their teammates.   1   2   3   4   5   6   7

16. Effective teams should have the ability
to clarify situations that seem unclear.   1   2   3   4   5   6   7

ORGANIZATIONAL I-BOUNDARY INVENTORY SCORING SHEET

Instructions: Transfer responses from the inventory to the scoring grid below, circling your personal responses to distinguish them from organizational responses. (Note that there are eight polarities represented in the sixteen items; items 1 and 3 are opposite, items 2 and 4 are opposite, and so on.) Next connect the circles. This will yield your individual Organizational I-Boundary (your personal values) in reference to your own Bear Fighter/Cave Dweller capacities. Repeat the procedure for your assessment of your organization's values on each characteristic, using Xs to indicate each score. Connect the Xs to yield an Organizational S-Boundary (S-system) and then compare the two sets of values.

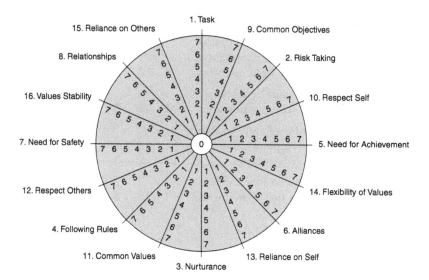

The eight polarities going clockwise from 1, "Task," through 13, "Reliance on Self," are "Bear Fighter" characteristics. These characteristics include: Concern with Task Accomplishment; Commitment to Common Objectives; Willingness To Take Risks; Taking Responsibility for Oneself; Need for Achievement; Valuing Flexibility; Need for Alliances; and Self-Reliance. These are geared to task accomplishment, teamwork, and organizational effectiveness.

Continuing to move clockwise, the remaining eight polarities, beginning with 3, "Nurturance," and ending with 15, "Reliance on Others," are

"Cave Dweller" characteristics. These include: the Need To Be Nurturant; Commitment to Commonly Held Values; Following Rules; Respect and Responsibility for Others; the Need for Safety; Valuing Stability; a Need for Close Relationships; and Reliance on Others. These characteristics are geared to providing for the needs of safety, belonging, and caring for others.

Your position on each sub-boundary, for both the Bear Fighting and the Cave Dwelling characteristics, reflects your capacity for responding to that characteristic. Remember that there is no good or bad or right or wrong way to be! Everyone has some needs on both sides.

By connecting the "O"s representing your own view, you obtain an Organizational I-Boundary that describes your "organizational self." By connecting the "X"s you make an Organizational S-Boundary that describes your system. Compare the two boundaries to see where your values are consistent with the organization's and where they may not be.

ORGANIZATIONAL I-BOUNDARY INVENTORY INTERPRETATION SHEET

The purpose of this inventory is to increase your awareness. Do not make any plans for change yet. If you are taking this survey with other members of your group, department, or organization, compare your perceptions of the organization with theirs. As this inventory and its interpretation are basically subjective in nature, it is up to you to determine their relevance and implications for you. What you intend to do, if anything, is best determined by looking at the results from your survey within the context of your organizational culture. The following points may assist you in deciding what to do with your results.

High Degree of Overlap

Complete, or near complete, overlap between the I-Boundary and the S-Boundary might mean that there is congruence between you and the organization. That is, there is an excellent match between your characteristics and those of the system. If things are progressing well and you have a strong sense of self, then this condition is all to the good.

There are, however, other possible interpretations of such results. For example, if there is a great deal of overlap, it could also indicate the lack of a strong sense of self and that you identify strongly with the organization, at least in terms of functioning within it. This is most typified by the term "Company Man" that was coined in the early 1960s. Typically, these people identify very strongly with the system, are fierce defenders of its values, and look askance at anyone who does not share their views about the organization.

Another interpretation might be that you see yourself as an "outsider." Here the tendency is to mimic the company values, rather than to internalize them, in an attempt to be included more fully by other members of the organization. You will need to determine whether the expression of individual capacities and values you gave is authentic or not.

Little Overlap

A great deal of disparity between the I-Boundary and the S-Boundary might suggest that you do not clearly understand the organization's values. On the other hand, it might indicate that there is too great a difference between your needs and capacities and those of the system. In this situation it may be difficult for you to make a significant contribution. That is, the difference is so great that the organization represents a hostile environment and you may spend more time in self-protection and hiding than in contributing to the organizational objectives.

Issues To Consider

Although there is no prescribed method for analyzing the results of the inventory, there are a few simple ways of being. First, three points disparity between your score ("O") and the system's ("X") on any of the sixteen individual characteristics would indicate the high likelihood of a problem and you should look at those items first. A few of the more obvious possible areas of disparity are listed below.

Alliances Versus Relationships. What does the organization value as opposed to what you are seeking in the work setting? It may be that you are trying to develop more supportive relationships when what is being demanded are more effective alliances among people who need one another to do the job.

Controlling the Environment Versus Adapting to It. Understanding the difference between adaptation and control is critical to attaining objectives. Most people in an organization have limited control over conditions and must rely on their ability to adapt to existing conditions, making the best choices from there. However, it is appropriate to challenge rules if they are impeding progress.

Willingness Versus Unwillingness To Negotiate. Negotiating is an essential set of bear fighting skills that provides a means for attaining a group objective. Cave dwellers are frequently more concerned with liking or disliking the other person, rather than looking at what negotiation with the other person could produce. Often, cave dwellers would prefer not attaining the end if it means dealing with someone they do not like or hold in high personal regard. Bear fighters, in contrast, will engage in negotiation when necessary, regardless of whether they like or dislike the other person.

Risk Taking Versus Risk Avoidance. Bear fighters attempt to minimize risk, but they are willing to confront it; cave dwellers attempt to avoid it altogether. Rarely can an objective be successfully accomplished without taking some risk.

Teams Versus Friends. Operating as a team is a necessity when pursuing an object that an individual cannot meet alone. For bear fighters, the sole purpose is goal attainment. Cave dwellers put more emphasis on the process than on the outcome; for them, the purpose of a team is to develop trust, get along well, and work well together. Be clear about the compatibility of assumptions that you make about the nature of teams and those that your organization makes.

A STRATEGIC HUMAN RESOURCES AUDIT

Sophie Oberstein

Abstract: In today's business environment organizations need to manage the financial as well as the
human implications of their business strategies.
Companies that have the best results in productivity, customer service, and profitability have used
their human resource (HR) departments as strategic partners to achieve this balance. The Strategic
Human Resources Audit assesses the capability of
an organization and its human resource professionals to escalate HR to the role of business partner.
The audit can be used as an organizational survey.
It provides a straightforward method for a group to
explore the organizational dimensions of the role
of human resources and to initiate a process for improving it. The audit is based on extensive research
and practical experience in companies that have
seen positive results when they positioned HR as a
strategic player.

Too often people are not considered corporate assets of the same magnitude as cash and net worth. Furthermore, the belief that leveraging all of a company's assets will lead to increased profitability, service, and productivity is not widespread.

Yet, organizations that have created partnerships between HR and the business—such as AT&T, Hewlett-Packard, British Airways, and Electronic Data Systems—have seen numerous positive results. A strategic HR partnership exists when the human resource department is a crucial contributor to the development and execution of business strategy and when all of the department's efforts and initiatives support this strategy. The benefits of such alliances are shown in Figure 1.

Before any of these positive outcomes can be realized, both beneficiaries must examine their prevailing attitudes, structures, and roles.

Benefits to the Organization	Benefits to the HR Professional
• Maximizes the talents of an increasingly diverse workforce.	• Professionalizes the HR role; HR becomes:
• Ensures transfer of an organization's core competencies worldwide.	• A value-added contributor.
• Lends a long-term focus to the day-to-day operations of the organization.	• A performance consultant.
• Can create a shared mind-set/culture among employees.	• A problem solver.
	• A business partner, not a messenger.
• Avoids the surprises that certain human implications of business strategies can bring.	• Provides HR with direction for its efforts; HR does not work in a vacuum.
• Ensures legal compliance.	• Provides HR with support/funding for its programs.
• Improves employee morale and retention.	• Provides some job security for HR professionals.
	• Allows HR to deal with happy "customers."

Figure 1. Benefits of a Strategic Partnership Between HR and the Business

Many companies claim to recognize the importance of human resources but do not recognize the bottom-line results of HR initiatives. These companies separate HR from what they consider to be revenue-producing business units, which keeps them from transforming the HR function into a strategic one.

Human resource professionals and departments are prevented from becoming strategic partners for a number of reasons. Most of these have to do with the traditional role of HR. Often, either no one thinks to change the status quo or no one is able to invest the time and energy to do so. Human resource departments often are asked to implement programs or processes that they were not involved in creating (and may disagree with). If they fail in such undertakings, the HR departments' reputations are tarnished. Political forces (such as unions) also keep HR from taking on a partnership role, and most organizations do not have internal champions for transformations of this kind.

It is not until both the HR department and the organization make an effort to circumvent these obstacles that a partnership can be formed and its benefits realized.

DESCRIPTION OF THE AUDIT

The Strategic Human Resources Audit is designed to help individuals in organizations assess the current status of the human resource department with an eye toward moving it into the role of strategic partner. The audit should be completed by representatives of the human resource department and the department's internal customers. The thirty-six items assess an organization's capacity for utilizing HR as a strategic partner by measuring the presence of characteristics that have been proven to promote this relationship. Each item is rated on a four-point scale that describes the extent to which the item is perceived to be true.

Validity

The items in the audit are drawn from research and case studies that address the preconditions for partnership. At present, no universally agreed-on model for effectively utilizing HR in a strategic manner exists. The Strategic Human Resources Audit is designed to be an action-research tool rather than a rigorous data-gathering instrument. Used in this manner, the items are hypotheses that have high levels of face validity.

Administration

The total time required to administer, score, and interpret the Strategic Human Resources Audit is approximately thirty minutes. Additional time is necessary to facilitate group action-planning activities. Each participant will need a copy of each of the elements of the audit: Strategic Human Resources Audit, Strategic Human Resources Audit Scoring Sheet, Strategic Human Resources Audit Interpretation Sheet, and Strategic Human Resources Audit Work Sheet. To best facilitate this session, human resource professionals should follow these steps:

1. *Introduce the session* by asking the participants their views of the role of HR in their organization. Questions might include:

   ■ What has the HR department done for the organization's employees lately?

   ■ What has the department done to assist the organization in meeting its strategic goals?

   ■ What do the participants wish HR were doing to assist in either of these areas?

2. *Distribute the Strategic Human Resources Audit* and ask each participant to complete it.

3. *Present a brief lecturette* on the characteristics of a strategic HR partnership. The content for this lecturette may be drawn from material in the Strategic Human Resources Audit Interpretation Sheet.

4. *Distribute the Strategic Human Resources Audit Scoring Sheet, the Strategic Human Resources Audit Interpretation Sheet, and the Strategic Human Resources Audit Work Sheet,* and review their instructions. Ask the participants to form cross-functional subgroups (homogeneous groups if only one department is present) of two to five people. Ask the subgroups to complete the analysis of the audit results.

5. *Invite each subgroup to share at least one insight* gained from the session. These insights should be recorded and posted on a newsprint flip chart and used for action planning.

References

de Geus, A. (1997). *The living company*. Boston, MA: Harvard Business School Press.

Fisher, C., Schoenfeldt, L., & Shaw, J. (1996). Making the change to strategic human resource management. In S. Kahn (Ed.), *Human resource management*. Boston, MA: Houghton Mifflin.

Fitz-Enz, J. (1997). *The eight practices of exceptional companies: How great organizations make the most of their human assets*. New York: AMACOM.

Miles, R.E., & Snow, C.C. (1978). *Organizational strategy, structure, and process*. New York: McGraw-Hill.

Ulrich, D. (1998, January-February). A new mandate for human resources. In *Harvard Business Review*, as quoted on their website at http://www.HBS.edu.

Sophie Oberstein, M.S., is founder of Targeted Training Solutions, a human resources and training consultancy in Maple Glen, Pennsylvania. She is also a professor of human resources in the M.B.A. program at Drexel University. She has contributed to numerous professional publications, including McGraw-Hill's Team and Organization Development Sourcebooks *and has written an* InfoLine *for the American Society for Training & Development (ASTD) describing her own technique for creative training design.*

STRATEGIC HUMAN RESOURCES AUDIT

Sophie Oberstein

Instructions: A strategic partnership between human resource departments and traditional business units is vital, and this audit will help to provide information needed to create such a partnership in your organization. Please answer each item with care and honesty; the intention is to benefit everyone. Individual results are strictly confidential and will never be identified by name.

You may feel that you do not have sufficient knowledge to answer an item. In this case, select the "don't know" option. However, an opinion, even if it is subjective, is better than a "don't know" response.

Choose your response based on the following scale:

This statement is true:

1 = To no extent   2 = To a slight extent   3 = To a moderate extent   4 = To a great extent   dk = don't know

1. This organization is focused on using internal resources to solve business problems.   1   2   3   4   dk

2. This organization's human resource (HR) department's day-to-day work is driven by the organization's mission and business strategy.   1   2   3   4   dk

3. Representatives from the HR department are present during the organization's strategic planning efforts.   1   2   3   4   dk

4. Communication in this organization is consistent and encompasses all stakeholders and employees.   1   2   3   4   dk

5. The HR department is seen as a central clearinghouse for communications in this organization.   1   2   3   4   dk

6. Representatives from the HR department are present on any task forces or cross-functional work teams in this organization.   1   2   3   4   dk

7. This organization provides resources to support HR initiatives.	1	2	3	4	dk
8. The HR department focuses on results, not procedures.	1	2	3	4	dk
9. The value of its employees is mentioned in this organization's mission and value statements.	1	2	3	4	dk
10. This organization wants to be known as a premier employer.	1	2	3	4	dk
11. The HR department has identified its internal customers and determined their needs.	1	2	3	4	dk
12. When this organization adopts a new business strategy, the HR department is given tasks to implement.	1	2	3	4	dk
13. This organization has a long-term focus.	1	2	3	4	dk
14. Members of the HR department speak the language of business.	1	2	3	4	dk
15. This organization's annual report (or progress reports) includes human resource results.	1	2	3	4	dk
16. This organization has been successful in change efforts and/or is regarded as flexible.	1	2	3	4	dk
17. The HR department is seen as an internal change leader.	1	2	3	4	dk
18. Human and financial values are balanced in this organization.	1	2	3	4	dk
19. Teams or other alternative work structures are being utilized in this organization.	1	2	3	4	dk
20. The HR department, or functions within it, have been renamed to reflect a performance-enhancing role.	1	2	3	4	dk

21. The HR department contributes best-
    practice and market data to the
    organization.   1   2   3   4   dk

22. This organization utilizes some form of
    performance-based, flexible pay.   1   2   3   4   dk

23. The HR department recommends or
    implements solutions to organizational
    problems.   1   2   3   4   dk

24. The HR department is consulted for,
    or involved in, all decisions to hire
    external vendors.   1   2   3   4   dk

25. This organization is willing to "shake
    things up," to take risks.   1   2   3   4   dk

26. HR initiatives and successes are highly
    visible internally.   1   2   3   4   dk

27. The HR department helps to equip all
    executives to perform critical HR func-
    tions, such as performance management,
    forecasting, and selection.   1   2   3   4   dk

28. This organization has a strong corporate
    culture that has been communicated to
    the employees.   1   2   3   4   dk

29. This organization's HR initiatives have
    been recognized in the external press.   1   2   3   4   dk

30. Individuals from the HR department are
    highly visible internally and/or the
    director of HR reports to the CEO or
    president of the organization.   1   2   3   4   dk

31. This organization practices financial
    conservatism (fiscal prudence).   1   2   3   4   dk

32. Members of the HR department receive
    professional development and necessary
    resources.   1   2   3   4   dk

33. External vendors are hired to handle
    some of the more administrative HR tasks.   1   2   3   4   dk

34. This organization is in, or plans to enter,
    the international market in the next
    two years.   1   2   3   4   dk

35. The members of the HR department
    are generalists, not specialists.   1   2   3   4   dk

36. Senior management vocally endorses
    HR initiatives formally and informally.   1   2   3   4   dk

STRATEGIC HUMAN RESOURCES AUDIT SCORING SHEET

Instructions: Transfer the numbers you have circled for each item on the Strategic Human Resources Audit to the scoring grid that follows. All "dk" responses should receive a score of zero.

Next add the scores in each vertical column and enter them in the "Total" row at the bottom of the sheet.

Category: Forward-Thinking Organization		Category: HR Partner		Category: Strategic Partnership	
Question #	Your rating	Question #	Your rating	Question #	Your rating
1		2		3	
4		5		6	
7		8		9	
10		11		12	
13		14		15	
16		17		18	
19		20		21	
22		23		24	
25		26		27	
28		29		30	
31		32		33	
34		35		36	
Total		Total		Total	

STRATEGIC HUMAN RESOURCES AUDIT INTERPRETATION SHEET

The Strategic Partnership Equation

The three scores from your Audit Scoring Sheet assess how close your organization is to achieving a beneficial strategic partnership with its HR department. If your organization is forward thinking, it is likely that a partnership already has been initiated. A forward-thinking organization is one that is focused on the "big picture" and has explored how all of its departments work together to produce results. Each department is then empowered not only to perform its own functions, but also to suggest organizational improvements to enhance quality and efficiency.

The HR department that is ready to become a partner has established itself as competent and trustworthy. Its traditional focus (specialized, transactional, and monolingual—speaking "HR-ese") has been replaced by a more generalized, proactive, and integrated approach.

The sum of these two parts produces a partnership that is aligned to bring about mutually desired outcomes, as shown in Figure 1 below.

Forward-Thinking Organization	p	HR Partner
The organization's focus provides fertile ground for a productive business partnership with HR, including recognizing HR's potential.	l u s	The human resource department is structured and equipped to serve as a value-added business partner in the organization.

equals

Strategic Partnership
Human resources is a critical function—like operations, research & development, or marketing—in increasing the organization's productivity, profitability, or service.

Figure 1. Strategic Partnerships

Interpretation Guidelines

Instructions: Begin reading the descriptions that follow for each of three parts of the equation. Share your scores from the Strategic Human Resources Audit Scoring Sheet with the other members of your subgroup. Look at the lowest scoring category as well as the particular items that have consistently received low scores from you and others in your group. You and your group will do some action planning later to help move your organization toward a partnership between the business units and HR.

The Forward-Thinking Organization

Several of the factors that ensure that an organization makes the most of its human assets are also factors that ensure its general ongoing health and success. A forward-thinking organization knows the importance of long-term, big-picture thinking and of involving all stakeholders. These factors include the following:

■ The organization is focused on using internal resources to solve business problems.

■ Communication in the organization is consistent and encompasses all stakeholders and employees.

■ The organization provides resources to support HR initiatives.

■ The organization has a strong corporate culture that has been communicated to the employees.

■ The organization is willing to "shake things up," to take risks.

■ The organization has a long-term focus.

■ The organization practices financial conservatism (fiscal prudence).

Whatever business strategy an organization decides to pursue, there will be implications for the HR function. For example, if an organization wishes to grow through acquisition, the HR department can assist with selection from the new firm, training, establishing an equitable compensation package, and implementing outplacement for those employees whose positions become obsolete. Even if a plan is simply to add new types of equipment in the coming year, training efforts will probably be involved. Some business decisions may rely on the HR department's expertise to make them work. These include:

- The organization wants to be known as a premier employer.
- The organization is in, or plans to enter, the international market in the next two years.

Like future plans, several current workplace trends will require the input and skills of an HR professional. If the organization already has any of these present, it is ripe for a partnership. These include:

- Teams or other alternative work structures are being utilized in the organization.
- The organization utilizes some form of performance-based, flexible pay.
- The organization has been successful in change efforts and/or is regarded as flexible.

The HR Partner

An HR department is positioned to become a partner when it has shown that it is credible and trustworthy. The department's results prove its credibility and competence. The individuals within the department can create trust through their own professional development. If both credibility and trust are present, the reputation of the department will be strong.

If the HR department has achieved good results, it will be seen as a value-added function, not as a drain on the business. Good results are those that contribute to the overall goals of the organization or that help other areas to work more effectively. Good results come from the HR department:

- Tying its day-to-day work to the organization's mission and business strategy.
- Focusing on results, not on procedures.
- Identifying its internal customers and determining their needs.
- Recommending or implementing solutions to organizational problems.

To become credible and trustworthy, HR professionals need to expand their traditional roles. To do this, they must:

- Receive professional development and necessary resources.
- Become generalists, not specialists.
- Speak the language of the business.

The HR department's reputation is both internal and external. A positive external reputation creates a positive image of the organization as a whole. An HR department that has a good reputation:

- Is seen as a central clearinghouse for communications in the organization.
- Is seen as an internal change leader.
- Has been renamed to reflect a performance-enhancing role (or functions within it have been).
- Has initiatives and successes that are highly visible internally.
- Has initiatives that have been recognized in the external press.

Strategic Partnerships

In an organization in which the HR department plays a strategic role, certain activities occur and the contributions of the HR department are deemed as important as the contributions of other money-making functions. This might mean that:

- Human and financial values are balanced in the organization.
- Representatives from the HR department are present during the organization's strategic planning efforts.
- Representatives from the HR department are present on any task forces or cross-functional work teams in the organization.
- When the organization adapts a new business strategy, the HR department is given tasks to implement.
- The HR department helps to equip all executives to perform critical HR functions, such as performance management, forecasting, and selection.
- The HR department contributes best-practice and market data to the organization.

Some characteristics of an HR partnership, although important, are more superficial, for example, when links between the HR department and the business have been acknowledged but not yet realized. A partnership may exist on paper, but if no one "walks the talk," it goes no further. Such characteristics of partnership include:

- The value of its employees is mentioned in the organization's mission and value statements.

- The organization's annual report or (progress reports) includes human resource results.
- The HR department is consulted for, or involved in, all decisions to hire external vendors.
- Individuals from the HR department are highly visible internally and/or the director of HR reports to the CEO or president of the organization.
- External vendors are hired to handle some of the more administrative HR tasks.
- Senior management vocally endorses HR initiatives formally and informally.

Which Did You Rate the Highest?

You transferred scores on individual items from the Strategic Human Resource Audit into three columns on the Audit Scoring Sheet. Each one represented one of the components of the partnership equation. There is significance in how your total scores in each column compare with one another. Find the order listed below that describes your highest to lowest scoring categories and study the descriptions to understand this significance.

Forward-Thinking Organization, HR Partner, Strategic Partnership. This sequence represents what is perhaps the most natural progression when it comes to creating a strategic HR partnership. If an organization is led effectively, it follows that the HR department within that organization would also be effective. In such situations, there usually is an internal champion promoting the importance of the HR function, and the HR department does not let that champion down. A caution in this situation is that for HR to remain a true partner the department must be value-added and not just follow the organization's lead.

Forward-Thinking Organization, Strategic Partnership, HR Partner. In this sequence, HR is not a strategic partner. In fact, the department may be in jeopardy. The organization is leading effectively and has made efforts to bring the HR department into a partnership, but the department has not held up its end. It may be working on its own initiatives and not integrating with the organization. In all probability, the HR department's customers do not regard it highly.

HR Partner, Forward-Thinking Organization, Strategic Partnership. This sequence also represents a natural progression when it comes to forming a strategic partnership. When there is a strong HR department that does what it can to be a professional asset, it follows that the overall organization will positively be affected. In such cases, the HR department effectively documents its potential impact on the bottom line, and its successes are visible throughout the organization. The caution in this situation is that the strong organization and the strong HR department might prefer to work independently, butting heads when it comes to partnering. Also, because the organization is usually more powerful than a single department, the partnership can become unequal.

HR Partner, Strategic Partnership, Forward-Thinking Organization. This sequence is the most frustrating for forward-thinking HR professionals. The HR department operates in an organization that is not aware of the value that it is adding or could potentially add. As organizational principles and operations are probably the most difficult of the three categories to change, this is the hardest sequence to rectify. However, because some partnering is happening despite the organization's reluctance, the HR department can capitalize on it by promoting the resulting benefits.

Strategic Partnership, Forward-Thinking Organization, HR Partner or Strategic Partner, HR Partner, Forward-Thinking Organization. When elements of a partnership are present but the organization and HR department behind it are not practicing the necessary behaviors, the partnership is generally not genuine. This is the kind of situation in which the organization's mission statement says, "Employees are our most valuable asset," yet the employees don't feel or believe it to be true. Both the organization and the HR department need to establish trust and credibility to move beyond this superficial partnership and to realize the benefits of a true one.

STRATEGIC HUMAN RESOURCES AUDIT WORK SHEET

Instructions: Determine the category with the lowest score for yourself and for your subgroup. To determine your subgroup's lowest scoring category, convert your scores according to the formula below. Then combine the individual converted scores for each category and divide by the number of members in the subgroup, as follows:

Category	My score	Converted score (Highest scoring category = 1; Mid-scoring category = 2; Lowest scoring category = 3)	Total of subgroup converted scores (My converted score + converted scores of other subgroup members)	Average converted score (Total divided by number of subgroup members)
Forward-Thinking Organization				
HR Partner				
Strategic Partnership				

Twelve items on the Strategic Human Resources Audit are associated with the category to which your subgroup has given the lowest average score. These twelve items are listed in separate columns on the Strategic Human Resources Audit Scoring Sheet. For each item, tally the number of subgroup members who rated the item a "1." Select the *three* items from the category that received the lowest scores from the most members of your subgroup.

If more than three items receive the most number-1 responses, simply use more than three, or vote for the top three to use.

Item #s in subgroup's lowest scoring category	# of subgroup members rating this item with a 1 (including yourself)

The items with ratings of 1 from the most subgroup members are probably the best places to begin to enhance the role of HR in your organization. These results need to be verified by discussion and further evaluation. In your subgroup, select three items that the highest number of subgroup members rated 1 and discuss them. Answer the questions that follow and fill in the grid to create a strategic partnership action plan.

1. Why isn't this currently happening in our organization?
2. Who benefits when this does not happen in our organization? In what way?
3. Who suffers when this does not happen in our organization? How?
4. What must the organization do to make this happen?
5. What must the HR department do to make this happen?
6. What are the next steps? Who will do what by when?

Issue #1: _____

Positive consequences of the issue: _____

_____

_____

_____

Negative consequences of the issue: _____

_____

_____

_____

What must HR do to remedy the issue? _____

_____

_____

_____

What must the organization do to remedy the issue? _____

_____

_____

_____

By when will these steps be taken? _____

_____

Issue #2: _____

Positive consequences of the issue: _____

_____

_____

_____

Negative consequences of the issue: _____

_____

_____

_____

What must HR do to remedy the issue? _____

_____

_____

_____

What must the organization do to remedy the issue? _____

_____

_____

_____

By when will these steps be taken? _____

_____

Issue #3: _____

Positive consequences of the issue: _____

_____

_____

_____

Negative consequences of the issue: _____

_____

_____

_____

What must HR do to remedy the issue? _____

_____

_____

_____

What must the organization do to remedy the issue? _____

_____

_____

_____

By when will these steps be taken? _____

_____

QUALITY PRINCIPLES MEASURE

Joe Willmore

Abstract: Efforts to improve internal quality and service are priorities for most public and private sector organizations. Although organizations should be able to assess progress in this arena when the process is further along by measuring improvements in customer satisfaction or reduced waste or defects, determining progress in the early stages of a quality effort may often be difficult. Additionally, many organizations claim to be committed to quality initiatives while providing only service-level actions that do little to adjust the system. The Quality Principles Measure is a tool for assessing individual perceptions of the degree of consistency within the organization's efforts to achieve Deming's Fourteen Principles. More specifically, this tool asks individuals to assess to what degree they perceive that the organization emphasizes each of the Fourteen Principles of quality.

INTRODUCTION

Dr. W. Edwards Deming, a major figure in the quality movement worldwide, formulated fourteen basic principles essential to any effort to improve quality and service within an organization. Deming referred to these as the Fourteen Principles (Deming, 1986). According to Deming, any serious quality initiative must be consistent with these Fourteen Principles. Failure to do so will either derail the quality effort before it starts or eventually result in its failure as inconsistent elements within the system compete against one another and actions are at cross-purposes. The Fourteen Principles follow:

1. *Constancy of purpose.* How clear is the organization about its purpose? Does the organization sometimes act in inconsistent ways or with actions that are tangential to its true mission? Additionally, does the organization view its primary role as to make money or to refine service continually?

2. *Commitment to quality as an essential way of operating.* Is the organization clear that quality involves a change in the basic and fundamental ways that organizations do business?

3. *End reliance on inspection as a quality compliance tool.* Does the organization design quality into the system to minimize mistakes and keep waste from happening or does it depend on work review after the work has been completed?

4. *Reliance on single suppliers, ending the focus on low-bid systems.* Does the organization seek to establish long-term relationships with vendors rather than emphasizing low prices? Does the organization operate with a wide range of vendors or does it seek opportunities to use the same vendors for multiple needs?

5. *Commitment to ongoing improvement.* Is the quality initiative treated as a dynamic and perpetual activity or is it viewed as a one-time action?

6. *Institute training on the job.* Does the organization have an extensive effort to promote learning from the work process? Are workers provided with clear instructions about the nature of their jobs and effective instruction to build key skills?

7. *Managers who empower rather than rely on control.* Does the organization encourage personnel initiatives unilaterally to prevent problems and utilize

their own judgment? To what extent do managers limit the discretion of employees?

8. *Eliminate fear and coercion within the organization.* To what extent is it possible for people to admit (and thus learn from) mistakes? Does the organization fix the blame or fix the problem?

9. *Break down barriers within the organization.* How much compartmentalization and stovepiping occur? Does the organization maximize information sharing between departments?

10. *Eliminate internal competition among personnel.* Are employees forced or encouraged to compete against one another or are there incentives for collaboration?

11. *Eliminate work standards and quotas.* Does the organization set output standards?

12. *Eliminate individual review/appraisal systems.* Are employees evaluated within their work groups or by overall organizational performance?

13. *Institute a vigorous program of training and self-improvement.* Does the organization recognize the need to support skill building? Is everyone committed to improving his or her own skill levels? Has the organization provided the training (such as statistical process control and teamwork) in the key areas to improve quality?

14. *Everyone in the organization is responsible for quality.* Is quality "owned" by a specific office within the organization? Does everyone have the ability and responsibility to intervene when they see opportunities to improve performance?

DESCRIPTION OF THE INSTRUMENT

The Quality Principles Measure (QPM) is a self-scoring instrument that may be used individually or within groups. The QPM asks participants their perceptions of how committed or consistent they perceive their organization to be with Deming's Fourteen Principles. Participants assess the degree to which each of the Fourteen Principles is emphasized within the organization on a five-point scale.

The QPM can be used effectively for three purposes. First, it is an effective tool for assessing employees' perceptions of commitment and progress within the organization. If employees perceive little or no emphasis (or a consistent response of little emphasis on the same principles), that information is useful to the organization. If employees' perceptions reflect reality, then the organization has an assessment of areas they must work on to improve their quality initiative. If employees' perceptions do not reflect organizational reality, this tells the organization that the quality initiative is still relatively invisible. Without action to improve employee involvement and awareness of the initiative, it will ultimately fail.

Second, the QPM is a useful tool for assessing the degree to which participants understand quality principles and Deming's Fourteen Principles. If managers do not completely grasp their role within the quality initiative, it will fail because of their insistence on control or internal competition. Consequently, the QPM can be a valuable tool for highlighting discrepancies between participant knowledge and the principles inherent to the quality initiative.

Finally, the QPM is a useful tool for stimulating discussion and analysis about quality. It is an ideal means for engaging participants in a discussion prior to or at the start of a company quality initiative. Participants can use the discussion to gain a better understanding of what the initiative will involve, the degree of changes the initiative requires, and the depth and intensity required for a successful quality initiative. Consequently, the QPM can be helpful in developing shared expectations within the organization prior to a quality initiative.

ADMINISTERING THE INSTRUMENT

Begin by explaining to participants that the purpose of the QPM is to assess their perceptions about the organization's commitment to key quality principles. Say that you are not asking participants to put their names on their copies of the QPM—they may choose to keep their responses anonymous if they wish.

Next, provide some brief background on Deming's Fourteen Principles. Additional background on these principles can be obtained from any of Dr. Deming's writings, those of Mary Walton (such as *The Deming Management Method*), or from the official Deming Institute Website at http://www.Deming.org.

Then provide information about assessment tools. Key points to emphasize to participants include: There are no right or wrong answers; the QPM is not a test—it measures perceptions; and results may change over time as perceptions and exposure to new information changes. Say that you are asking them for their individual perceptions, not what they believe others perceive. Explain to participants that they are being asked their individual *perceptions of how committed or consistent the organization is on each of the Fourteen Principles*. You are not asking participants for how much progress the organization has achieved (for instance, there may be few direct results from the quality initiative to this point). Say that you are asking them to assess how consistent and committed the organization is toward the principles that will ultimately determine how successful the quality initiative will be.

Make sure that all participants are thinking of the *same* organizational level (so that some do not assess only their immediate office or team, others their division, and others all offices across the world). Choose and verbalize which level you want participants to assess. Point out that participants will be asked to assess organizational commitment on a five-point scale.

Participants should assess the degree to which they perceive the organization is committed to or emphasizing each of the Fourteen Principles. The evaluation scale for each principle ranges from 1 to 5 and is listed at the top of the instrument.

After participants have had an opportunity to assess the Fourteen Principles, have them answer the two open-ended questions on the QPM. Specifically, participants are asked to write a paragraph describing an incident within the organization that exemplifies the organization's consistency or commitment to one of the Fourteen Principles and to write a paragraph describing an incident within the organization that violates one of the Fourteen Principles.

Participants will need ten to fifteen minutes to complete the QPM. Once they have completed it, you have several options:

1. Participants can discuss the results in groups, looking for principles where everyone was aligned, or discuss why some points demonstrated a very wide perspective (some people may have scored the organization a "1" while others scored it a "5").

2. You can also ask participants to disclose what examples they used in their answers to the questions and then use these examples to generate a discussion about the Fourteen Principles or to discuss areas within the quality initiative in which the organization is doing well and areas that lack commitment.

3. You can also use these examples to gain insight into how knowledgeable the participants are about the quality principles. The questions serve as a reflection of how accurately participants scored their organization on the Fourteen Principles. The examples generated by participants may show

that they do not really understand the Fourteen Principles, in which case the organization clearly needs to work harder on providing knowledge and skills training about the quality initiative.

4. You may want individuals to total their own responses to the fourteen questions and discuss them in groups. Alternatively, you could add all the individual scores for each principle, then divide by the number of participants to reach an "average" score for each principle. Create an overhead or a flip-chart page using the Quality Principles Measure Scoring Graph and post the averages and ranges for each item.

5. You may want to have participants discuss the results and discuss these and other questions: "What surprises emerged?" "What follow-up actions are necessary?"

References

Deming, W.E. (1982). *Quality, productivity, and competitive position.* Cambridge, MA: MIT.

Deming, W.E. (1986). *Out of crisis.* Cambridge, MA: MIT.

Walton, M. (1986). *The Deming management method.* New York: Dodd, Mead.

Walton, M. (1990). *Deming management at work.* New York: Putnam.

Official Deming Institute Website: http://www.Deming.org.

Joe Willmore is president of the Willmore Consulting Group, located in Annandale, Virginia. He specializes in the areas of team building, facilitation, strategic planning, and creative problem solving. He is an adjunct faculty member of the University of Virginia and served as the 1997 president of the Metro DC Chapter of ASTD. He was a presenter at the 1998 ASTD International Conference on the subject of scenario planning.

QUALITY PRINCIPLES MEASURE

Joe Willmore

Instructions: Indicate the degree to which each of the fourteen quality principles listed below is being emphasized in your organization. Focus only on your own perceptions (not what you believe other people's perceptions to be) about the organization's degree of commitment to or emphasis on each principle. The evaluation scale for each principle ranges from 1 to 5, with 5 being high.

1 = no emphasis or commitment whatsoever
2 = weak emphasis, more talk than walk
3 = mixed performance, some emphasis but glaring inconsistencies
4 = good emphasis, but commitment is not complete
5 = consistent and strong emphasis—very committed

Circle the number for each principle that you believe reflects the degree of emphasis and commitment you see organizationally.

1. Constancy of purpose.	1	2	3	4	5
2. Commit to quality as a means of operation/doing business.	1	2	3	4	5
3. End reliance on inspection as a quality compliance tool.	1	2	3	4	5
4. Reliance on single suppliers, end reliance on the low bid or lowest price as a means of selecting vendors.	1	2	3	4	5
5. Commitment to ongoing improvement— the quality initiative never ends.	1	2	3	4	5
6. Institute formal job training rather than ad hoc on-the-job training.	1	2	3	4	5
7. Managers empower and lead instead of focusing on control.	1	2	3	4	5
8. Eliminate fear and coercion within the organization.	1	2	3	4	5
9. Break down barriers within and between departments.	1	2	3	4	5

10. Eliminate internal competition among personnel.   1   2   3   4   5

11. Eliminate work standards and quotas.   1   2   3   4   5

12. Eliminate individual review/appraisal systems.   1   2   3   4   5

13. Institute a vigorous program of training and self-improvement so that all individuals gain specific quality initiative skills and everyone works to improve.   1   2   3   4   5

14. Everyone in the organization is responsible for quality.   1   2   3   4   5

When you have completed your assessment, write a paragraph about each of the items below:

1. Describe an incident that occurred in your organization that you consider to be an example consistent with or supportive of one of the fourteen principles above.

_____

_____

_____

_____

_____

_____

_____

_____

_____

_____

2. Describe an incident that occurred in your organization that you consider to be an example of omission or inconsistency with one of the fourteen principles.

_____

_____

_____

_____

_____

_____

_____

_____

_____

_____

_____

Quality Principles Measure Scoring Sheet

	Average	Range
1. Constancy of purpose	_____	_____
2. Quality as a way of operating	_____	_____
3. End reliance on inspection	_____	_____
4. End reliance on low bid	_____	_____
5. Continuous improvement	_____	_____
6. Formalized job training	_____	_____
7. Empowerment instead of control	_____	_____
8. Eliminate fear and coercion	_____	_____
9. Break down internal barriers	_____	_____
10. Eliminate internal competition	_____	_____
11. Eliminate work standards	_____	_____
12. Eliminate individual reviews	_____	_____
13. Vigorous training and self-improvement	_____	_____
14. Everyone is responsible for quality	_____	_____

Introduction
to the Presentation and Discussion Resources Section

The Presentation and Discussion Resources Section is a collection of articles of use to every facilitator—theories, background, models, and methods to challenge facilitators' thinking, enrich their professional development, and assist their clients (internal and external) with productive change. These articles may be used as a basis for lecturettes, as handouts in training sessions, or as background reading material.

This section will provide you with a variety of useful ideas, theoretical opinions, teachable models, practical strategies, and proven intervention methods. The articles will add richness and depth to your training and consulting knowledge and skills. They will challenge you to think differently, explore new concepts, and experiment with new interventions. The articles will continue to add a fresh perspective to your work.

The 1999 Annual: Volume 2, Consulting includes ten articles in the following categories:

Individual Development: Personal Growth

Bolster Your Brain Power with Memory and Mind Mapping
by Jeanne Baer

Individual Development: Life/Career Planning

The Professional Pairing Program: A New Way To Mentor
by Nancy Vogel Mueller

Problem Solving: Models, Methods, and Techniques

Making Team Decisions by Kristin Arnold

Consulting: OD Theory and Practice

Organization Development Resource Guide by Homer H. Johnson, Lynette A. Hurta, Valerie Revelle Medina, and Joan H. Wrenn

Successful Implementation of ISO-9000 by Michael Danahy

Facilitating: Theories and Models of Facilitating

Focus Groups: A Qualitative Research Tool by Pamela J. Schmidt

Facilitating: Evaluating

How To Generate Real-Time Data for Designing Effective Interventions by Robert Merritt and Richard Whelan

As with previous *Annuals*, this volume covers a wide variety of topics. The range of articles presented should encourage a good deal of thought-provoking discussion about the present and future of HRD. Other articles on specific subjects can be located by using our comprehensive *Reference Guide to Handbooks and Annuals*. This book, which is updated regularly, indexes the contents of all the *Annuals* and the *Handbooks of Structured Experiences*. With each revision, the *Reference Guide* becomes a complete, up-to-date, and easy-to-use resource for selecting appropriate materials from the *Annuals* and *Handbooks*.

Here and in the *Reference Guide*, we have done our best to categorize the articles for easy reference; however, many of the articles encompass a range of topics, disciplines, and applications. If you do not find what you are looking for under one category, we encourage you to look under a related category. In come cases we may place an article in the "Training" *Annual* that also has implications for "Consulting," and vice versa. As the field of HRD becomes more sophisticated, what is done in a training context is based on the needs of, and affects, the organization. Similarly, from a systemic viewpoint, anything that affects individuals in an organization has repercussions throughout the organization, and vice versa.

It is for this reason that the new "Organization" category has been added to the 1999 volumes. We encourage you not to limit yourself by the categorization system that we have developed, but to explore all the contents of both volumes of the *Annual* in order to realize the full potential for learning and development that each offers.

BOLSTER YOUR BRAIN POWER
WITH MEMORY AND MIND MAPPING

Jeanne Baer

Abstract: The simple diagramming technique presented here was developed by Tony and Barry Buzan
in the 1960s and 1970s. The technique is currently
being used all over the world to allow people to explore and retain ideas more successfully. Tony Buzan
called the method "mind mapping" and applied it
both to brainstorming and also to aiding the recall of
concepts and facts. "Memory mapping" is the same
technique, but used for a different purpose.

This article explains how one can increase retention through memory mapping and effectively
explore ideas, alone or with a team, through mind
mapping. As a consultant you can train your clients
or teams to use the techniques; help a group to create a group memory; or use the techniques yourself
for taking notes during a briefing, while reading, or
in many other situations.

Imagine that you have to learn and remember the locations of the fifty states and of the topographical features of the United States. Further imagine that instead of learning this material by looking at a map, you have to learn it by someone *describing* the map to you!

While the person details the arrangement of fifty states stretched over the land mass, the mountains that punctuate, and the rivers that flow through the country, you begin to feel a little panic-stricken, trying to grasp and remember it all.

Now imagine someone showing you a map of the United States in a giant atlas. Ah—now you can see it all, from sea to shining sea, at a glance! After taking time to study it, you know you understand and can recall what you've seen.

MEMORY MAPPING: A PICTURE IS WORTH A THOUSAND WORDS

A memory map is similar to a geographical map in that it helps you grasp and recall material more clearly. It is a diagram that features key words and simple pictures to remind you of the concepts you want to learn or remember.

An alternate method of taking notes, it is also a helpful way to review your learning. What makes it even more memorable is that you create it yourself—you do not have to study and try to make sense of someone else's interpretation of important concepts.

If you are like most people, you are probably accustomed to taking notes in a linear or outline format. But your brain does not work that way! As you are learning and recalling, your brain creates connections between bits of information organized around a central theme. Memory mapping is a way of taking notes in this same natural, interconnected way.

Also, you may have noticed that you are more likely to grasp and remember pictures than actual words. How many times have you heard that pictures are worth a thousand words? Scientists theorize that it is because the right hemisphere of your brain, which stores pictures so accurately, works 1,500 times faster than the left hemisphere, which stores words less accurately.

Memory mapping takes advantage of both hemispheres. As you draw quick pictures or symbols on your map to accompany your key words, the facts and concepts become firmly anchored in your mind, ready for recall when you need them.

Once you learn how to "map" your learning, you will find that it is fun, creative—even relaxing! And you won't dread reviewing your notes when they are in the form of imaginative memory maps!

Let Your Right Brain Out to Play: Making a Memory Map

How do you create a memory map?

1. Begin by writing the subject in the middle of a sheet of paper. Enclose the subject in a circle, square, or other shape.

2. Add a branch extending out from the center for each key point or main idea you want to remember. The number will vary with the number of ideas or segments presented.

3. Write a key word or phrase on each branch, adding other branches from the main branches for additional details. Do not write whole sentences on your branches; your memory will have difficulty storing and later "seeing" long strings of words.

4. Add symbols, cartoons, or any illustrations for better recall. Be creative and outrageous. Remember, your brain is more likely to remember ludicrous images than sensible ones!

Figure 1 shows a memory map on the topic, "How To Avoid Public Speaking Anxiety." The map creator has drawn pictures, such as a muu-muu clad speaker, that will be very memorable to him or her.

Mapping Tips To Strengthen Recall

Here are a few tips for making a memorable map.

1. Turn your paper horizontally; it gives you more useable space.

2. If you are mapping a chapter of a book or manual, consider giving branches the same titles as the headings or subheads.

3. In addition to key words, jot down abbreviations on your memory map, but use only those you are really familiar with, so you will recognize them days or weeks later. As you become more skilled at mapping, you will develop your own "shorthand" of commonly used abbreviations and symbols.

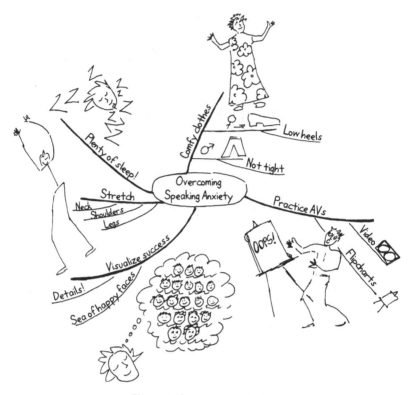

Figure 1. Sample Memory Map

4. Make important ideas stand out by underlining them, making them larger, or making them especially bold.

5. If you have several colors available, use a different color for each branch. This color coding will help your brain lock in learning.

6. If possible, play pleasant, refreshing music while you memory map. Experiment to find the type of music that works best for you.

Engaging with Reading Material

Memory mapping will not only help you remember what you have already read, but it will also help you "get into" what you need to read!

Before you begin an assigned reading, take a few minutes to scan the text. What piques your interest? What questions would you like to find answers to? What questions might you be tested on? Make a map of those questions, with the chapter title or main topic encircled in the center of the page.

Then read specifically for answers to your questions, jotting down your findings on the memory map. This technique will help you stay focused on the reading and prevent your mind from wandering.

An Aid to Taking Notes

It may look odd to the uninitiated, but skilled memory mappers draw maps instead of taking notes as they listen to a lecture. That way, if a speaker suddenly remembers to make a point about a previous thought, they can easily add it to the appropriate place on the map. Other people prefer to take more traditional notes and translate them into a memory map afterward.

Memory maps are also an effective way to record discussions and decisions at meetings. You might have a branch for action items, one for discussions, one for who has been assigned what tasks, etc. After the meeting you can use your map to remind you of your own assignments and note their completion on that same page.

Throw Away Your Speech!

As you can imagine, memory mapping a speech you plan to deliver will boost your recall quite a lot. You may never write and memorize a speech word for word again!

Here's how: After you have decided what to say, make a memory map of your key points, spicing up the map with colorful pictures to symbolize your points. Consider color-coding entire branches, or subtopics of your speech.

Even the process of making the map will help you retain your speech later on! When you practice the speech, if you forget a point, simply glance momentarily at your map, with its key words and symbols. When you actually deliver the presentation, you will easily recall your key words, evocative pictures, and color-coded branches.

Many memory mappers are able to speak entirely without notes; some carry only one page (the map!) to the podium; and a few make a poster-sized memory map and have it tacked at the back of the room, out of audience view.

Shortcut to Presentation Development

If you design training packages or make client presentations, you will find that memory mapping is a quick and easy way to help you organize your material. After you have gathered information from all your sources, jot down your topic in a center circle and your subtopics on branches.

If the topic is continuous quality improvement, for instance, you may have branches labeled, "Why?," "Evolution of CQI," "Success Stories," "Quotes," "Tools," "Our Goals," and others. Branches coming off from these main branches will let you explore each topic in more detail. As you work, you may even begin drawing some icons that symbolize AV support and training activities that occur to you to enliven your presentation.

Once you have many of your abbreviated thoughts on your map, you will see that, because your thoughts are organized onto branches, it will be easy to convert them into a more formal outline. However, in a pinch, you can train straight from your map!

MIND MAPPING: CAPTURE IDEAS, PROJECTS, AND MORE

Mind mapping uses the same diagramming technique as memory mapping, but for a different purpose. People use mind maps to brainstorm (alone or with a group), to manage projects, to make plans and decisions, or to manage or take notes at meetings. In other words, mind mapping is useful any time you work with people, information, or problems!

Better Brainstorming for Teams and Individuals

Mind mapping takes advantage of how our brains work—more like pinball machines, with ideas ricocheting and flashing, than like staid soldiers marching in order. Because mind mapping captures ideas and connects them to others quickly, most people believe that mind mapping enhances creativity by allowing for an unbroken stream of ideas.

Mind mapping is easy and flexible. If your team wants to brainstorm via mind mapping, here is what to do:

1. Write your topic or your problem statement in a circle in the middle of a huge sheet of paper attached to the wall.

2. As ideas are suggested, jot them down on main or subordinate lines radiating from the center circle. Think of the lines as main branches and

smaller branches or even "twigs" that extend from and split off from previous branches.

As you can imagine, when people offer ideas literally and figuratively "all over the map," you have plenty of space in which to add their ideas. An advantage of mind mapping over listing ideas on a flip chart is that, because you add new ideas near similar ones, the eventual sorting of ideas is quite easy. When people have finished suggesting ideas, the map shows the results of the brainstorming session at a glance—both the "forest" and the "trees."

Figure 2 shows a mind map that was drawn to generate ideas about what might be causing bad-tasting coffee in an office.

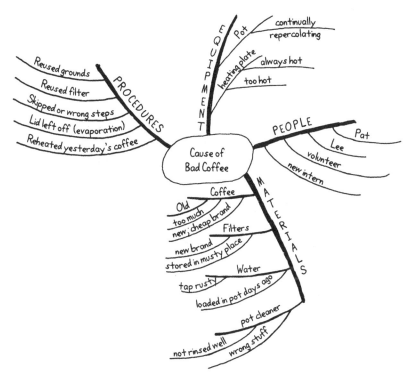

Figure 2. Sample Mind Map

Here are some ways to maximize your team's mapping success:

- Because you want people's suggestions to be as visible as possible, avoid rotating your giant map and/or writing upside down.

- Write as quickly as possible, or have others write, shout, and hand you ideas to stick onto the map. If possible, use Post-it® Notes or static-cling notes. Later, if ideas do need to be put in a different category, they can be peeled off one area and stuck elsewhere.

- When the team seems to be out of ideas, add some blank branches. Just as nature abhors a vacuum, brains hate to see a line without an idea on it; more ideas may come bubbling to the surface!

- Use as large a piece of paper as possible, so that you have plenty of room for all the ideas that will be generated. Use a huge sheet of butcher paper or many flip-chart pages taped together.

- Use color to jazz up the map. The use of several colors, especially wild ones, encourages wild ideas to match, and those wild ideas may give birth to great practical ideas once the original ideas are refined! You can also use different colors to organize concepts.

- Do not bring the flow of ideas to a screeching halt by arguing about which branch an idea belongs under ("I think that should go under 'methods,' not 'tools!'") Just write the idea anywhere and move on. You can always put it elsewhere when you begin to consider the merit of ideas.

Drawing icons is not nearly as important with mind mapping as it is with memory mapping, as your goal is not to remember every phrase on the map. However, because ideas come so fast and furiously during a lively session, a skilled recorder may develop and use a "shorthand" of certain icons to keep up with the team's enthusiastic participation. Figure 3 shows several examples of simple icons you might use when brainstorming.

From Fishbone to Octopus

Does this "great circle route" seem too foreign for you to try? If you use the problem-solving and decision-making tools that are often a part of quality initiatives, you are already using a similar technique. The Ishikawa Diagram, or "fishbone" diagram as it is often called, is used to brainstorm both the possible causes for a problem and also potential solutions.

With a mind map, your topic is in the middle instead of at the "head" of the diagram. Thus, the lines coming from it produce more of an octopus shape than a fishbone shape.

Figure 3. Some Common Mapping Symbols

Better Meetings

If your team members like to use mind mapping to generate ideas, they may also enjoy mapping as a method for recording meeting transactions. You might suggest having one branch for action items, one for discussions, one for who has been assigned what tasks, etc. People have discovered that mapping their notes during meetings helps them remember more about the meeting, create more concise notes, and easily spot action items. Afterward, they add branches and track the status of action items on the same map.

Explore Your Mental Jungle

As you can imagine, mind mapping is an excellent way to explore your own thoughts on any topic. You can develop plans for projects, training programs, speeches, and more. Some people chart their goals and objectives on a mind map, enjoying the radial, expansive approach versus the more controlled approach offered by planning books.

Other people map what they are thinking and feeling instead of writing in a diary; once again, the way space is used on a mind map seems to promote creative reflection.

Some people even draw mind maps to guide them through a day full of errands, clustering their "to do's" according to geographical area.

To construct your own personal mind map, use paper at least 8½" by 11". Then simply follow the traditional brainstorming rules below:

- Go for quantity, not quality; let your imagination run wild!

- Write as quickly and nonjudgmentally as possible, so you do not stop the natural flow of your ideas.

- If, while you are brainstorming, you suddenly think of something completely unrelated that you must do or remember, start a new branch off to one side and quickly jot down a key word expressing it. That way, you can return to your creative ideas without the need to remember the other thought.

- When you are mind mapping alone, you may wish to rotate the paper as you add branches and key words.

- Don't worry if your mind map looks or sounds silly; no one else needs to understand or even see your mind map.

- Stop when your ideas stop. Rest, and perhaps later you will want to build on some of the ideas you have already mapped.

Later, you can take a more analytical look at your map. You can sort, refine, and discard, just as teams do as they begin to make decisions. By this time, thanks to the mind-mapping process, you will have the makings of a solid, innovative plan!

To learn more about mind mapping, I recommend the books in the Resources section at the end of this article. Several of the more popular mind-mapping software packages and their websites are also listed. Each package has different strengths, so check the sites, try the demos, and then decide.

However, do not forget about the best mind-mapping system—one that is highly portable, powerful, intuitive, and adaptable. It can work with pens, markers, or whatever is available. And the best part is the price: it is free! You already own this bio-super-computer, housed squarely between your shoulders, and it is ready for your commands!

As the father of mind mapping, Tony Buzan, says, "Whoever, wherever, you are, you are using—to read these words—the most beautiful, intricate, complex, mysterious, and powerful object in the known universe: your brain."

Resources

Books

Buzan, T. (1974). *Use both sides of your brain.* New York: Dutton.

Buzan, T., with B. Buzan (1994). *The mind map book: How to use radiant thinking to maximize your brain's untapped potential.* New York: Dutton.

DePorter, B. (1992). *Quantum learning.* New York: Dell.

Margulies, N. (1991). *Mapping inner space.* Tucson, AZ: Zephyr Press.

Wycoff, J. (1991). *Mindmapping.* New York: Berkley.

Software

Axon—http://web.singnet.com.sg/~axon2000/article.htm

Inspiration—http://www.inspiration.com

Mindman—http://www.mindman.com

Smart Ideas—http://www.smarttech.com

VisiMap—http://www.coco.co.uk/

Visio Technical—http://www.visio.com

Jeanne Baer is the president of Creative Training Solutions, which has provided performance improvements through training, facilitation, and program design services since 1990. Clients include Chrysler, Campbell's Soup, DuPont Pharmaceutical, Cliffs Notes, and the U.S. Navy. A past president of the Lincoln, Nebraska, chapter of ASTD, Jeanne also teaches at two colleges in Lincoln. Jeanne's work has been published in five McGraw-Hill sourcebooks, in two Harvard Business Press guidebooks, and in Jossey-Bass/Pfeiffer's 20 Active Training Programs, Vol. III.

THE PROFESSIONAL PAIRING PROGRAM: A NEW WAY TO MENTOR

Nancy Vogel Mueller

Abstract: The Professional Pairing Program is less formal, more flexible, easier to implement, and requires fewer financial, time, and human resources than a traditional mentoring program. The intent is the same: matching a more experienced employee with a less experienced one in order to provide guidance and information to the mentee. A program coordinator announces the program and encourages participation, gathers information about potential participants, suggests pairings, coordinates the program, and evaluates the results.

$\mathbf{M}$entoring is based on a one-on-one relationship between someone who is wiser, more experienced, more powerful, and typically older and someone who is less experienced, less powerful, and typically younger. At its best, it is a close, intense, and mutually beneficial relationship.

HISTORICAL PERSPECTIVE

The word mentor has its origin in *The Odyssey*. Mentor was a close friend of Odysseus and cared for his son Telemachus while Odysseus traveled for ten years. Mentor was a parent substitute, teacher, friend, guide, and protector. These are still the characteristics one looks for in a mentor—a wise and trusted advisor.

Historically, the act of mentoring consisted of one man partnering with another man to learn about a business or trade over his lifetime. Today, employees (both men and women) typically change jobs more than ten times during their careers. They think and travel globally and, with today's technology, expect information immediately. Because of these changes, the conventional method of mentoring may no longer be appropriate.

TODAY'S PERSPECTIVE

Formal developmental programs such as mentoring enhance employee growth and change, improve retention of skills and knowledge, and strengthen overall employee performance. Therefore, today's best organizations are taking steps to nurture their employees, viewing them as resources and assets.

It takes significant time to establish and maintain a formal, structured mentoring program. People must design and develop the system, monitor and improve it, train the mentors, and deal with unique situations in which the mentoring relationships are not working smoothly. The organization must create a culture to support the mentoring process and must be committed to it for the long term.

A NEW WAY TO MENTOR

The Professional Pairing Program (PPP) has the same objective as mentoring: to establish a relationship between a more experienced person and a less experienced person for the benefit of both. It has these advantages over traditional mentoring:

- Limited time commitment,
- Simpler implementation,
- Less bureaucracy,
- Lower costs,
- Focus on the needs of the mentee, and
- Ownership of the process with the mentee.

The Professional Pairing Program offers employees a chance to network with other employees within an organization while learning more about a specific department and exploring potential career options. The first meeting is arranged by a PPP coordinator. The members of the pair determine whether they want to schedule future meetings. If they do not, the process can be replicated by the mentee to seek further contacts that are perceived to be a better fit.

The following are quotations from participants in a Professional Pairing Program.

- "It was informative, personalized, and focused."
- "I learned that this area is not one in which I want to work."
- "Everything was valuable, especially learning more about my partner and her department and expanding my network of contacts."

THE PPP PROCESS

To start, a champion within the organization introduces the idea of a pairing program, selling the idea to the organization's top management.

Next, a program coordinator is appointed. This often is someone from the human resources department but could be someone who is designated because of other internal affiliations. Someone contracted from outside is less likely to be successful in this role because a thorough knowledge of the organization's structure and internal relationships with potential partners are helpful in setting up the pairings.

The program coordinator creates the tools to communicate about and monitor the program. These tools include an announcement about the program and invitation to participate, the instrument used to gather information about the mentees, the guidelines that are shared with mentees and mentors, and the evaluation form. Samples of each are provided at the end of this article.

The announcement is a marketing tool for the program. It informs potential mentees about the program and highlights the fact that participation is voluntary. Information is solicited about a potential mentee's expertise, areas of interest, and (perhaps) a specific employee with whom the potential mentee would like to be paired.

Potential mentees may be concerned about the confidentiality of participation, especially those who may be investigating changes of career. Although there cannot be complete confidentially, it is advisable to limit the information that is distributed about the pairings.

The coordinator then sets up the pair by contacting the employee named by the mentee or another individual from the department of interest (preferably the highest ranking employee possible, depending on the organization's culture). The program is explained and the commitment outlined. The initial commitment is for a one- or two-hour meeting. Employees rarely say "no" when they are asked, "Would you be willing to spend one to two hours with another employee and share the benefits of your experience? Would you mind being an advisor and coach for a limited time?"

The coordinator contacts both the mentor and the mentee with the names of the other partner. The coordinator provides a set of written guidelines about how to proceed. The rest is up to the individual pairs. The intent of the PPP is to provide flexibility, encourage informality, maintain ease of implementation, and take little time.

The PPP provides flexibility. It is entirely up to individual pairs to determine how many times they will meet. Typically a pair decides to meet several times on a regularly scheduled basis. Other pairs may decide the need has been met with one meeting. The final decision is entirely up to each pair.

The PPP is informal. The mentees prepare lists of questions based on suggested guidelines they receive as participants in the program. Sample guidelines appear at the end of this article. The experience can take on whatever direction or focus the mentee decides.

The PPP is easy to implement. The guidelines help the mentee stay focused. The backbone of the program is the list of questions the mentee creates that focus on the mentor's background, education, and job; careers and career paths; and the mentor's advice, observations, and recommendations desired. These questions form the basis of an effective and productive relationship.

The PPP takes little time and few resources. Once pairs are determined, little administrative time is required. Most pairs meet for about an hour the first time. Subsequent meetings are set to accommodate both people's schedules. The guidelines help the mentee focus the content of each meeting, ensuring wise time use.

The coordinator also is responsible for evaluating the program, in terms of the participants' satisfaction and the process. Questions may focus on whether the participants' expectations were met, whether the participants found value in the program, and ways to improve the program.

The PPP works especially well when it is implemented on an annual cycle. It can be done more frequently, depending on the number of employees and participants and the time that the program coordinator can allocate to the process.

Employees want to do the best work they can. A Professional Pairing Program can provide a way to attract and retain great employees. In addition, pairing relationships leave long-lasting impressions and create memories. They may even leave legacies.

Nancy Vogel Mueller, M.B.A., is the principal of Opportunities for Transition. She played an instrumental role in developing this mentoring initiative. It was used successfully for three years by a Midwestern utility to link women with senior-level management employees. Ms. Mueller has over fifteen years' experience in training and development. Her areas of expertise include training for trainers, quality improvement, presentation skills, and diversity. She is a certified DACUM (Developing a Curriculum) facilitator and a Distinguished Toastmaster.*

Sample PPP Announcement and Invitation

Announcing a Professional Pairing Program

Because of the continued interest of our employees, we are pleased to offer the Professional Pairing Program (PPP) once again.

What Is the Professional Pairing Program?

The PPP provides an opportunity for you to meet with more experienced employees in an area of particular interest to you. The Professional Pairing Program offers you the chance to network with other company employees while learning more about a specific department and exploring potential career options. You can request a particular person to be your partner, or we will make a recommendation for you based on your areas of interest.

What Should I Expect if I Participate?

Your first meeting (similar to an informational interview) generally consists of you—the "interviewer"—asking questions you have previously prepared of your partner. We will provide you with some typical questions and guidelines after your pairing is confirmed to help you to prepare for your first meeting. The first meeting usually lasts about an hour, but you and your partner can make it however long or short you want it to be.

I'm Interested, so What's Next?

Participation is easy. Simply complete the attached PPP Interest Profile, outlining your current professional experience and area(s) of interest, and return it to [name], in [location], by [date]. We encourage you to indicate the person with whom you would like to be paired.

The PPP coordinator will then act as liaison between you and your partner. We will help to arrange your first meeting; then, if you and your partner choose, you can schedule future meetings as well.

Please Join Us!

We hope you'll consider taking part in the program this year. Participants from years past have given rave reviews of their experiences, and we believe that you can enjoy the same satisfaction. Give it a try!

If you have any questions about this program, please call [name], at [telephone number].

Sample PPP Interest Profile

In order to set up a Professional Pairing Program partner for you, we need more information about you and your needs. Please complete the following:

Name: _____ Extension: _____ Date: _____

Department: _____ Location: _____

Current primary job responsibilities (limit five):

_____

_____

_____

_____

_____

_____

_____

Areas of expertise (not necessarily part of your current responsibilities):

_____

_____

_____

_____

_____

_____

Area(s) of interest for Professional Pairing Program (rank by level of interest; maximum of three):

_____ Community Development

_____ Corporate Communications

_____ Customer Relations

_____ Engineering

_____ Finance

_____ Human Relations

_____ Information Technology

_____ Labor Relations

_____ Management

_____ Market Research

_____ Marketing

_____ Purchasing

_____ Risk Management

_____ Sales

_____ Other (specify)

Is there a particular employee with whom you would like to be paired?

_____ Yes (specify) _____

_____ No, please choose an appropriate partner for me.

Return to [name], at [location], by [date].

Sample PPP Guidelines

Prepare

What do you already know (or what can you find out) about your partner?

- Name
- Position/Title
- Department
- Employment History

What about you?

- Skills, knowledge, training
- Areas of interest
- Short-term objectives
- Long-term objectives
- Reason for participation in the Professional Pairing Program

Create a List of Questions

Suggestions:

- What do I want to learn about my partner?
- What do I want to learn about my partner's job?
- What do I want to learn about my partner's department?
- How does my partner's department fit into the corporate picture?
- How did my partner reach his/her current position?
- How did my partner get started?
- What education and/or training has my partner had?
- What is a typical career path in my partner's area of expertise?
- What skills, knowledge, and attitudes does my partner think are necessary for me to achieve my objective(s)?
- What recommendations does my partner have for me?
- Are there any other observations my partner could share with me?
- Are there other employees my partner would suggest I contact or speak with? If so, whom?

Set Up Mutually Convenient Meeting Time

Your partner has been told that you will be calling shortly (within the next week or so) to set up a meeting and is expecting your call. It is best to call as soon as possible to minimize scheduling hassles.

Meet with Your Partner

It is important that you be on time to your meeting. Because scheduling concerns are among the foremost reasons for lack of desire to participate in the Paired Professional Program, the courtesy you show by a timely arrival will help this program to succeed.

During your meeting:

- Share some information about yourself.
- Tell your partner about your objectives.
- Ask your questions.
- Stay focused on the task so that you can accomplish your objectives.
- Honor your time commitments (don't take more than an hour or so unless your partner has previously agreed).
- If you desire (and your partner agrees), arrange future meetings.

Remember:

- Be yourself.
- The more you share, the more you will receive in return.
- Kind words can be short and easy to speak, but their echoes are endless.

Thank Your Partner

Please send a written thank-you note to your partner. The Professional Pairing Program is strictly voluntary, and it often is difficult for individuals to make time to participate. Besides, it's a good business practice.

Complete the Paired Professional Program Evaluation

Send your completed evaluation form to [name], at [location], by [date].

SAMPLE PPP EVALUATION FORM

In order to ensure the best use of time and resources, it is important for us to receive your input on the success of this program.

Please take a moment to complete this form and return it to [name], at [location], by [date]. Your responses will be kept anonymous, so please answer freely!

1. Were you an: _____ Interviewer _____ Partner
   (The Interviewer is the one who requested the pairing by completing an Interest Profile.)

2. Did this program meet your expectations? _____ Yes _____ No
   If it did not, please explain:

   _____

   _____

   _____

   _____

3. Was this a valuable experience overall? _____ Yes _____ No
   If yes, why? If no, why not?

   _____

   _____

   _____

4. Did you accomplish your objectives? _____ Yes _____ No
   If not, why?

   _____

   _____

   _____

5. Do you think your meeting was worth the effort? _____ Yes _____ No

6. What was the most valuable aspect of your meeting?

   _____

   _____

   _____

7. How would you improve this program and/or the pairing process?

_____

_____

_____

8. Would you participate in this program again?   _____ Yes _____ No
   Why or why not?

_____

_____

_____

9. Do you think this program should be
   continued next year?   _____ Yes _____ No

10. Please list any suggestions you have for expanding or changing the program:

_____

_____

_____

11. Would you recommend this program to
    another employee?   _____ Yes _____ No

12. Is this your first year of participation in the
    program?   _____ Yes _____ No

13. Additional comments, please:

_____

_____

_____

_____

_____

_____

_____

MAKING TEAM DECISIONS

Kristin Arnold

Abstract: Making decisions is one of the most important team responsibilities. Team members must not
only make the most effective and appropriate decisions, but they must make decisions that will be supported by everyone on the team. This article presents
seven decision-making methods for teams. It focuses
on consensus, the most misunderstood, yet often
the most needed method, providing suggestions for
more efficiently reaching consensus.

How do teams make decisions? If you took a poll, most team members would say "by consensus"—without really knowing what consensus is or how to build a true team consensus. Most traditional teams use only one or two strategies to make decisions. However, high performing teams use a wide range of decision-making options, from one person (usually the team leader or expert) deciding to the entire team agreeing wholeheartedly, depending on the time available, involvement desired, expertise available within the team, and the need to develop the team. Several methods and the advantages and disadvantages of each are shown in Figure 1. Let's define each of these ways teams make decisions and some reasons why each may be successful.

Command Decisions. With this method, the team leader or expert decides. This method is useful when a decision must be made quickly and the leader is in control of the situation. The key here is for the leader to explain the decision and the reasons for making the decision to other team members as soon as possible.

Leader Decides with Input from Individuals. The advantage of obtaining input is that the leader does not have to bring all the team members together; yet he or she does collect information from them before making a decision. As information is collected, the key is for the leader to explain the criteria for making the decision, how others will be involved, and what type of input is needed (ideas, suggestions, information).

Leader Decides with Input from Team. By gathering the team together, the leader creates opportunities for creativity, synergy, and buy-in. However, the process does take more time and may create conflict if the leader makes a decision that is against the team's recommendation. The key is for the leader to explain the criteria for making the decision, how the team will be involved, what type of input is wanted, and the time available for discussion. In addition, the leader must clearly state up front that he or she will make the decision.

Majority Vote. Majority vote is useful when the issue is relatively inconsequential or the team is stuck. The advantage is that Americans are fairly comfortable with a hand vote. The key is for the leader to ensure that everyone understands what they are voting on and the rules involved *before* the actual vote is taken.

Method	Disadvantages	Advantages
Command decisions	• May not consider expertise in the group. • Limited implementation commitment. • Disagreement and resentment may decrease effectiveness.	• Efficient when leader has all information. • Fastest of all methods.
Leader decides with input from individuals	• Leader must explain criteria and input multiple times, resulting in increased chance for miscommunication. • No chance for group brainstorming of new ideas. • May not have complete buy-in from team members after decision.	• Do not have to gather all team members together. • Not much time needed from members.
Leader decides with input from team	• May not create commitment to implementation. • May create competition among group members. • Members may tell leader what they think he or she wants to hear. • Potential for group think.	• Uses entire group as a resource. • Gains benefit of group discussion. • Members can play off one another's ideas. • Takes less time.
Majority vote	• May leave minority dissatisfied. • Decision lacks total commitment. • May not utilize resources of team.	• Good for fast decision when consensus is not important. • Closes discussions that are not important.
Minority rule	• No widespread commitment. • Unresolved conflict may have future implications.	• Useful when all cannot meet. • May be opportunity for delegation. • Useful for simple, routine decisions. • Opportunity to use experts.
Unanimous agreement	• Very difficult to reach.	• May be necessary for most critical decisions.
Consensus	• Takes a great deal of time and psychological energy. • Time pressure must be minimal. • Potential for weak decision.	• Produces innovative, high-quality decisions when done well. • Elicits commitment from all. • Uses all resources. • Future decision-making ability of group is enhanced.

Figure 1. Decision-Making Methods Employed by Teams

If the team must make a decision among many choices, ¾-inch round labels can be used to prioritize. The leader can post the list on a flip chart and give each participant one vote per item. If the leader desires, team members can be given more than one label and allowed to vote for more than one item or to place all labels beside just one item. This produces a more dramatic visual representation of the team's preferences. Also, the leader could use two different colors of label so that team members could vote for first and second preferences. The results in this case could resemble Figure 2.

Minority Rule. Minority rule is a standard default for routine team decision making and useful for less important issues. It does, however, require a team member to have the courage to speak up with an opposing viewpoint. From a positive perspective, the team may request a subject-matter "expert" in the group to make a decision. The key is that the team must support this method of decision making and the decision reached.

Unanimous Agreement. The hardest way to reach a decision is by unanimous agreement. This strategy is not recommended unless all team members must agree, as in matters of life or death.

Consensus. When there is consensus, everyone can live with *and* support the decision, but it is not necessarily everyone's first choice. Leaders use consensus for important issues when the team must learn about all the alternatives and issues, and then implement the decision. Reaching consensus increases the likelihood and ease of successfully implementing a decision.

Consensus is not the same as unanimity, wherein a decision is everyone's first choice. Nor is it a compromise, whereby each person makes con-

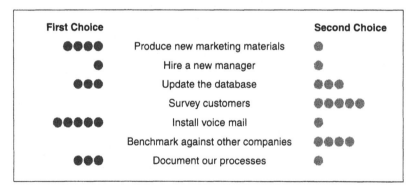

Figure 2. Making a Team Decision by Affixing Labels

cessions to achieve a team decision. As Robert Ludlum said, a compromise is "a decision which pleases no one, except in knowing that no one else got what they wanted either." Consensus is a process. The team *builds* a consensus—striving to reach a decision that best reflects the thinking of *all* team members. Consensus is a bigger, better decision that is built from the input of each and every team member.

When a team decides to make a decision by consensus, the leader must explain exactly what consensus means and why it is important for the team to reach it. The leader must ensure that all team members understand the issue and the most important aspects of the decision. To prevent confusion, he or she must take the time to define terms, as well as identify and outline any constraints (e.g., time, financial, resources, political). The leader must remind each member to participate fully in the discussion and that each has equal power to support or block any proposals. Finally, the team must agree on a "fallback" decision-making strategy in case consensus cannot be reached. For a group of peers, the fallback strategy is usually to use majority vote. When the leader is part of the group, the fallback strategy may be to defer to the leader.

To build a consensus, the leader *must* hear from everyone on the team. Many teams do this by soliciting opinions from everyone in the group or by brainstorming every possible option and then looking for opportunities to combine, create, and synergize the items into a better idea.

The following questions can be used to help a team be more creative before trying to reach consensus:

- "All of these items are possible. Do we have to choose only one?"

- "Is there any way we can use the best features of all of our options?"

- "What would happen if we added/deleted features of several options. Would that move us closer to what we want?"

- "Could we try out several options in parallel before we commit to just one?"

Team energy increases as new ideas and possibilities surface. Using a trial-and-error approach appears chaotic; however, it is well worth it if a team builds a new, synergistic alternative based on the best of the best.

When it appears that a team has reached a decision, the leader usually takes a "straw poll" to see how close or how far apart the team members are. The leader reminds the team at this point that this is not a final vote, but simply a way to determine how much work must be done to build consensus. These sentence starters can be used:

- "It sounds as though we are making progress. Let's check that out with a quick straw poll to see how close we are to a consensus. We'll go right around the table. Sally?"

- "Let's see if everyone either can agree with or can agree to support the most popular alternative. Let's start with Emile and go around the room."

Record the responses and summarize the results. If everyone can live with and support the alternative, then the team has reached a consensus.

Try this quick, fun approach to testing for consensus: the "Five L Straw Poll." Give each person a Post-it™ Tape Flag. Draw the "Five L" scale on a flip chart, as shown in Figure 3. Describe each "L" as you write it. Say something like "You *loathe* it or hate it. You will *lament* it and moan about it in the parking lot. You can *live* with it. You can *like* it. Or you can really *love* it."

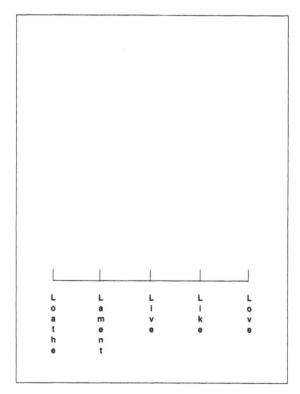

Figure 3. Sample Five L Scale

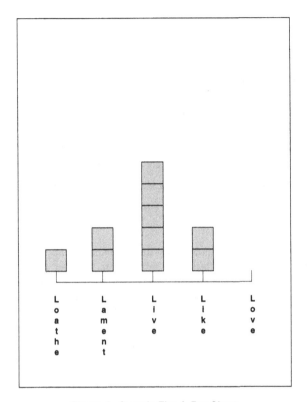

Figure 4. Sample Five L Bar Chart

Now ask the team members to think silently about the proposed alternative. Then ask them to place their tape flags on the flip chart, building a bar chart, such as the one in Figure 4.

Ask if the team believes there is a consensus, that is, the alternative received at least a "live with" or better vote. In the event there are votes that are in the "loathe" or "lament" categories, the leader must check with the team to see why people have voted that way, being careful not to pick on a specific person, but hearing feedback from team members.

If your team cannot reach consensus, try these sentence starters:

■ "There seems to be a lot of support for this alternative. What would it take for *everyone* to support it?"

- "What is getting in the way of some team members' ability to support this alternative? What could we do to meet those needs?"

Integrate the feedback and create another, better alternative! Continue to build agreement for the decision until there is true consensus, that is, when everyone can live with *and* support the decision. Four criteria must be met before a decision can be declared to have been made by consensus.

1. All team members must have had an opportunity to provide input.

2. All team members must believe that they were heard and understood.

3. Everyone must be able to state the decision clearly.

4. All team members must agree to support the decision in what they say and what they do.

If time runs out, the leader must decide whether to postpone the decision for another time or whether to fall back to another decision-making method. If a leader uses the fallback decision option frequently or for many key decisions, something is happening that must be addressed. Many times, the "something" is happening outside of the group or is beyond the team's control.

By building a consensus, team leaders have a greater chance of producing a better quality decision, a more cohesive team, and smoother implementation of the decisions that are made.

Kristin Arnold maintains a private consulting practice specializing in facilitation services and training, with an emphasis on strategic planning, strategic partnerships, collaborative problem solving, and team building. Ms. Arnold has extensive experience as both an internal and external consultant with a wide variety of manufacturing and service industries, as well as the government sector.

ORGANIZATION DEVELOPMENT RESOURCE GUIDE

Homer H. Johnson, Lynette A. Hurta,
Valerie Revelle Medina, and Joan H. Wrenn

Table of Contents for OD Resource Guide

About this Guide

"Do you know of any good books on team building?" "What is ODN's address?" "Are there any websites that focus on coaching?" "Where can I find information on the search conference?" "What's a good journal for OD?" These are some of the frequently asked questions that we receive.

To answer these and many other questions people have, we asked some 200 organization development (OD) practitioners and students to identify the most useful books, journals, organizations, and websites about organization development. The only restriction placed on the request was that the resource be practical and easily accessible. The resulting guide has the following characteristics:

- The focus is on practical, how-to-do-it resources for a new or experienced consultant.
- Material falls into both recent and classic references.
- The guide is intended as a starting point for information in a given content area and is not intended to be comprehensive.
- The material reflects what the respondents said they found useful in learning and practicing organization development.
- The material is readily accessed through general library or computer resources.
- Each reference is followed by a brief description of its contents.

RESOURCES BY SUBJECT

Action Learning

Froiland, P. (1994, January). Action learning: Taming problems in real time. *Training*, pp. 27–34.

A good overview of action learning approaches in the U.S., with examples from Corning, Whirlpool, and others. At AT&T, seven managers, each from different units, meet for seven days. On each day, one of the managers presents a business problem for two hours, and the rest of the group questions him or her and discusses the problem for the rest of the day. The manager is held accountable for the results. Also discusses combining action learning with personal development such as Outward Bound and visits to soup kitchens.

Raelin, J.A. (1997, Summer). Action learning and action science: Are they different? *Organizational Dynamics*, pp. 21–34.

The article describes both action learning and action science and points out the similarities and differences. Both approaches focus on the individual and question the issues and assumptions that lie behind an individual's decision making. Uses a case from Argyris to illustrate how each of the action technologies might approach the problem raised in the case. An easy-to-read and clear explanation of each approach. Good overview of action learning.

Action Research Model

(See also Organization Development, Introductory Materials for discussion of model.)

Beer, M., & Eisenstat, R.A. (1996). Developing an organization capable of implementing strategy and learning. *Human Relations, 49*(5), 597–619.

An interesting adaptation of the Action Research Model to change in a large organization, using a five-box diagnostic model. At each site, an employee task force conducts interviews inside and outside the organization about specific management practices and organizational arrangements that help or hinder the implementation of strategy. The data are presented to management in a three-day meeting designed to promote personal and organizational learning.

Action Science

(See Argyris references under Organization Development, Classics.)

Appreciative Inquiry

Bushe, G.R. (1995). Advances in appreciative inquiry as an organization development intervention. *Organization Development, 13*(3), 14–22.

An introduction to the theory behind appreciative inquiry as well as a description of the process. While noting that there is no standard procedure, the author discusses how he has used the technique, including some innovations to the basic process.

Srivasta, S., & Cooperrider, D. (Eds.). (1990). *Appreciative management and leadership.* San Francisco, CA: Jossey-Bass.

Book of readings on appreciative management. Chapter 4 is often quoted and is titled "Positive Image, Positive Action: The Affirmative Basis for Organizing." This chapter outlines the basic logic for focusing on the positive, rather than focusing on problems (via the action research model). The chapter concludes with a discussion on the affirmative organization.

Watkins, J.M., & Cooperrider, D. (1996). Organizational inquiry model for global social change organizations. *Organization Development, 14*(4), 97–112.

Describes the application of the appreciative inquiry methodology to a "global social change organization" (international development organization). Contains an overview of a three-phase model (ABC).

Change Management, General Resources

Ackerman-Anderson, L.S., with Anderson, D., & Marquardt, M. (1996). Development, transition, or transformation: Bringing change leadership into the 21st century. *OD Practitioner, 28*(4), 5–16.

Describes four major types of change: developmental, transitional, reactive transformational, and conscious transformational. Additionally, the article details the unique elements of each type of change and provides implementation strategies for each type.

Beer, M., Eisenstadt, R.A., & Spector, B. (1990). *The critical path of corporate renewal.* Boston, MA: Harvard Business School Press.

Contains business strategy implementation processes. The book focuses on group processes for examining barriers to implementation rather than asking for "look good" reports.

Bridges, W. (1991). *Managing transitions: Making the most of change.* Reading, MA: Addison-Wesley.

Explains in vivid terms why the human transitions that accompany change are difficult and what leaders and OD professionals can do to facilitate more productive change. Checklists are included for each step of the change process. Terrific tool for teaching leaders in client organizations about leading change.

Duck, J.D. (1993, November/December). Managing change: The art of balancing. *Harvard Business Review, 71,* 109–118.

An article containing many insights and examples of the change process. A large part of the article deals with the communication process and the importance of the actions of managers as "messages."

Imparato, N., & Harari, O. (1994). *Jumping the curve: Innovation and strategic choice in an age of transition.* San Francisco, CA: Jossey-Bass.

Four major imperatives that enable organizations to manage accelerated change, necessary for survival in the future, are identified and outlined: innovation, intelligence, coherence, and responsibility.

Kilmann, R.H. (1989). *Managing beyond the quick fix: A completely integrated program for creating and marketing organizational success.* San Francisco, CA: Jossey-Bass.

A perennial question in change implementation has been which piece of the implementation should be first, second, etc. This book provides one answer to this question. The unique feature of this book is that the author presents an integrated (and sequential) framework for organizational improvement. The five-track model suggests that successful change can take place by implementing five tracks in a designated sequence: (1) culture track, (2) management-skills track, (3) team-building track, (4) strategy-structure track, and (5) reward-system track. Each track is described and a case example (Eastman Kodak) is provided to illustrate implementation.

Nevis, E.C., Lancourt, J., & Vassallo, H. (1996). *Intentional revolutions: A seven point strategy for transforming organizations.* San Francisco, CA: Jossey-Bass.

Addresses how today's organizations need to make multiple discontinuous changes in significant aspects of their identity—transformational change. A key approach to making these changes is to create new organizational realities.

Nolan, R.C., & Croson, D.C. (1995). *Creative destruction: A six-stage process for transforming the organization.* Boston, MA: Harvard University Press.

Deals with transformations occurring at the enterprise level across the corporate and not-for-profit landscape. This book is a useful resource for consultants engaged in enterprise or business-unit change initiatives, especially in multinational corporations. This book integrates the business need for change with a model for managing the process on a macro scale.

Change Management, Methods and Tools

Conner, D.R. (1993). *Managing at the speed of change: How resilient managers succeed and prosper when others fail.* New York: Villard.

Practical description of the effect of change on individuals and how to manage that change. The chapters on resistance and gaining commitment to change are particularly good.

D'Aprix, R. (1996). *Communicating for change: Connecting the workplace with the marketplace.* San Francisco, CA: Jossey-Bass.

Entire book deals with communication and change. In the author's view, communication is a tool for accomplishing change that often is used poorly and confuses people. The book contains step-by-step advice for linking communication to the marketplace, along with communication models and real-life examples on how to communicate effectively for change.

Galpin, T.J. (1996). *The human side of change: A practical guide to organization redesign.* San Francisco, CA: Jossey-Bass.

A how-to manual for organizations currently undergoing or planning a major change effort. Tool kits for strategy and implementation are included. Topics addressed include: communication, culture, leadership, performance feedback and coaching, rewards, and recognition.

Galpin, T.J. (1995). Pruning the grapevine. *Training & Development, 49*(4), 28–33.

Practical article for change agents on how to deal with rumors. Uses an organizational Johari window and a variation of Maslow's hierarchy of needs, called the "resistance" pyramid. Also presents methods for analyzing stakeholder needs.

Johnston, K.B. (1993). *Busting bureaucracy: How to conquer your organization's worst enemy*. Burr Ridge, IL: Irwin Professional.

Puts bureaucracy in perspective as an inhibitor to productivity, customer service, and positive employee relations and provides lessons in mission-driven management and cultural change.

Kotter, J.P. (1996). *Leading change*. Boston, MA: Harvard Business School Press.

Clear and easy-to-follow change process supported by theory. An excellent up-to-date resource.

Price Waterhouse Change Integration Team. (1996). *The paradox principles: How high-performance companies manage chaos, complexity, and contradiction to achieve superior results*. Burr Ridge, IL: Irwin Professional.

Covers the five paradoxes facing modern organizations undergoing or contemplating change. Especially helpful for OD professionals working at the enterprise level in large organizations, although the techniques in this book could easily be applied to the creation or management of a small business. Additionally, this book is an excellent primer on how large consulting organizations perceive their organizational markets and how they position their expertise relative to "pure OD" firms.

Coaching

Bell, C. (1996). *Managers as mentors: Building partnerships for learning*. San Francisco, CA: Berrett-Koehler.

Clear and practical guide to mentoring, focusing on a partnership philosophy between mentor and protege. Author provides an entire chapter explaining what mentoring is and is not. Unique features include a case study illustrating an effective "mentor-mentee" relationship and an instrument for assessing one's own "mentoring talents." Interesting chapter on how to give advice and feedback without getting resistance and/or resentment.

Hargrove, R. (1995). *Masterful coaching*. San Francisco, CA: Jossey-Bass/Pfeiffer.

A guidebook for the manager who would like to develop a coaching-style management. Provides a model and tools.

Hendricks, W. (Ed.). (1996). *Coaching, mentoring, and managing.* Franklin Lakes, NJ: Career Press.

> Short book that outlines a five-step coaching model. Begins with performance assessment, then discusses when to be a coach, when to be a mentor, when to be a counselor. The fifth step is team integration. Written in workbook format with cases and activities.

Hutcheson, P.G. (1996, March). Ten tips for coaches. *Training & Development, 50,* 15–16.

> Brief article on tips for coaches: accepting that the coach is not in control, listening with full attention, paying attention to what is not being said as well as what is heard, probing for information without conducting an inquisition, coaching without judging, guiding the other person to his or her own solutions, helping to uncover the causes of problems without using personal expertise, not allowing past experiences with the other person or personal doubts to interfere with the coaching, being cautious about what is communicated by coaching actions, and using a structure for the coaching session.

Koonce, R. (1994, February). One on one. *Training & Development, 48,* 34–40.

> Brief but step-by-step description of how to coach executives. Before coaching begins, the coach identifies the issues that coaching should address through interviews and data gathering with the executive to be coached, as well as with the executive's colleagues, boss, and subordinates. Coaching sessions between coach and executive consist of regular meetings during a seven-to-twelve month period. Follow-up monitoring and consulting take place once the formal coaching period ends.

Peterson, D.B., & Hicks, M.D. (1996) *Leader as coach.* Minneapolis, MN: Personnel Decisions International.

> Very readable and brief book that outlines the principles of coaching. Authors define coaching as the process of equipping people with the tools, knowledge, and opportunities they need to develop themselves and become more effective. Book is organized around five coaching strategies: forge a partnership, inspire commitment, grow skills, promote persistence, and shape the environment. Plenty of practical advice and personal action steps for the coach to take.

Compensation

Lawler, E.E., III. (1990). *Strategic pay*. San Francisco, CA: Jossey-Bass.

Lawler is one of the gurus of pay systems, and this book is one of the best in the field. It examines a wide range of performance-based pay systems, from piece work to merit and skill-based systems, and shows how these systems can be tailored to fit the organization's business strategy. Lawler's preference is participatory management and those pay systems that support it, and he is strongest in this area. But, all in all, this is a nice review of the link between pay and performance.

McAdams, J.L. (1993). *The reward plan advantage*. San Francisco, CA: Jossey-Bass.

A very popular book by a consultant in the area of rewards and performance. Outlines in a very clear and how-to manner the steps in linking the reward plan with corporate goals such as profits, customer satisfaction, and cost reduction.

Consulting, Establishing a Practice

Biech, E. (1998). *The business of consulting*. San Francisco: CA: Jossey-Bass/Pfeiffer.

A practical, comprehensive work that explains how to run a consulting firm day by day. A diskette in the back of the book enables readers to customize invoices, financial worksheets, and correspondence.

Cohen, W. (1994). *How to make it big as a consultant* (2nd ed.). New York: AMACOM.

Interesting chapters on project planning and how to solve a client's problem. Includes a sample proposal and additional chapters on marketing, selling, pricing, etc.

Holtz, H. (1993). *How to succeed as an independent consultant* (3rd ed.). New York: Berkley Business.

Probably the most comprehensive of the how-to consulting books, now in its third edition. Covers all aspects of the business, including marketing and sales, brochures, proposal writing, initial client meeting, fee negotiations, final reports and presentations, and collection. Also, sections on seminars and public speaking. Good chapter on additional references. Highly recommended.

Holtz, H. (1995). *The independent consultant's brochure and letter handbook*. New York: John Wiley.

Advice on how to produce letters and brochures that demand attention and get results. It comes with a diskette of representative examples.

Kelley, R.E. (1986). *Consulting: The complete guide to a profitable career.* New York: Charles Scribner.

Good background for owning and running your own business, though not necessarily specific to organization development consulting. The book contains chapters on starting a practice, outfitting an office, fee collecting, selling/marketing, and writing reports.

Maister, D.H. (1993). *Managing the professional services firm.* New York: The Free Press.

Interesting book for two reasons: (1) OD professionals may find themselves consulting to a professional services firm, or (2) OD professionals may find themselves working in or setting up such a firm. Book covers client issues, including practice development packaging, marketing, and attracting new clients. Includes chapters on people issues, partnership issues (including compensation), and issues related to multiple sites. Good basic book for understanding these types of firms.

Tepper, R. (1995). *The 10 hottest consulting practices: What they are, how to get into them.* New York: John Wiley.

Highly practical examination of the field of consulting, its current state, and the author's vision of the profession's future. Of particular interest, he writes of the reorganization/organization emergence and the opportunities within this niche.

Shenson, H.L. (1990). *The contract and fee-setting guide for consultants and professionals.* New York: John Wiley.

Probably the best practical guide on the topic. Explains and gives examples of the different ways to set and collect fees as well as how to write proposals, contracts, and final reports.

Werner, T.J., & Lynch, R.F. (1994). *The consultant's handbook.* Littleton, CO: Qual-Team, Inc.

Handbook written for beginning OD consultants or students considering entering the field. Explains the basics of consulting and stages of change, and proposes three models for change: (1) reengineering processes and people systems, (2) targeted process improvement, and (3) total team systems. Great chapter on resistance (both client and consultant) and how to identify and deal with it.

Consulting, Personal Reflections

Freedman, A.M. (1996, September). The value and legacy of the founders of NTL: An interview with Ken Benne. *The Journal of Applied Behavioral Science, 32,* 332–344.

An interview with Ken Benne—the last surviving founder of NTL until his death in 1993. The author interviewed Ken during the summer of 1988 at Benne's home in Bethel, Maine. The article is a transcript of the interview and summarizes Benne's legacy to behavioral science.

Harrison, R. (1995). *Consultant's journey: A dance of work and spirit.* San Francisco, CA: Jossey-Bass.

Autobiography of one of the founders of organization development; easy and interesting reading. On one level it provides a rich history of OD starting in the mid-1950s. On another, it documents the author's struggles as he tries to live according to OD values in his life and consulting practice.

Kaplan, K.L. (1995). Women's voices in organization development: Questions, stories, and implications. *Journal of Organizational Change Management, 8*(1), 52–80.

Analysis of in-depth interviews with thirty-two women who have extensive experience as OD consultants. Interesting discussion of their perceptions of male and female perspectives: male seen as strategic, rational, analytic; female seen as voice of inclusion, recognition of differences, and making all people feel valued. Other topics: perception of some participants that they failed to receive appropriate recognition and issues of authenticity. Excellent study of women in consulting.

Page, T. (1996). *Diary of a change agent.* Hampshire, England: Gower.

A journal covering three years in the life of the author, a change management consultant, who works as a sole practitioner. This book is a candid account of the challenges the author faced in seeking a balance among personal, professional, and commercial value. It is recommended reading for anyone considering a career as an independent OD consultant.

Consulting, Skills

Bellman, G. (1990). *The consultant's calling.* San Francisco, CA: Jossey-Bass.

Great overall discussion on issues related to being an OD consultant. This book answers the "How To" in finding meaning and value in your life and work as well as how to add meaning to organizations through consulting.

Block, P. (1981). *Flawless consulting: A guide to getting your expertise used.* San Francisco, CA: Jossey-Bass/Pfeiffer.

A classic book on the steps of the consulting process: entry, contracting, data collection and diagnosis, feedback and decision to act, and implementation. The Appendix contains checklists on how to do things "flawlessly." A nice chapter on techniques for dealing with resistance.

Golembiewski, R.T. (Ed.). (1993). *Handbook of organizational consultation.* New York: Marcel Dekker.

Compendium of 101 short articles on various areas of OD practice, some original and some reprinted. Articles are introductions to the many areas in OD, rather than detailed descriptions on how to do it.

Miller/Howard Consulting Group. (1996). *The internal consultant's guide: Tools and techniques to create and sustain a team-based organization.* Atlanta, GA: Author.

Comprehensive tool kit for internal consultants—helpful for experienced consultants as well as those new to the role. Discusses role of the internal consultant, implementation, managing client relationships, influencing skills, providing feedback, and providing advice, and contains an extensive reading list.

Schaffer, R.H. (1997). *High-impact consulting.* San Francisco, CA: Jossey-Bass.

Author is a very successful management consultant who uses a collaborative and unique approach based on designing projects for specific results. His five steps are (1) define projects by targeting client results; (2) match scope to readiness; (3) get quick results; (4) partnership and mutual learning; and (5) leverage resources (i.e., use client resources). Although the author's approach is collaborative, his work is relatively unknown among OD professionals, probably due to his background in management consulting. However, he has produced some impressive results and seems more in line with OD values than many OD practitioners.

Culture

Adizes, I. (1988). *Corporate life cycles: How and why corporations grow and die and what to do about it.* Englewood Cliffs, NJ: Prentice Hall.

A powerful guide to the causes and effects of organizational growing and aging. The book presents a therapeutic approach to organizational renewal and a contingency approach to intervention design. Essential reading for OD professionals working at the enterprise or departmental level.

Adizes, I. (1995). *The pursuit of prime: Maximize your company's success with the Adizes program.* Santa Monica, CA: Knowledge Exchange.

This book updates *Corporate Life Cycles* but aims its message more toward leaders running organizations than to OD professionals assisting organizations. As a result, it has less of the theoretical background found in the earlier book. Recommended as a teaching tool or reference for a client organization using the Adizes framework.

Egan, G. (1994). *Working the shadow side: A guide to positive behind-the-scenes management.* San Francisco, CA: Jossey-Bass.

Details Egan's "Model C" framework for understanding the hidden or "shadow side" of an organization. The book provides methods for identifying and constructively dealing with shadow-side aspects of organizational culture. Of particular interest is a section on organizational culture that offers a primer of beliefs, values, and norms.

Green, A. (1996). *A company discovers its soul: A year in the life of a transforming organization.* San Francisco, CA: Berrett-Koehler.

Excellent story of how a consultant worked with a company to help change its culture; a very practical and insightful case study. It includes dialogue from meetings, correspondence, and people's reactions, as well as how attitudes did or did not change throughout the process.

Hofstede, G. (1997). *Cultures and organizations: Software of the mind.* New York: McGraw-Hill.

Written by one of the leading experts in culture. Not a step-by-step guide, but rather a review of the culture field using the author's more than twenty years' of research findings as illustrations. Contains sections discussing differences in culture at the national and organizational levels. Discusses the practical implications, including culture shock, ethnocentrism, language, stereotyping, and humor.

Kilmann, R.H., Saxton, M.J., & Serpa, R. (Eds.). (1985). *Gaining control of the corporate culture.* San Francisco, CA: Jossey-Bass.

Interesting mix of chapters on organizational culture, ranging from the highly theoretical to the practical. Each chapter is written by one of the leaders in organizational culture. Major sections include: what culture is, general approaches to understanding and managing culture, and dynamic of culture. For practical application, see Allen's chapter on the four phases of bringing about cultural change and Kilmann's chapter on the five-step model.

Kotter, J.P., & Heskitt, J.L. (1992). *Corporate culture and performance*. New York: The Free Press.

Interesting study and discussion on the relationship between organizational culture and performance. Presents data that demonstrates that organizations with "strong cultures" (e.g., Proctor & Gamble, IBM, Time, Quaker Oats, etc.) outperform firms with weaker cultures. However, the authors point out that a strong culture could be a deterrent to change and discuss other important characteristics, such as strategic alignment and adaptability. The book also discusses the issues of how corporate cultures can be adapted to be more performance-enhancing. Uses several cases.

Ryan, K.D., & Oestreich, D.K. (1991). *Driving fear out of the workplace: How to overcome the invisible barriers to quality, productivity, and innovation*. San Francisco, CA: Jossey-Bass.

Discusses the dynamics of fear in the workplace and the problems that it causes for employees and the organization. The book covers strategies for creating a high-trust work environment through knowing what to look for and how best to handle the situation.

Ulrich, D., & Lake, D. (1990). *Organizational capability: Competing from the inside out*. New York: John Wiley.

Based on the idea that a company's competitive advantage comes from organizational capability—its ability to improve management processes and satisfy the customer by building a dynamic culture in which everyone is keyed into market demands and devoted to customer service.

Data Feedback

Nadler, D.A. (1977). *Feedback and organizational development: Using data-based methods*. Reading, MA: Addison-Wesley.

A three-step approach to data and its use in organization development, focusing primarily on understanding how the use of data brings about changes in behavior; discusses various approaches and techniques for collecting data and using it to bring about change. The author believes that any intervention should include systematic data collection, analysis, and feedback of the data. The book emphasizes the importance of planning the intervention as well as step-by-step guidelines and questions to ask your client and yourself as practitioner. It also includes a number of major systematic approaches to feedback and feedback meetings.

Empowerment

Block, P. (1987). *The empowered manager.* San Francisco, CA: Jossey-Bass.

One of the pioneer books on empowerment and still popular today. First part of book deals with bureaucracy and proposes empowerment as the antidote. Book outlines a loosely connected series of steps to empowerment, including creating a vision of greatness, sharing the vision, building support, balancing autonomy and dependence, facing organizational reality, and enhancing the vision. Full of practical advice on forming relationships that foster openness and responsibility, how to deal with adversities in positive, nondefensive terms, and facing no-win situations. Enjoyable reading.

Block, P. (1996). *Stewardship: Choosing service over self-interest.* San Francisco, CA: Berrett-Koehler.

Stewardship is the "willingness to be accountable for the well-being of the larger organization by operating in service, rather than in control, of those around us." This is a fairly radical concept in most (paternal) organizations. Block lays out the conditions of stewardship, including that every person join in defining purpose and deciding what kind of culture the organization will develop. Interesting and provocative discussion and questions.

Cloke, K., & Goldsmith, J. (1996). *Thank God it's Monday: 14 values we need to humanize the way we work.* Burr Ridge, IL: Irwin Professional.

Addresses the most forgotten component of the change process, the human factor, through fourteen specific values. With years of experience in conflict resolution and organizational change, the authors have identified practical ways to satisfy human needs and alter the paradigms and contexts that define our work. Includes skill-building activities.

Ketchum, L.D., & Trist, E. (1992). *All teams are not created equal: How employee empowerment really works.* Thousand Oaks, CA: Sage.

Identifies the principles of effective work: team structuring, employee empowerment, open communication, and active innovation. Authors provide many case examples of companies that have applied these principles.

Vogt, J.F., & Murrell, K.L. (1990). *Empowerment in organizations: How to spark exceptional performance.* San Francisco, CA: Jossey-Bass/Pfeiffer.

A brief introduction to empowerment. Includes the history and definition; empowerment interventions; enacting empowerment; and future of empowerment. Appendix contains a management styles survey with focus on empowerment issues.

Ethics and Values, OD

Burke, W.W. (1997, Summer). The new agenda for organization development. *Organization Dynamics*, pp. 7–20.

Burke argues that "If organization development practitioners want to sleep better at night, they need to love the basic values of their profession, challenge actions they know are immoral, and play a more expansive role in organizational life." OD was founded as a value-based discipline, but may have lost its way in the past few years as practitioners have become part of the new corporate trends, such as downsizing and reengineering. Burke discusses some of the current consulting issues, including downsizing and reengineering, mergers, and corporate power, and suggests that the OD practitioner's agenda might be discovering how to live the basic values as part of the change effort.

DeVogel, S.H. (1995). OD values-clarification instrument. In J.W. Pfeiffer (Ed.), *The 1995 annual: Volume 2, consulting*. San Francisco, CA: Jossey-Bass/Pfeiffer.

A thirty-six-question instrument for OD professionals to gain insight into OD values such as autonomy, informed consent, collaboration, confidentiality, and professional development; helpful in identifying personal values and understanding the role values play when faced with dilemmas.

Gellermann, W., Frankel, M.S., & Ladenson, R.F. (1990). *Values and ethics in organization and human systems development*. San Francisco, CA: Jossey-Bass.

Discussion of the values and ethics surrounding the field of OD; contains a history of OD's ethical origins. Discusses the development of the OD code of ethics. Contains perspectives on ethics by experts in the field. Useful chapter on the ethics of contracting.

Facilitation

(See also Teams)

Hart, L.B. (1996). *Faultless facilitation: The new, complete resource guide for leaders and facilitators* (2nd ed.). Amherst, MA: HRD Press.

Contains the basics of facilitation: group dynamics, decision-making and problem-solving techniques, room logistics. Can be used as both a self-study guide and a participant's workbook. Separate instructor's manual contains training designs, lesson plans, and examples of handouts.

Kinlaw, D.C. (1996). *Facilitation skills: The ASTD trainer's sourcebook.* New York: McGraw-Hill.

Contains tools for creating and conducting workshops ranging in length from one hour to two days. Complete source for questionnaires, exercises, handouts, overheads, and a variety of other material.

Parry, S.B. (1994). *From managing to empowering: An action guide to developing winning facilitation skills.* White Plains, NY: Quality Resources.

Focuses on changing one's management style from command and control to facilitation; includes many skill-building exercises, self-quizzes, and checklists. Chapters include response styles, leadership skills, effective use of questions, decision making, teams, coaching, and counseling.

Schwarz, R. (1994). *The skilled facilitator: Practical wisdom for developing effective groups.* San Francisco, CA: Jossey-Bass.

Discussion of what makes a group effective and how a facilitator can improve group effectiveness by (1) identifying patterns of behavior that are getting in the way, (2) helping the group stick to a few critical ground rules, (3) utilizing practical methods for handling emotions when they arise in a group, and (4) using a diagnostic approach to help both facilitators and group members identify and solve problems that can undermine the group process.

Focus Groups

Kormanski, C. (1997). Designing, facilitating, and analyzing focus groups. In *The 1997 annual: Volume 2, consulting.* San Francisco, CA: Jossey-Bass/Pfeiffer.

Reviews the steps of conducting a focus group: selecting participants, outlining the process, constructing the questions, facilitating the group, analyzing the data, and preparing the report. This book contains several checklists and an example of a focus group report.

Krueger, R.H. (1994). *Focus groups: A practical guide for applied research* (2nd ed.). Thousand Oaks, CA: Sage.

Easy-to-read, comprehensive, and practical guide; covers all aspects of focus groups, including when to do them, selecting participants, developing a chronological and fiscal plan, what questions to ask, how to moderate the group, and how to analyze and report results. The book covers details such as sample invitation letters, screening questions, sample reports, and ways of estimating time required to write the report.

Morgan, D.L. (1997). *Focus groups as qualitative research*. Thousand Oaks, CA: Sage.

Very brief (80 pages with references) introductory book on focus groups. It covers the basics, such as deciding whether to use focus groups, determining the size of the group and who should participate, conducting the focus group session, and analyzing and reporting the data.

Industrial Engineering

Salvendy, G. (1992). *Handbook of industrial engineering*. New York: Wiley InterScience.

A handbook covering all major areas of industrial engineering, including job design, human factors, management systems design, and management engineering. The author is the chairman of the Human Factors program at Purdue University and is an expert in ergonomics. Although this book was written primarily for industrial engineers, it was designed for use by other managers, including OD practitioners.

Large Group Interventions

Bunker, B.B., & Alban, B.T. (1997). *Large group interventions*. San Francisco, CA: Jossey-Bass.

This is *the* book to read on large group techniques. It briefly describes eleven such approaches, including those focused on creating the future (e.g., search conference and future search); on work design (e.g.. the conference model and participative design); and on whole-system participative work (e.g., simu-real, and work-out). Also describes dynamics of large groups.

Bunker, B.B., & Alban, B.T. (Eds.). (1992). Large group interventions. *Journal of Applied Behavioral Science, 28*(4).

This is a special issue that covers large group interventions, many of which appear in a book written by the editors. Contains articles (with examples) written by Axelrod, Danemiller and Jacobs, Emery, Hirschhorn, Klein, and others. Although the book covers much of the same material in an easy-to-read format, the articles are written by the designers rather than summarized by the authors of the book.

Emery, M., & Purser, R. (1996). *The search conference: A powerful method for planning and organizing change and community action*. San Francisco, CA: Jossey-Bass.

A guide to the search conference method—a specific large group technique originally developed by Fred Emery in the 1950s. The book describes the principles and research on which the method is based, provides examples of search conferences, and details the steps for conducting a search conference.

Jacobs, R.W. (1994). *Real time strategic change*. San Francisco, CA: Berrett-Koehler.

An explanation of one technique of the search conference, using a process developed by Dannemiller-Tyson. The technique involves bringing the whole organization together for a three-day conference in which participants share important information, diagnose, vision, and plan change of the organization.

Spencer, L.J. (1989). *Learning through participation*. Dubuque, IA: Kendall/Hunt.

The Institute for Cultural Affairs has been conducting large group interventions for more than twenty-five years, both in the U.S. and abroad (serving seventy-five international centers). Over the years, the Institute has developed a set of group facilitation methods that are easy to use and quite effective. This book describes several of these Technology of Participation (TOP) techniques. The TOP Focused Conversation Method, the TOP Workshop Method, the TOP Strategic Planning Process, the TOP Mission and Philosophy Retreat, and TOP Leadership Development. Methods are for use in both community and organizational settings, as well as in profit and not-for-profit organizations.

Organization Design

Galbraith, J.R. (1994). *Competing with flexible lateral organizations* (2nd ed.). Reading, MA: Addison-Wesley.

Galbraith's model has been quite influential in organization design. The book focuses on creating a competitive advantage by building a lateral capability that enables a firm to respond flexibly in an uncertain world. Introduces the Star Model: task, structure, processes, rewards, and people. Capability is created when all of the elements of the Star Model are aligned and support task performance. Discusses the application to different forms of the lateral organization, including international.

Lucas, H.C. (1995). *The T-form organization: Using technology to design organizations for the 21st century*. San Francisco, CA: Jossey-Bass.

Describes how technology enables organizations to flatten hierarchies and become more customer responsive. This book provides case studies of companies such as Mrs. Field's and Calyx and Corrolla, who have achieved superior business results through alignment of technology and organizational structure.

Nadler, D.H., Gerstein, M.S., Shaw, R., and Associates. (1992). *Organizational architecture: Designs for changing organizations.* San Francisco, CA: Jossey-Bass.

A series of short chapters on various aspects of organization design, covering the congruence model, acquisitions, partnerships, high-performance work systems, TQM, empowerment, and learning. Three chapters deal with designing senior management, which is rarely discussed elsewhere. The final chapters discuss how to improve competitive performance and organizational architectures for the 21st Century.

Wheatley, M. (1994). *Leadership and the new science.* San Francisco, CA: Berrett-Koehler.

Discusses how business principles are built on 17th Century Newtonian principles of structure and force, but that business should upgrade its thinking to 20th Century science (e.g., fields: invisible forces that help guide outcomes). The book is useful in explaining a new science-based way of thinking to organizations working on older principles.

Wheatley, M., & Kellner-Rogers, M. (1996). *A simpler way.* San Francisco, CA: Berrett-Koehler.

Building on Wheatley's trail-blazing *Leadership and the New Science,* this book examines the impact of the Evolutionary Paradigm, a theory generated by modern biology and physics, on our notions about work, organization, and change. Crafting engaging metaphors with literature, spiritual teachings, and personal experiences, the authors guide readers toward a simpler and more experiential way of viewing and structuring their endeavors based on evolutionary tenets.

Organization Development, Classics

Argyris, C. (1970). *Intervention theory and method: A behavioral science view.* Reading, MA: Addison-Wesley.

One of the first books to present a theory of "intervention." Part One discusses the goals of intervention, conditions under which decisions can be made, resources used to solve problems, implications of organizational deficiencies and ways to overcome them, and applications. Part Two contains a series of cases illustrating the issues that need to be dealt with to ensure continuity within a total development effort.

Argyris, C., & Schon, D.A. (1978). *Organizational learning: A theory of action perspective* (2nd ed.). Reading, MA: Addison-Wesley.

This is a classic on organizational learning. The authors introduce the concepts of "espoused theory," which is what organizations or people say they do or believe, and "theory-in-use," which is how they actually behave. Another key concept is "single-loop learning" in which a problem is corrected without challenging or changing the basic assumptions, policies, and procedures of the organization. "Double-loop learning" is problem solving that questions and changes basic assumptions and policies. Authors argue that organizations and people may be unaware of their theory-in-use and typically practice single-loop learning, which prohibits organizational learning on any large scale. Authors provide examples of how to move organizations and people to double-loop learning.

Beckhard, R., & Harris, R.T. (1977). *Organizational transitions: Managing complex change*. Reading, MA: Addison-Wesley.

One of the first OD books on change management. It looks at three states: the present state, the future state, and the transitions state. Much of the book focuses on steps in the transition state, as one moves from the present to the desired state. Although twenty years old, the model is still used and the book contains helpful ideas on change.

Blake, R.R., & Mouton, J.S. (1964). *The managerial grid*. Houston, TX: Gulf.

The Managerial Grid was the first "packaged" OD program. The program, regarded as successful by many, generated criticism from purists who believed that all OD interventions should be tailored to the specific client situation. In the grid, managers can be rated on two dimensions—concern for people, and concern for production. The ideal manager is one who is high on both of these dimensions. The authors developed a training program to assist managers to move toward the ideal. The book referenced here is the authors' first, and it outlines the assumptions of the grid. In later books, the grid is extended to apply to organizations, and the authors developed a program for organizational change based on grid principles.

French, W.L., & Bell, C.H., Jr. (1993). *Organization development: Behavioral science interventions for organization improvement* (5th ed.). Englewood Cliffs, NJ: Prentice Hall.

One of the first comprehensive textbooks in OD, now in its fifth edition. Presents the action research model as the basic consulting model. Most of the book is organized around interventions such as T-groups, sociotech, team building, etc. This book is used widely by universities as an introductory textbook in OD.

Lippitt, G., & Lippitt, R. (1978). *The consulting process in action.* San Francisco, CA: Jossey-Bass/Pfeiffer.

Written by pioneers in the OD field who trained many OD consultants in the 1960s and 1970s. This book describes their six-step model: entry, contract, diagnosis, setting goals, taking action, and contract completion. Additionally, the book is distinguished by its discussion on consulting "dilemmas" and an OD approach to managing them.

McGregor, D. (1960). *The human side of enterprise.* New York: McGraw-Hill.

A book considered to be as relevant today as it was when written in 1960. McGregor's theory is that an organization's performance is directly related to its ability to tap human potential. This means rejecting the Theory X view (people cannot be fully trusted and don't like to work that hard) in favor of the Theory Y view (people view work as natural and desirable and will actively seek responsibility).

Schein, E. (1969). *Process consultation: Its role in organization development.* Reading, MA: Addison-Wesley.

More than any other, this book helped define a consulting approach used in OD. In contrast to the expert or doctor-patient approach, the process consultant works with the client in a collaborative manner to assist the client to perceive, understand, and act on process events that occur in the client's environment. The author describes the model, the process, and examples of how to use this approach.

Van Eynde, D.F., Hoy, J.C., & Van Eynde, D.C. (Eds.). (1997). *Organization development classics.* San Francisco, CA: Jossey-Bass.

A collection of twenty-eight articles reprinted from the *Organization Development Practitioner,* the journal of the Organization Development Network, a professional organization. The articles are brief, four to eight pages in length, and cover many of the "classics" in OD. Authors are the well-known people in the field such as Marv Weisbord ("The organization development contract"), Warner Burke ("Who is the client?"), Herb Shepard ("Rules of thumb for change agents"), Geoff Bellman ("Bringing who you are to what you do"), Jerry Harvey ("Eight myths OD consultants believe in. . .and die by"), Dick Beckhard ("Who needs us? Some hard thoughts about a moving target—the future"), and Roger Harrison ("Strategy guidelines for an internal organization development unit").

Walton, R.E. (1969). *Interpersonal peacemaking: Confrontations and third-party consultation.* Reading, MA: Addison-Wesley.

This book is a "must" for OD practitioners who want to understand conflict management. It presents a model for diagnosing recurrent conflict between two persons. Based on the author's understanding of the dynamics of interpersonal conflict, the book includes several strategic interventions that can facilitate a constructive confrontation.

Organization Development, General Resources

The *Annual* series, 1972 through 1999. San Francisco, CA: Jossey-Bass/Pfeiffer.

This series started in 1972, as the *Annual Handbook for Group Facilitators*, edited by J.W. Pfeiffer and J.E. Jones, and gradually evolved into what is now two volumes: one focusing on training and the other on consulting. The series is an excellent source of short articles on OD theory and practice, questionnaires and other tools, as well as experiential activities. Materials presented in the *Annuals* may be reproduced for training without permission and are a good source for workshops as well as for ideas about techniques.

Pfeiffer, J.W. (Ed.). (1988). *Instrumentation kit.* San Francisco, CA: Jossey-Bass/Pfeiffer.

This is a three-volume collection of 114 instruments that appeared in the *Annual* and other Pfeiffer publications. The range of instruments is broad, including an Assertion Rights Questionnaire, Blockages Survey, Conflict Management Instrument, Disclosure/Feedback Instrument, Feedback Rating Scales, Group Climate Inventory, Group Leadership Questionnaire, Interpersonal Communications Inventory, Learning Style Inventory, etc. The advantage of this kit is that it brings a large number of diverse instruments under the same cover. (See Appendix for listing of commercial instruments.)

Pfeiffer, J.W. (Ed.). (1991). *Theories and models in applied behavioral science, Vols. 1-4.* San Francisco, CA: Jossey-Bass/Pfeiffer.

An introduction to the many theories and models in OD: Volume I focuses on theories and models related to individuals; Volume II on group level models; Volume III on organization level models; and Volume IV on management and leadership. Each theory or model (over 200 in all) is described in a two- to four-page article. As an example, the organization volume contains some 60 entries, including action research, scientific management, six-box model, stream analysis, work redesign, and others. Excellent resource for a quick introduction on just about any OD topic.

Pfeiffer, J.W. (Ed.). (1989). *The encyclopedia of group activities.* San Francisco, CA: Jossey-Bass/Pfeiffer.

Contains 150 group experiential activities categorized into five sections: personal awareness, values clarification, communication, group process, feedback, and miscellaneous. Most activities are brief, averaging one hour or less in length. Covers many of the key types of experiential exercises.

Organization Development, Introductory Materials

Burke, W.W. (1987). *Organization development: A normative view*. Reading, MA: Addison-Wesley.

A concise and very easy-to-read introduction to organization development. Begins with a history and an explanation of OD, describes the steps of OD as a change process, reviews several diagnostic models, discusses the role of the OD consultant and finally looks at the future of OD.

Cummings, T.G., & Worley, C.G. (1993). *Organization development and change* (5th ed.). St. Paul, MN: West.

Probably the most popular textbook used in introductory organization development courses. A very comprehensive survey of OD techniques as well as applications in different types of organizations. There are several hundred references, which in themselves are a valuable resource. Each chapter provides one or more short, real-life cases that illustrate the technique described.

French, W.L, & Bell, C.H., Jr. (1994). *Organization development: Behavioral science interventions for organization improvement* (5th ed.). Englewood Cliffs, NJ: Prentice Hall.

A comprehensive review of the OD field. Includes history, definition, assumptions, values, foundations, and the action research model. Reviews types of interventions: team, intergroup, personal and interpersonal, structural, and comprehensive. Also discusses conditions for success, issues in consulting, research in OD, and the future of OD. Widely used in universities as an introductory textbook in OD, it has a companion book of readings.

French, W.L., Zawacki, R.A., & Bell, C.H., Jr. (1994). *Organization development and transformation: Managing effective change* (4th ed.). Burr Ridge, IL: Irwin Professional.

A compilation of readings by some of the greats in OD. From the basics of OD to the intricacies of the field, Schein, Argyris, Weisbord, Burke, and others address topics such as appreciative inquiry, consultant behavior, TQM, OD, and organizational culture. Text also cites cases and challenges of OD and Organization Transformation.

Hanson, P.G., & Lubin, B. (1995). *Answers to questions most frequently asked about organization development.* Thousand Oaks, CA: Sage.

> A comprehensive introduction to the theory and practice of organization development; written in question-and-answer format; an excellent reference book for novices as well as experienced practitioners. Chapter topics include: basic concepts, values, interventions, OD compared to other change technologies, consultation, and evaluation. Appendices include sample diagnostic instruments for team effectiveness, survey data feedback case examples, and a self-assessment monitoring checklist.

Rothwell, W.J., Sullivan, R., & McLean, G.N. (Eds.). (1995). *Practicing organization development: A guide for consultants.* San Francisco, CA: Jossey-Bass/Pfeiffer.

> A good introduction to OD, written in a very clear and nontechnical language. Consists of fifteen chapters, each written by a different expert. Covers the action research model, including entry, start-up, assessment, feedback, and action planning. Chapters on large system interventions, small group interventions, person-focused interventions, evaluation, adoption, and separation. Ends with international OD, ethics, and OD competence for the future. Also includes a sample consulting proposal and an OD ethics statement.

Weisbord, M.R. (1987). *Productive workplaces: Organizing and managing for dignity, meaning, and community.* San Francisco, CA: Jossey-Bass.

> The first part of this book is an excellent history of work and OD, including scientific management, Lewin, McGregor, Trist and Emery, and action research. The final part of the book outlines "third wave" management and consulting. Good examples of large group intervention in designing or redesigning a work system. Should be required reading for any student of OD, as it covers the basic theorists and paradigms in OD in a fun and interesting manner. Provides the history and logic behind current large group interventions.

Organization Development, Skills and Competencies

Church, A.H., Waclawski, J., & Burke, W.W. (1996). OD practitioners as facilitators of change: An analysis of survey results. *Group & Organization Management, 21*(1), 22–66.

> Results of a study undertaken to determine the degree of knowledge and understanding that organization development practitioners have regarding key issues in the management of change in organizations. Responses were compared with previous findings from managers and

executives; then, differences of categories among practitioners were identified. Overall, OD practitioners were found to be quite knowledgeable about the concepts covered in the questionnaire, more likely to be transformational (vision for future) than transactional (status quo) in their consulting approach, and relatively tolerant of ambiguous situations.

Head, T.C., Armstrong, T., & Preston, J.C. (1996). The role of graduate education in becoming a competent OD professional. *OD Practitioner, 28*, 1–2.

Two panels of OD educators and consultants reviewed Warrick and Donovan's list of forty OD skills (see separate reference below) to identify the preferred mechanism for acquiring each skill. Personal growth and understanding, internships, and college education were identified as the preferred mechanisms. Recommends a graduate curriculum with both required and elective courses that emphasizes internships and other applied experiences.

Warrick, P., & Donovan, T. (1979). Surveying organization development skills. *Training & Development, 76*, 22–25.

A comprehensive and sound study performed in the late 1970s; identifies forty general skills of the OD practitioner, ranked in importance. High-ranking human skills include: integrity, helping skills, sensitivity to organization needs, and general concern for people. High-ranking conceptual needs include: sound philosophical base, systems perspective, and ability to innovate. High-ranked knowledge skills include: organizational behavior, organization development, and behavioral sciences. High-ranked consulting skills include: problem solving, capability for identifying and responding to real needs, diagnostic skills, ability to adapt quickly, and ability to establish trust.

Organization Diagnosis

Burke, W.W., & Litwin, G.W. (1992). A causal model of organizational performance and change. *Journal of Management, 18*(3), 532–545.

The Burke-Litwin Model has a rich history of research and application. It specifies the causal relationships between categories of the model. Looks at twelve categories: external environment, leadership, mission and strategy, culture, structure, management practices, systems, work unit, climate, task requirements, motivation, individual needs, and individual and organizational performance. In addition, some work has been done on the causal chains linking the categories to outcome variables. (Also published in the Jossey-Bass/Pfeiffer *1989 Annual: Developing Human Resources.*)

Egan, G. (1993). *Adding value: A systematic guide to business-driven management and leadership.* San Francisco, CA: Jossey-Bass.

Describes a business-based diagnostic approach based on three frameworks: Models A, B, and C. Model A deals with the overall management of the business: strategy, operations, structure, human resources, management, and leadership. Model B presents a framework for initiating and managing change. Model C focuses on the hidden (shadow side) activities that influence the processes and tasks of Models A and B.

Harrison, M.I. (1994). *Diagnosing organizations: Methods, models and processes.* Thousand Oaks, CA: Sage.

This book offers an excellent overview of how to go about making an organizational diagnosis. It clearly presents the open systems model and follows this with a variety of specific approaches and techniques. Also, it provides a useful entry questionnaire/interview format.

Weisbord, M.R. (1976). Organization diagnosis: Six places to look for trouble with or without a theory. *Group & Organization Studies, 1,* 430–447.

Contains a useful model to get a quick read on where the issues are—Purpose: What business are we in?; Structure: How do we divide the work?; Rewards: Do all needed tasks have incentives?; Helpful mechanisms: Have we adequate coordinating mechanisms?; Relationships: How do we manage conflict between people?; Leadership: Does someone keep the boxes in balance?

Participative Design

(See also Large Group Interventions)

Cabana, S. (1995, January-February). Participative design works, partially participative doesn't. *Journal for Quality and Participation,* pp. 10–19.

Good introduction to the purpose and implementation of participative design (PD). Discusses the "democratic" way of organizing things and the traits of a self-managed group. Notes the six critical human requirements for effective work—adequate elbow room, opportunity to learn, variety, mutual support and respect, meaningfulness, and a desirable future. Describes in some detail the agenda for a two- or three-day PD workshop. Brief, clear, and to-the-point introduction to this topic.

Van Eijnatten, F. (1993). *The paradigm that changed the world.* Assen, The Netherlands: Van Goreum.

This is not an easy book to find nor is it easy to read, but it frequently appears on lists of recommended reading. It is a comprehensive work on the history and practice of the sociotechnical system approach to organization design. Chapter Four discusses participative design (PD) and is of interest because it treats PD as a "variant" of the basic sociotechnical system design (STSD) and discusses it in that context, together with Integral Organizational Renewal, Democratic Dialogue, and Modern STSD in North America.

Process Consultation

Reddy, B.W. (1994). *Intervention skills: Process consultation for small groups and teams.* San Francisco, CA: Jossey-Bass/Pfeiffer.

For the seasoned consultant or the new process consultant, this guide presents a framework for intervening in groups to help you (1) make impactful group interventions that lead to desired outcomes; (2) determine the appropriate type and depth of intervention—concepts critical to understanding group process consultation; and (3) understand the style, role, and competencies required of the leader or facilitator.

Schein, E.H. (1988). *Process consultation, Volume I: Its role in organization development* (2nd ed.). Reading, MA: Addison-Wesley.

Part of the Addison-Wesley OD series, this book outlines basic concepts and techniques for process consultation. Contains a basic definition of process consultation, how it differs from other types of consultation, and how to do it; supported by case examples.

Schein, E.H. (1988). *Process consultation, Volume II: Lessons for managers and consultants* (2nd ed.). Reading, MA: Addison-Wesley.

Part of the Addison-Wesley OD series, this book further refines the concepts presented in Volume I. This volume is directed at managers and consultants and uses numerous case examples that add to the reader's understanding of the major pitfalls in process consultation.

Strategic Planning

Fogg, C.D. (1994). *Team-based strategic planning: A complete guide to structuring, facilitating, and implementing the process.* New York: AMACOM.

Comprehensive guide on how to tailor the strategic planning process to an organization, how to prepare the organization, and then implement the process. Contains meeting agendas, facilitator notes, sample forms, and plenty of examples and cases.

Goldberg, B.G., & Silfons, J.G. (1994). *Dynamic planning: The art of managing beyond tomorrow.* New York: Oxford University Press.

Based on twenty years' experience with clients in the public and private sectors, this book discusses strategic alignment as the focal point of a framework for business and technology planning. Based on the concepts of complex adaptive systems and chaos theory as applied to business.

Kaplan, R.S., & Norton, D.P. (1992). The balanced scorecard: Measures that drive performance. *Harvard Business Review, 70,* 71–79.

Article that explains the balanced scorecard framework. It describes the four perspectives: financial, organizational, business process, and customer. Gives examples of translating a company's strategy and mission statement into specific goals and measures.

Kaplan, R.S., & Norton, D.P. (1993). Putting the balanced scorecard to work. *Harvard Business Review, 71,* 134–147.

More than a measurement exercise, the balanced scorecard is a management system that can motivate breakthrough improvements in critical areas.

Kaplan, R.S., & Norton, D.P. (1996). Using the balanced scorecard as a strategic management system. *Harvard Business Review, 74,* 75–85.

The balanced scorecard enables a company to align its management processes and focuses the entire organization on implementing long-term strategy.

Mintzberg, H. (1994). *The rise and fall of strategic planning: Reconceiving roles for planning, plans, planners.* New York: The Free Press.

Based on the author's view that strategy cannot be planned because planning is about analysis and strategy is about synthesis. In a light, humorous style, the book explains the different approaches to strategy and how to become a strategic thinker.

Morrisey, G.L. (1996). *Morrisey on planning. A guide to strategic thinking: Building your planning foundation.* San Francisco, CA: Jossey-Bass.

Deals with how to get started in the strategic planning process by determining an organization's principles and values as well as its strategic direction.

Worley, C.G., Hitchin, D.E., & Ross, W.L. (1996). *Integrated strategic change: How OD builds competitive advantage.* Reading, MA: Addison-Wesley.

A model of step-by-step strategic change that brings all parts of the organization into the process. Describes how the processes of strategic management, such as formulating and implementing new strategic orientation, can be implemented by integrating the principles of OD. Traditionally, these two disciplines have been separate, with the former being externally focused and the latter being internally focused. Contains numerous case examples.

Survey Feedback

Born, D.H., & Mathieu, J.E. (1996). Differential effects of survey-guided feedback: The rich get richer and the poor get poorer. *Group & Organizational Management, 21*(4), 388–403.

This article highlights results of an OD survey administered to members of a military organization where supervisors received feedback. A follow-up survey was administered one year later indicating that the perceptions of management/supervision and supervisory communications and work climate changed significantly as a result of the feedback, but differentially—consistent with the authors' hypotheses. Results are discussed in terms of meta-analytic reviews of OD interventions and practice in organizations.

Heinrichs, J.H. (1996). Feedback, action planning, and follow-through. In A. Kraut (Ed.), *Organizational surveys: Tools for assessment and change.* San Francisco, CA: Jossey-Bass.

It is difficult to find current materials on survey feedback. This chapter is one of the most recent and provides an overview of the process, and covers (very briefly) the purpose, history, and steps of this technique.

Surveys

Alreck, P.L., & Settle, R.B. (1995). *The survey research handbook* (2nd ed.). Burr Ridge, IL: Irwin Professional.

Comprehensive and easy-to-follow textbook on how to do survey research. The book begins with a chapter on planning, then goes through designing samples, creating items, building the questionnaire, collecting data, processing data, analyzing data, reporting data, etc.

DeVellis, R.F. (1991). *Scale development: Theory and applications.* Thousand Oaks, CA: Sage.

The focus of this book is how to develop measurement scales of the type used in surveys, job satisfaction questionnaires, and other similar instruments. Book starts with an introduction to measurement, then covers reliability and validity; provides a step-by-step process for scale development; and discusses factor analytic strategies.

Edwards, J.E., Thomas, M.D., Rosenkid, P., & Booth, S. (1997). *How to conduct organizational surveys: A step-by-step guide.* Thousand Oaks, CA: Sage.

Practical guide to the use of surveys to resolve organizational issues; covers survey development, respondent selection, administration, and results interpretation.

Kraut, A.I. (Ed.). (1996). *Organizational surveys: Tools for assessment and change.* San Francisco, CA: Jossey-Bass.

The most recent up-to-date summary of survey methods. Fifteen chapters, each written by an expert, cover all aspects of organizational surveys, including purposes and use, the survey process, and special applications.

Tactical Planning

Morrisey, G.L. (1996). *Morrisey on planning. A guide to tactical planning: Producing your short-term results.* San Francisco, CA: Jossey-Bass.

Provides all managers (executives, middle managers, first-line supervisors, and individual contributors alike) with a methodology for achieving meaningful short-term results on both a planned and ad-hoc basis.

Teams, Designing Team-Based Organizations

Graham, M.A., & LeBaron, M. (1994). *The horizontal revolution: Reengineering your organization through teams.* San Francisco, CA: Jossey-Bass.

An applied approach to creating a team-based organization. The first part of the book presents a four-stage model for the "revolution"—pioneering; settling in; tilting; and transforming. The second part focuses on how to lead a team-powered organization. The third part outlines how to keep the "revolution" alive and well once the transition is completed. Additionally, it contains a comprehensive list of recommended readings.

Gross, S.E. (1995). *Compensation for teams: How to design and implement team-based rewards programs.* New York: AMACOM.

Author is associated with the Hay Group and has many years of practical experience in compensation. Looks at three types of teams—parallel, process, and project—and describes how to set up a compensation program for each. Excellent chapter on competencies, which describes twenty-one competencies of teams. Competencies can be used for appraisal, development, or evaluation. Chapter 9 covers base pay, performance appraisal, recognition awards, incentive compensation, and the architecture of team pay. Concludes with a three-phase model, composed of thirteen steps, for implementing team pay. Very practical.

Harshman, C.L., & Phillips, S.L. (1994). *Teaming up: Achieving organizational transformation.* San Francisco, CA: Jossey-Bass/Pfeiffer.

A brief easy-to-read book on how to implement a team-based structure in an organization. It provides a step-by-step process, supported by checklists and lists of insider tips. Interesting section on how to overcome the major barriers to establishing a team-based structure.

Mohrman, S.A., Cohen, S.G., & Mohrman, A., Jr. (1995). *Designing team-based organizations: New forms for knowledge work.* San Francisco, CA: Jossey-Bass.

A comprehensive book with emphasis on the design of team-based organizations for knowledge work (although applicable to other work). It is based on a four-year research study of organizations that have adopted a team-based structure. Contains easy-to-understand models supported by examples of how to design an effective organization structure for teams. This book should be a "must" read for organizations moving to team-based structures.

Mohrman, S.A., & Mohrman, A.M., Jr. (1997). *Designing and leading team-based organizations: A workbook for organizational self-design.* San Francisco, CA: Jossey-Bass.

A companion guide to *Designing Team-Based Organizations.* The workbook details the steps in the process of tailoring the design of team organizational structures to an organization's specific needs and environments. Easy-to-read workbook format. Also available is a separate facilitator's guide.

Teams, Executive

Nadler, D.A., Spence, J.L., & The Delta Consulting Group, Inc. (1998). *Executive teams.* San Francisco, CA: Jossey-Bass.

There is a lot of talk about executive teams but there does not seem to be much information on the subject. This volume highlights the authors' vast experience in working with such teams in many of the leading corporations and provides plenty of valuable advice on how to bring teams up to their full potential.

Teams, Team Building

Katzenbach, J.R., & Smith, D.K. (1993). *The wisdom of teams: Creating the high-performance organization.* New York: HarperCollins.

Discusses the various types of teams and what it takes to become a high-performance team. Interesting discussions of the challenges of teams whose members are executives and teams whose members are geographically dispersed. Contains a team performance model that can be used by a team to assess its progress in becoming a high-performance team.

Kayser, T.A. (1990). *Mining group gold: How to cash in on the collaborative brain power of a group.* El Segundo, CA: Serif Publishing.

Deals with how managers can develop facilitative leadership skills. This book explores the process of managing people and ideas to achieve dramatic results in a rapidly changing, global economy. As a guide to changing the culture through building and maintaining collaboration within and across work teams, it defines the tools and processes that can make a difference in team productivity and can be applied in many environments.

Mankin, D., Cohen, S.G., & Bikson, T.K. (1996). *Teams and technology: Fulfilling the promises of the new organization.* Boston, MA: Harvard Business School Press.

The importance of teams and technology working together is paramount for an organization's success. The authors develop their own framework for creating mutual design efforts between teams and technology. Additionally, the book discusses the challenges of succeeding.

Phillips, S.L., & Elledge, R.L. (1989). *The team-building sourcebook.* San Francisco, CA: Jossey-Bass/Pfeiffer.

A hands-on tool that educates managers on the definition and concepts of team building and team effectiveness. In addition, it contains modules and instructions for data collection, data analysis, data feedback, design implementation/evaluation. Traditional and non-traditional data-collection methods are addressed.

Teams, Virtual

Asher, F., Freedman, S., & Stroud, A. (1996). Remote team connectivity: The next best thing to being there. *1996 ODN Conference Proceedings* (pp. 34–39). South Orange, NJ: Organization Development Network.

Discusses strategies for building an effective remote team, includes typical problems of remote teams and some ideas for solving them, and presents an overview of several technical tools available to remote teams. Contains a bibliography of recommended readings.

Geber, B. (1995). Virtual teams. *Training, 32*(4), 36–40.

Provides examples of the methods that real-life virtual teams can use to increase their productivity. The article discusses major pitfalls and how actual teams have overcome the pitfalls.

Lipnack, J., & Stamps, J. (1997). *Virtual teams: Reaching across space times, and organizations with technology.* New York: John Wiley.

Brief, yet complete, guide to virtual teams; written in plain, nontechnical language. Begins with an overview of history and nature of virtual teams. A major portion of the book discusses case studies of six companies that have successfully used virtual teams—includes NCR, Eastman Chemical, and Sun Microsystems. Concludes with step-by-step process for setting up virtual teams. Refer to the authors' website at *www.netage.com* for more information on terminology and networks.

Townsend, A.M., DeMarie, S.M., & Hendrickson, A.R. (1996, September). Are you ready for virtual teams? *HRM Magazine, 41,* 123–126.

Brief article that describes the characteristics of a virtual team and the factors that make it a powerful form of work organization: bringing people together regardless of geographical proximity, access to resources outside the organization, expansion of potential labor markets, and speed in responding to customer needs.

Values

Fairholm, G.W. (1991). *Values leadership: Toward a new philosophy of leadership.* New York: Praeger.

Clearly written and convincing book that calls for a new model of leadership based on values. Defines value leadership and explains why it is important; sets forth the six principles of value leaders and devotes a chapter to each one. The book offers many suggestions in the principles sections on how to implement the model.

Johnson, H.H. (1995). Implementing values. *Organization Development Journal, 13*(3), 27–32.

A method for quickly developing and implementing organization value statements is described using a small manufacturing company as an example. The initial statement was formulated by the management team and then reviewed by the managers and employees in each unit. Revisions were made on the basis of unit feedback. Using a survey feedback technique, each unit then evaluated the extent to which the values were practiced in the company, and corrective action was taken where problems were evident.

Lewis, H. (1990). *A question of values: Six ways we make the personal choices that shape our lives.* New York: HarperCollins.

A framework for comparing, contrasting, and evaluating values through six modes of moral reasoning: authority, deductive logic, sense experience, emotion, intuition, and science. Framework is useful for thinking through personal, business, and family issues.

Malcolm, H., & Sokoloff, C. (1989). Values, human relations, and organization development. In D. Sikes (Ed.), *The emerging practice of organization development.* Alexandria, VA: NTL.

An article on the Get-Ahead simulation about competition versus cooperation. (Available from NTL at 800-777-5227 or 703-548-1500.)

McDonald, P., & Ganz, J. (1992, Winter). Getting value from shared values. *Organizational Dynamics, 20,* 64–77.

Interesting approach to use of values. The author believes that an organization can turn values into competitive advantage by developing value measurement profiles relevant to the modern corporation. The article suggests different value profiles for different organization strategies, e.g., relationship-oriented organizations, change-oriented organizations, task-oriented organizations, and maintenance-oriented organizations. Additionally, the article describes a model that links vision with values.

Virtual Organizations

Davidow, W., & Malone, M. (1992). *The virtual corporation: Structuring and revitalizing the corporation of the 21st century.* New York: Harper Business.

Although it doesn't deal with "how-to," this book is considered a classic because it was one of the earliest books written about the virtual corporation. The author defines a virtual corporation as a company that makes virtual products—customized products for individual customers. It focuses on strategies and philosophies of the virtual company.

Grenier, R., & Metes, G. (1995). *Going virtual: Moving your organization into the 21st century.* Englewood Cliffs, NJ: Prentice Hall.

Practical advice about how to implement the virtual organization. This book contains chapters on how virtual teams work together using networked information and communication systems. Also discusses operational aspects and cultural implications and learning.

Handy, C. (1995, May-June). Trust and the virtual organization. *Harvard Business Review, 73,* 40–50.

Discusses basic principles of trust that Handy believes are necessary for making a virtual organization work. "If we are to enjoy the efficiencies and other benefits of the virtual organization, we will have to rediscover how to run organizations based more on trust than on control. Virtuality requires trust to make it work; technology alone is not enough."

Work Environment, High Performance

Becker, F., & Fritz, S. (1995). *Workplace by design: Mapping the high-performance workscape.* San Francisco, CA: Jossey-Bass.

Deals with a seldom-discussed aspect of a high-performance workplace: the physical environment. The book describes the high-performance workplace as a system that integrates four elements: work processes, organization culture, information technology, and physical facilities. Then it presents examples of some of the new ways of working, including team environments, home-based telecommuting, telework centers, and nonterritorial offices.

Hamilton, J., Baker, S., & Vlasic, B. (1996, April 29). The new workplace. *Business Week,* pp. 106–115.

An overview of the trends in workplace office design, including hoteling, personal harbors, and "cave and commons." This article describes companies that are adopting such new office designs and the challenges that the designs present.

INTERNET RESOURCES

Coaching

www.thecoach.com

> Contains book reviews, a coaching quiz, and text of a talk presented in April 1996 entitled "Coaching of Behaviors and Skills Utilized by Empowering Managers."

Facilitation

www.hsb.baylor.edu/fuller/iaf

> International Association of Facilitators. The purpose of the IAF is to promote, support, and advance the art and practice of ethical facilitation. Right now the website contains membership information for the IAF and links to facilitator central, which contains a list of facilitator references.

www.news/misc.business.facilitators

> Group Facilitators Newsgroup. The electronic discussion on group facilitation process expertise for group effectiveness. This moderated forum focuses on the practical aspects of group facilitation. Participants share ideas and advice on situations, methods, resources, and more. This group focuses on facilitation, rather than on training issues.

Focus Groups

www.uth.tmc.edu:80ut_general/admin_fin/cqi/resource/tools/focusgroup.html

> Information and references on conducting focus group interviews.

Instrumentation

www.unl.edu/buros

> Buros Institute of Mental Measurement provides professional assistance, expertise, and information to users of commercially published tests and also provides help with locating tests and giving a review of them. The Education Testing Service Test Collection contains records on over 10,000 tests and research instruments. These records describe the instruments and provide availability information. Test

Review Locator allows you to search to find citations to reviews of education and psychological tests and measures.

Organization Development and Change

www.aom.pace.edu/lists/l-odcnet.html

The Academy of Management Online Organizational Development and Change Division. Has information on the following: conflict management, entrepreneurship, management education and development, managerial consultation, organization and management theory, OD and change, organizational behavior, and many more.

Teams

www.on.ca/~bwillard/ideateam.htm

Ideas on Teams and Teamwork. This site is divided into three main subject areas: (1) leadership, empowerment, and delegation; (2) teamwork and teams; and (3) empowered teams. Main subject areas are further divided into subtopics, such as team player styles, signs of trouble in teams, etc. These subtopics provide valuable insight into the inner workings of successful teams. The site also contains an extensive bibliography.

www.gpsi.com

Group Performance Systems. Source for human-to-human communication and the technologies used to support it. At this site there is valuable information on interpersonal communication, learning organizations, and teamwork. Includes a list of related resources.

www.workteams.unt.edu

Center for the Study of Work Teams. The Center for the Study of Work Teams is sponsored by the University of North Texas. This website contains the center's mission, conferences, information and editorials, research projects, conference proceedings, work team newsletter, and educational resources.

PROFESSIONAL JOURNALS

Journals dedicated to Organization Development Practice.

OD Practitioner
Organization Development Network
76 South Orange Avenue, Suite 101
South Orange, NJ 07079-1923
201-763-7337

> Published by the National Organization Development Network, this journal contains short articles on the theory and practice of OD, plus letters to the editor, Network reports, occasional interviews, and conference announcements. (Quarterly)

Organization Development Journal
1234 Walnut Ridge Road
Chesterland, OH 44021
216-461-4333

> Published by the Organization Development Institute, this journal is solely devoted to OD issues. Emphasis is more on theory and practice with an occasional research study. Contains short articles, OD practitioner interviews, column on OD issues, letters to the editor and conference announcements. (Quarterly)

Journals with a focus on original data-based research studies in organization development.

Group and Organization Management
Sage Publications
2455 Teller Road
Thousand Oaks, CA 91320
805-499-0721

> Publishes original data-based research articles of practical interest to managers, teachers, consultants, and facilitators. Covers topics such as empowerment, group mentoring, value congruence, organizational politics, upward influence attempts, and employee attitudes. (Quarterly)

Journal of Applied Behavioral Science
Sage Publications
2455 Teller Road
Thousand Oaks, CA 91320
805-499-0721

> Published by the National Training Laboratory (NTL), this journal focuses on research and theoretical articles on personal satisfaction and quality of life. Topics include learning organizations, injury prevention at work, community research, teaching leadership, mergers, ethics, and conflict in teams. (Quarterly)

Journal of Organizational Change Management
CB University Press
P.O. Box 10812
Birmingham, AL 35201-0812
800-633-4931

> This journal takes a broad perspective and includes both theoretical and practical articles on topics such as gender issues, globalization, consulting in schools, self-awareness and consulting, environmentalism, learning through feelings, postmodern organizational paradigms, organizational renewal, and the Shamonic perspective on organizational change. (Bi-Monthly)

Leadership and Organization Development Journal
MCB Publications
198/200 Keighley Road-Bradford
West Yorkshire BD9 4JQ
England

> Tries to achieve a balance of articles involved in theory, and the practice (especially case studies) of organizational change and organizational leadership. The emphasis is on leadership and management, as well as on change, diversity, culture, quality, conflict, downsizing, etc. Also includes short news items and book reviews. (Bi-Monthly)

Journals with occasional articles related to OD.

Academy of Management Journal
Anne S. Tsui, Editor
c/o Pace University
861 Bedford Road
Pleasantville, NY 10570-2799
405-624-5086

Academy of Management Review
Ken Smith, Editor
University of Maryland
College of Business Management
College Park, MD 20742
405-624-5086

> Published by the Academy of Management (which has an OD division), the *Journal* publishes only research articles and the *Review* publishes only theoretical articles. Although few of the articles are directly related to OD practice, several are related to issues covered by OD such as diversity, the "learning organization," quality, and organizational culture. (The *Journal* is bi-monthly and the *Review* is quarterly.)

Administrative Science Quarterly
Cornell University
20 Thornwood Drive, Suite 100
Ithaca, NY 14850-1265
607-254-7143

> Published by the School of Management at Cornell University, this journal contains articles "advancing the understanding of administration through empirical investigation and theoretical analysis." Contains articles focused on general management issues, book reviews, and occasionally on OD. (Quarterly)

California Management Review
University of California at Berkeley
School of Business Administration
350 Barrows Hall
Berkeley, CA 94720
510-642-7154

> Published by the School of Business, University of California at Berkeley, this journal covers some of the latest in business theory and ideas (similar to the *Harvard Business Review*). (Quarterly)

Harvard Business Review
Harvard Business School Publishing
60 Harvard Way
Boston, MA 02163
617-495-6800

> This is the number one business journal in the world, with top quality articles. It publishes an occasional OD-related article; however, a major reason for reading the HBR is its reputation as the source for the latest business theory and ideas. Although it is somewhat expensive, most libraries subscribe to it. (Bi-Monthly)

Organization Studies
Walter de Gruyter Inc.
200 Saw Mill River Road
Hawthorne, NY 10532
914-747-0110

An interdisciplinary and international journal that promotes "the understanding of organizations, organizing and the organized, and the social relevance of that understanding." Articles tend to be of research and/or theoretical nature, and occasionally there is an article of interest to the OD practitioner. Includes book reviews. (Bi-Monthly)

Organizational Dynamics
P.O. Box 319
Saranac Lake, NY 12983-0319
212-586-8100
amapubs@aol.com

Published by the American Management Association as "a forum for authoritative views on organizational behavior and the problems of business and management." The majority of the content focuses on business and management, with an occasional article on organizational behavior. Includes book reviews.

Sloan Management Review
Subscriber Services
P.O. Box 55254
Boulder, CO 80322
800-876-5764

An academic journal published by M.I.T.'s Sloan School of Management. Articles focus on general management theory and practice, emphasizing cross-functional perspectives of management issues, organizational change, management of technology, and international business.

Training & Development
1640 King Street
P.O. Box 1443
Alexandria, VA 22313-2043
703-683-8100

Published by the American Society for Training and Development (ASTD), the content consists of short, easy-to-read, practical articles in the training area with an occasional article on OD. ASTD has an Organization Development Division. (Monthly)

Graduate Study in OD

Antioch University
Organization Systems Renewal Program
1800 Ninth Avenue, Suite 1400
Seattle, WA 98101
206-626-6588

Benedictine University
5700 College Road
Lisle, IL 60532
630-829-6220
fax: 630-960-1126
Sorensen@eagle.ibu.edu

Bowling Green State University
College of Business
Organization Development
Bowling Green, OH 43403
419-372-2210

Brigham Young University
Department of Organizational Behavior
790 TNRB
Provo, UT 84602
801-378-2664

California School of Professional Psychology
Headquarters Office
2749 Hyde Street
San Francisco, CA 94109
415-346-4500
fax: 415-931-8322

Case Western Reserve University
Department of Organizational Behavior
Sears Library Building
Cleveland, OH 44106
216-368-2138

Central Washington University
Organizational Development Center
Ellensburg, WA 98926
509-963-2368

Eastern Michigan University
Department of Management
504 Pray-Harrold
Ypsilanti, MI 48197
313-487-3240

Fielding Institute
2112 Santa Barbara Street
Santa Barbara, CA 93105
805-687-1099

George Washington University
School of Business
2125 G Street, NW
Washington, DC 20052

Loyola University - Chicago
Center for Organization Development (CORD)
820 North Michigan Avenue
Chicago, IL 60611
312-915-7517
fax: 312-915-6231
GRAD-CORD@LUC.EDU
www.luc.edu/depts/cord/

Pepperdine University
MSOD Program Office
400 Corporate Pointe
Culver City, CA 90230
310-568-5598

Sonoma State University
OD Program, Psychology Department
Rohnert Park, CA 94928-3601
707-664-2411

University of Monterey
aestria En Dessarollo Organizacional
Ave. Morones Prieto #4500 Pte.
Garcza Garcia, N.L.
Mexico
8-338-5102 or 8-338-5050

University of San Francisco
College of Professional Studies
Ignatian Heights, HR & OD
San Francisco, CA 94117-1080
415-666-6650

University of South Florida
Department of Management
Tampa, FL 33520

University of West Florida
Department of Management
Pensacola, FL 32514
904-474-2206

PROFESSIONAL ORGANIZATIONS

American Management Association (AMA-National)
P.O. Box 319
Saranac Lake, NY 12983-0319
800-262-9699
www.amanet.org

American Psychological Association (APA)
750 First Street, NE
Washington, DC 20002-4242
202-336-5500
www.apa.org

American Society for Training and Development (ASTD-National)
1640 King Street
P.O. Box 1443
Alexandria, VA 22313-2043
703-683-8100
www.astd.org

International Association for HR Information Management (IHRIM)
4643 Dallas Parkway, Suite 625
Dallas, TX 75240
972-661-3727
www.ihrim.org

International Society of Performance and Improvement (ISPI)
1300 L Street NW, Suite 1250
Washington, DC 20005
202-408-7969
edweb:sdsu/ISPI-SD/ISPI.html

Organization Development Institute (ODI)
11234 Walnut Ridge Road
Chesterland, OH 44021
440-729-7419
doncole@aol.com

The Organization Development Network (ODN-National)
76 South Orange Avenue, Suite 101
South Orange, NJ 07079-1923
201-763-7337
www.odnet.org

The Society for Human Resource Management (SHRM)
606 North Washington Street
Alexandria, VA 22314
312-856-2964
www.shrm.org

Society for Industrial/Organizational Psychology (SIOP)
Administrative Office
P.O. Box 87
Bowling Green, OH 43402-0087
cmit.unomaha.edu/TIP/SIOP/SIOP/html

The Society of Human Resource Professionals (SHRP)
8 South Michigan Avenue, Suite 1000
Chicago, IL 60603-3313
312-368-0188

CAREER RESOURCES

www.astd.org

American Society for Training and Development-National.

www.coachfederation.org

Website for the International Coach Federation, a professional association; source of referrals and information on finding a career coach.

www.ispi.org

International Society of Performance Improvement. Lists jobs and how to apply.

www.msod.com/jobs

Mastering the Science of Organization Development. Lists OD jobs and how to apply.

www.tcm.com/trdev

Training and Development Job Mart. A listing of OD and training and development jobs and how to apply.

www.trainingnet.com

TrainingNet. The site for training, management development, and HR. Lists jobs and how to apply.

Homer H. Johnson, Ph.D., *is a professor in the Center for Organization Development at Loyola University in Chicago, where he teaches and consults in the areas of continuous improvement, strategic planning, change management, and consulting skills. He is the co-author (with Sander Smiles) of the forthcoming* Consulting Skills Fieldbook.

Lynette A. Hurta, M.S.OD, *is an independent consultant for several companies, where she provides coaching and other services to management in the area of customer service.*

Valerie Revelle Medina *is a consulting manager in human resources and staffing for an information technology firm. Ms. Medina is currently working on her M.S.OD at Loyola University in Chicago.*

Joan H. Wrenn, M.S.OD, *is a management consultant specializing in information technology and organizational change.*

SUCCESSFUL IMPLEMENTATION OF ISO-9000

Michael Danahy

Abstract: Many organizations are adopting the ISO-9000 standards as the basis of their quality management systems. Some organizations adopt the standard under duress, when top management or a key customer says, "Do it or else." On the other hand, more forward-looking managers see it as a unique opportunity to improve quality, profits, and employee satisfaction.

The difficulty many organizations face is how to apply the standards to fit their individual circumstances. As a result, they are turning to consultants to assist them with this challenge. This article provides consultants with a road map for the ISO-9000 implementation process. It also offers suggestions to overcome some common obstacles.

ISO-9000 IN A NUTSHELL

ISO-9000 is a series of three standards written by the International Standards Organization (ISO). Your client will select one of the standards, based on the scope of the work performed. Companies that perform design functions through servicing the final product are certified to ISO-9001, the most comprehensive of the three options. ISO-9001 has twenty system requirements, listed in Figure 1. ISO-9002 is for organizations that perform everything but the design function, and ISO-9003 is for organizations that perform only an inspection and test function.

Twenty Quality-System Requirements
1. Management responsibility
2. Quality system
3. Contract review
4. Design control
5. Document and data control
6. Purchasing
7. Control of customer-supplied product
8. Product identification and traceability
9. Process control
10. Inspection and testing
11. Control of inspection, measuring, and test equipment
12. Inspection and test status
13. Control of nonconforming product
14. Corrective and preventive action
15. Handling, storage, packaging, preservation, and delivery
16. Control of quality records
17. Internal quality audits
18. Training
19. Servicing
20. Statistical techniques

Figure 1. Quality System Requirements

Each of the twenty system requirements has additional requirements. For example, "Inspection and Testing" includes requirements for receiving, in-process, and final inspection and test, as well as for inspection and test records. The primary aim of the standard is to prevent an incidence of product or service nonconformance at each of the twenty listed stages. Nonconformance occurs when a product or service does not meet a requirement of the customer.

Nonconformance is prevented by adhering to a now-famous ISO adage: "Say what you do, do what you say, and review the system to correct and prevent problems." For example, assume that one of the services provided by your client's organization is "taking reservations over the phone." To "say what it does," the organization describes how it takes reservations in the form of either a procedure or a work instruction. This description would include, in either narrative form or through a flow chart, the steps involved in properly performing this function (for example, answering the phone, greeting the customer, making the reservation, providing a confirmation number, etc.). There are generally three levels of documents in which the client organization will say what it does: the quality manual, quality procedures, and work instructions. These documents describe the quality system, addressing and conforming to the twenty system requirements.

To "do what it says," the organization ensures that the procedures are being followed. To illustrate with our example, your client would ensure that the people who are taking orders are following the procedures. Your client must also have records that provide objective evidence that the organization is doing what it says. For the reservation process, these records might include telephone logs and reservation records. To "review the system and correct and prevent problems," your client must make improvements to the system to reflect the changing needs of the organization as well as its customers.

How does your client become certified to the standard? Certification takes place through a third-party registration process. An independent company, called a registrar, performs an on-site audit of your client's quality system. If it meets the requirements of the standard, the registrar will issue a certificate. A governing body designates each registrar as qualified to perform registration audits. In the United States, this governing body is the Registrar Accreditation Board.

THE ISO-9000 IMPLEMENTATION PROCESS

Figure 2 outlines the seven steps of the ISO-9000 implementation process. These steps provide a road map for success.

1. Establish the Executive Team. The process starts with the executive team. This team consists of the senior person at the location (the president or the division, branch, or plant manager) and this person's direct reports. The responsibility of this team is to lead the implementation effort.

You, the consultant, will need to educate the client on what it will take to be successful. Your role includes overviewing the standard and what is involved in the implementation effort. The client must understand that it will take time, money, and patience—three things that may be in short supply in the organization. You will have to convince the client to stay involved, rather than hand the project off to someone else.

The scope of the effort will be extensive. Every work practice that impacts the final quality of the organization's products and services must be examined, changed if necessary to conform to the standard, documented as a procedure, verified with records, and audited.

You will work with the executive team to establish a quality policy and objectives and an implementation plan. The quality policy and objectives are a requirement of the standard. The quality policy must be stated in clear terms, and the objectives must explain what the client organization is trying to achieve with its quality system. The standard also requires the executive team to make the quality policy and objectives clear at all levels of the organization.

The implementation plan must include a proposed date for the registration audit, milestones to ensure that the plan is on track, and resources to accomplish the tasks involved in implementation. The plan should include selecting a registrar and making a preliminary contact with that registrar. It may seem early in the process to be contacting a registrar, but this should be done soon after the decision is made to pursue ISO registration. (Because of the demand, registrars are often scheduled months in advance. Be sure that when the client organization is ready for the registration audit, there is a registrar available to do it.)

Depending on the current condition of the quality system, the size of the location, and the complexity of the product or service, this implementation period usually ranges from six months to two years. Establishing milestones and then reaching them not only ensures that progress is being made but also helps those involved to be patient with the process and to celebrate

1. Establish the Executive Team
   - Overview the standard
   - Overview their role in the effort
   - Develop quality policy and objectives
   - Establish an implementation plan and milestones

2. Establish the Implementation Team
   - Overview the standard
   - Review their role in the effort
   - Team building for the implementation team

3. Develop the ISO-9000 System
   - Implementation team coordinates writing the quality manual, procedures, and work instructions
   - Train the work force on ISO and the new procedures
   - Issue quality manual, procedures, and work instructions
   - Document system compliance with records

4. Conduct an Internal Audit
   - Train internal auditors
   - Conduct the audit
   - Resolve findings

5. Registrar's Pre-Assessment Audit (Optional)
   - Resolve findings

6. Registration Audit
   - Resolve findings

7. Maintain the System
   - Management reviews, internal audits, and corrective and preventive action
   - Registrar's surveillance and registration audits

Figure 2. ISO-9000 Implementation Process

progress. The executive team should plan to meet at least quarterly during the implementation period to assess progress.

2. Establish the Implementation Team. In the second step of the process, the executive team establishes an implementation team to coordinate the day-to-day activities of the effort. Most of your consulting time will be spent with the implementation team and its members. It is best if this team is chosen from the next level down from the executive level and includes representatives from the parts of the organization that correspond to the twenty system requirements.

Start your work with the implementation team with an overview of the standard and a review of the team's role in the effort. As the team members will be working together for several months, conducting a team-building session beforehand is also advisable.

Your challenge is to help the implementation team determine how the generic standard will be applied to the unique needs of the organization. The team's role is to assign responsibility for writing procedures that comply with the standard and to make sure that the written procedures become actual work practices. Team members must also ensure that these practices are documented with records that provide objective evidence that the procedures are being followed.

3. Develop the ISO-9000 System. The third step in the implementation process is to develop the ISO system. This includes writing the procedures, providing training on the procedures, ensuring that work practices conform to the procedures, and documenting compliance. The implementation team coordinates writing the three levels of documents that will be the foundation of the ISO system—the quality manual, procedures, and work instructions.

Make sure that the implementation team members do not write all the procedures themselves. Instead, people should write the procedure and work instructions for their own processes. For example, sales people write the procedure and instructions for contract review, engineers write the procedure for and instructions for design review, and production workers write the procedure and work instructions for production control. Having the workers participate in writing their own procedure fosters ownership of the result, increasing the likelihood that the procedure will be followed.

After the three levels of documents are complete, the work force attends training on the ISO standard and the new work procedures. Workers cannot be expected to comply with the new procedures if they do not know what they are. It sounds simple, but it is surprising how many organizations make the mistake of not training employees in new procedures.

After the work force has been trained, the quality manual, procedures, and work instructions are issued as controlled documents. The quality manual is issued to the organization's executives and key managers. The procedures and work instructions go to all employees whose work is governed by them. For example, the documents that address "process control," especially the work instructions, should be accessible to production workers. The purchasing department would not receive documents on process control, unless the procedure or work instruction impacts purchasing. After the documents have been issued, everyone in the organization is expected to perform work in accordance with the published procedures and work instructions.

The final step in developing the ISO system is to document compliance with the procedures. The client organization's practices can be in complete compliance with the ISO standard and your written procedures, but unless these practices are supported by objective evidence it doesn't matter. The registrar's approach will be that "If it isn't documented, it didn't happen." Keeping records of action taken and tasks completed is the primary method for providing this objective evidence. For example, the ISO standard requires a final inspection on finished products. The organization must be able to produce final inspection records to demonstrate that such inspections actually occurred. Advise your client to have employees complete these records at the time the events occur rather than at some later time.

4. Conduct an Internal Audit. After your client's ISO system has been operating for at least six weeks, it is time to conduct an internal audit. This activity is an audit against the ISO standard, conducted by the organization's employees (internal auditors). Before the audit you should help your client select and train an internal audit team. Internal auditors should have good observation, listening, and analytical skills. They should be respected in the organization and should come from a variety of departments, not just the quality-assurance department.

Emphasize the fact that internal auditing is an excellent developmental opportunity, both for the individual team members and for the organization. It offers the individuals conducting the audit the opportunity to understand how other departments operate. It offers the client the opportunity to break down department barriers. This breakdown in barriers results when people from different departments work together as a team, establishing communication links with other employees.

Your client's auditors should receive training in both the ISO standard and auditing techniques. The training in auditing techniques should cover the information in the American National Standard, *Guidelines for Auditing Quality Systems* (the ANSI/ASQC Q-10011 series). The first audit is organization-wide, covering all twenty of the ISO elements. This audit is the organization's first objective—a systemic evaluation of its new quality system. When the auditors find an incidence of a nonconformance in the system, as they will, they document it by writing what is called a "finding." Each finding must be addressed and resolved. Do not let your client be disappointed if the audit uncovers many "findings." Stress that findings are opportunities to improve the system. Each resolved finding makes the quality system a little better—and is one less problem that the registrar will uncover. The organization runs internal audits until all major problems are resolved.

5. Registrar's Pre-Assessment Audit (Optional). After you and your client have decided that the major system problems have been identified and resolved, it is time to decide whether to have the registrar conduct a pre-assessment audit. The pre-assessment audit is a trial run of the registration audit. If you and your client believe that an outside expert will provide valuable insights and information, you should pursue this option. The pre-assessment audit provides face-to-face interaction with the registrar, giving your client the opportunity to learn how the auditors interpret the ISO standard.

Because the standard is generic, different registrars sometimes interpret the standard in slightly different ways and place more emphasis on some areas than others. The interpretation of corrective and preventive action is a good example. Some registrars have strict definitions of corrective action and preventive action and the differences between them. They may also have guidelines on how many examples of each are necessary to demonstrate a system. Other registrars may be more flexible in both their definition and their acceptance criteria. Having a pre-assessment audit can prepare your client for these differences in interpretation.

The big disadvantage to a pre-assessment audit is its cost. It can cost as much as a registration audit, and your client will not have a certificate at its conclusion! In general, if, as a result of the internal audits, you feel your client has eliminated all major system problems, you can advise him or her to skip the registrar's pre-assessment audit. If your client elects to have a pre-assessment audit, all of the registrar's findings must be resolved before the registration audit.

6. Registration Audit. During a registration audit, the registrar works independently to decide whether the ISO system complies with the standard. It is similar to an internal audit, except that it is much more thorough, as auditors who are experts on the standard conduct it. The registration audit starts with an off-site document review. The auditors who conduct the registration audit will review the quality manual to determine whether it meets the requirements of the standard. They may also request copies of some or all of your client's supporting procedures. They will write an assessment based on their review. If the quality manual meets the requirements of the standard, they will conduct the registration audit as planned.

Even with the best ISO systems, the auditors will uncover incidences of nonconformance, prompting written findings. Most registrars recognize two types of nonconformance: major and minor. In general, the registrar will issue the organization a certificate if the audit results in no major findings. A major finding occurs when a breakdown occurs in one of the twenty system requirements or when your client is unable to demonstrate that the organization has developed a system in one of these areas. For example, if your client has not held any management review meetings or has no records of them, your client will have a major finding, because management review is one of the twenty system elements. A major finding requires a revisit from the registrar so that the organization can demonstrate that the nonconformance has been resolved.

A minor finding is nonconformance that does not suggest a system problem. Most registrars will allow several minor findings, although the organization will have to resolve the nonconformance in a reasonable period of time, usually between thirty and sixty days. In general, minor findings do not require a revisit by the auditors; the organization sends documentation of the resolutions by mail. If the resolutions satisfy the auditors, the registrar will send the certificate indicating that the organization has achieved conformance with ISO standard. When your client receives the certificate, advise the executive team to recognize the people who were involved in making the effort a success.

7. Maintain the System. The organization's new quality system will not remain static. It is not something to achieve and then forget. It is a system that changes as the organization and customers change.

The ISO standard includes internal and external controls that require organizations to maintain their systems. The key internal controls are the requirements for management review, internal quality audits, and corrective and preventive action. These three system elements require the organization to take a look at its system to ensure its effectiveness.

The primary external control comes from the registrar in the form of surveillance and registration audits. The registrar conducts on-site surveillance audits twice a year. They are less thorough than a registration audit, generally involve fewer auditors, and take less time. They usually cover several, rather than all, of the twenty system requirements, often ones for which findings have occurred in the past. Every third year, the registrar will conduct a full registration audit to ensure compliance with the standard. The consequence for failing to maintain the system is serious: loss of the certification. This loss is particularly embarrassing if your client has advertised its previous success in obtaining it.

KEYS TO SUCCESSFUL IMPLEMENTATION

The implementation process just outlined provides a road map to help you lead your client to registration. But do not expect to complete the ISO journey without hitting a few bumps in the road. The nine suggestions that follow can be key to reducing the impact of some common problems. The first four apply to the executive team. This is fitting, as the team's leadership is essential for successful implementation.

1. Push the Executive Team To State Why They Are Seeking ISO Certification. Many organizations run headlong into an ISO certification process without a clear understanding of why they are doing it. When asked, they can usually come up with superficial reasons, such as "to improve quality" or "to remain competitive."

You will need a solid foundation to help your client build its ISO system. To do it, you will have to move the executive team beyond the superficial. At the first overview meeting, have the team decide what it wants to accomplish. Have team members bring data about customer complaints, rework rates, errors, cycle time, and costs. Ensure that their objectives in achieving ISO certification relate to the problems and issues they face every day.

For example, suppose that the executive team reviews data on dissatisfied customers and discovers that in the last three years 10 percent of customers have been dissatisfied. As a consultant, you may need to push them until they state that they want to reduce this by a specific rate, such as 1 percent each year. Pushing them to this level serves two purposes. First, specific objectives like this one provide focus for the ISO effort. Second, it helps the executive team see that ISO is not just an academic exercise. If they follow through, ISO can help them achieve results that will impact the bottom line. You can then use the management review process in the following months to monitor how well the organization is doing against its objectives.

2. Make Sure the Executive Team Provides Resources. A common problem is the lack of sufficient resources to do the job properly. Often, additional responsibilities are "dumped" onto existing ones, without thoughtful consideration of the consequences. For example, if the executive team simply adds ISO responsibilities to the implementation team members' regular job responsibilities, something will suffer—the work, the employees, or both. If you are an internal consultant, this will be particularly difficult because you will be continuously hearing the complaints of overwork from co-workers and peers.

The implementation plan, established early in the process, should address how the time and resources will be provided to make the effort successful. This plan may include hiring temporary, part-time employees or scheduling the peak workload times for the summer, when college students can be hired to help. When discussing resources, if you hear statements such as, "We just want to do the minimum amount so we can get certified," you know you still have more work to do in terms of fostering the executive team's understanding of the need for resources.

3. Keep the Executive Team Involved! As the implementation team will perform many of the day-to-day activities, there will be a tendency for the executive-team members to withdraw from the implementation effort (after the initial fanfare subsides, of course). It will take a special effort to maintain their involvement. Fortunately, the ISO requirement for management review ensures that the executive team will meet periodically to review the system. In addition to these meetings, you will keep them informed of roadblocks that may impact the implementation plan. Schedule regular one-on-one meetings with the senior executive team to review the implementation plan, discuss any emergent issues, and resolve problems as necessary.

4. Prepare the Executive Team for D-Day. During the ISO implementation process, there will come a time when the executive team's efforts to adopt ISO standards will be tested. You can look at this time as D-Day. Assume, for example, that your client has promised a product to a customer by a certain date. Your client is to receive a bonus if the deadline is met. However, when the deadline arrives, the product is not ready. Management wants to ship the product and complete the work in the field, but the inspection and test procedure states that no product can be shipped until all required work has been completed.

This D-Day scenario results in a battle between the way the client used to perform and the performance requirements of the new quality system. This is when you, the consultant, and everyone else in the organization learn whether the executive team's talk about the importance of ISO-9000 is for real. This will be a particularly difficult test if you are an internal consultant, as people whom you work for may be on the other side of the fence. If there is no preparation for D-Day, it is a good bet that the quality system will lose and the product will be shipped incomplete. The ISO naysayers will have their day, and a great deal of momentum will be lost.

Proper preparation can give the quality system a better chance of winning on D-Day. To prepare, you must talk about D-Day from your first interaction with the executive team. Tell them that there will come a time when their commitment will be tested. Call it D-Day. Tell them how difficult—and how important—it will be to make the right decision. Then, when D-Day arrives, you will be in a much stronger position to challenge them to comply with the new requirements.

5. Keep It Simple. Some companies that have completed the ISO process complain that it has created voluminous inflexible procedures and a large bureaucracy. If this happens, you have not served your client well. There is no requirement in the ISO standard for lengthy and rigid procedures or large bureaucracies. Yes, the system will require more paperwork in the form of procedures and records. And yes, the system will require additional responsibilities for some people. But there is no need to go overboard. Simple systems, procedures, forms, and practices usually meet the ISO requirements better than complex ones. So encourage your client to keep it as simple as possible.

For example, one of the requirements in the "training" section of the standard states that the organization must have a system for identifying the training needs of its employees. To keep it simple and still meet this requirement, your client could modify the performance appraisal form to include a section that assesses these needs. The supervisor completes this section with the rest of the form. Because most organizations already have a performance appraisal process, one small change in the process (keeping it simple) can meet this requirement. Note that "no additional training needed at this time" is an acceptable evaluation. Of course, if training is needed, there should be a record of how this training it to be provided.

6. Don't Throw Out the Baby with the Bath Water. Avoid reinventing things. Instead, when possible, work with what the client has. Many of your client's work practices will already conform to the standard. This makes sense, as they would probably not be in business if their products and services were of consistently poor quality. So, if they are already doing it right, you want to leave it alone.

The approach, when developing the quality system, is to review the current work practices and decide whether they already conform to the standard. If they do, just document (write a procedure for) the current work practice. That is working with what they have. This is the ideal situation, because the most difficult part of the ISO implementation effort is persuading people to change their work practices. The less often you have to change work practices, the less resistance you will encounter.

If the current work practices do not conform to the standard, you will have to change them to bring them into compliance. For example, a team of buyers from the purchasing department could flow chart the steps in the current purchasing process. The team could use the flow chart to identify areas in which their current process does not meet the requirements of the standard. Then the team could make the appropriate changes to the flow chart and work practices. The flow chart then becomes a tool to train new workers in (and remind experienced workers about) the improved practices.

7. Provide Training. There are two types of ISO training: training for those who are directly involved in the implementation effort and training for everyone else. The training for those involved in the implementation effort includes the overview sessions for the executive and implementation teams, team building for the implementation team, training in procedure writing for those who will write quality documents, and training in auditing for the internal auditors. Training for everyone else includes an overview of the ISO standard and training in the procedures and work instructions that will impact their work. The overview of the ISO standard for all employees covers why the client is pursuing certification, the client's quality policy and objectives, and a discussion of the employee's role in the effort.

Training in procedures and work instructions should be department specific. In other words, do not train everyone on every procedure in the organization or you will overwhelm them. Train them in the procedures that impact them. You may not feel that you have the technical background to provide some or all of this training. If so, help your client find someone who does.

8. Prepare the Client for "Loony Time." Loony time is the transition period when the organization is working in both the old and new way. As a consultant, you are probably familiar with this from previous interventions. The transition period brings fear, resistance, hostility, and all those other human feelings that accompany change. There is no way to make loony time completely disappear, but preparing for it can help to keep the mania at a manageable level.

Explaining from the beginning that the organization will go through this period will help people understand and accept it when it happens. Explain that it will not be permanent and that things will get better as the ISO system matures. Another important point to emphasize is that there is a clear dividing line between when it is acceptable to do things the old way and when things must be done the new way. That line is when the procedure is officially issued as a controlled document. Once the procedure is issued, people are expected to follow it. When they know this in advance, they accept it and adjust. Some organizations even issue all their procedures on the same day to help reduce the effect of loony time.

Loony time can be the most difficult stage of the implementation process. Do not blame people for honest mistakes, but also firmly insist that they follow the new procedures.

9. Avoid Delegating the Effort to Too Few People. The best ISO implementations use the team approach outlined in this article, which stresses involving many people and departments in the effort. Some organizations take the opposite approach and delegate the effort to one person (usually the quality manager), to one department (again, usually quality), or even to the consultant. If one person or department writes the procedures and is responsible for seeing that they are implemented, that person or department will battle resistance all the way. Because everyone else will be spectators, not players, they will not fully appreciate the need for the system or the requirements of the standard. They certainly will not want to change their work practices to satisfy "another quality initiative."

Similarly, if you as the consultant write the procedures, everyone will eagerly await the time when you leave, so they can go back to doing their jobs the way they always have.

This does not mean that the quality manager, the quality department, and a consultant should not be involved in the effort. Each is very helpful in implementing the ISO system. The problem occurs when one is given sole responsibility for the effort.

SUMMARY

Like most consulting projects, helping a client with an ISO-9000 implementation is a challenging and rewarding experience. Success requires a blend of traditional consulting skills and technical background and insights. The implementation process offers a proven road map to guide you on your journey. Also, the nine keys offer preventive actions to avoid common obstacles.

Recommending Reading

American Society for Quality Control. (1994). *Guidelines for auditing quality standards (ANSI/ASQC Q10011)*. Milwaukee, WI: Author.

American Society for Quality Control. (1994). *Quality management and quality assurance—vocabulary (ANSI/ASQC Q8402)*. Milwaukee, WI: Author.

American Society for Quality Control. (1994). *The ANSI/ASQC Q90 series of standards*. Milwaukee, WI: Author.

Hall, M. (1997). ISO implementation—Key success factors. *ASQC's 51st Annual Quality Congress Proceeding*. Milwaukee, WI: American Society for Quality Control.

Taylor, M. (1998). Preventive action vs. corrective action: The horse, the barn door, and the apple. *Quality Progress*. Milwaukee, WI: American Society for Quality Control.

Michael Danahy, founder and principal of Quality Innovations, Inc., helps organizations with total quality and ISO-9000 implementation efforts. Mr. Danahy is an American Society for Quality Senior Member and Certified Quality Engineer. He is also a Registrar Accreditation Board certified auditor for ISO-9000 systems. He earned his bachelor's degree from Georgetown University and his M.B.A. from the College of William and Mary.

FOCUS GROUPS:
A QUALITATIVE RESEARCH TOOL

Pamela J. Schmidt

Abstract: Focus groups are one of the most frequently
used forms of qualitative research. As business has
become more consumer-oriented, the focus group
has become a powerful tool for connecting with customers' perspectives and expectations. Introduced in
the 1930s, the focus group is a tried-and-true qualitative research tool when basic principles and concepts
are applied appropriately. This article discusses the
purpose of qualitative research, the strategic intent
of such research, and when focus groups are the best
bet. It cautions against abuses of focus groups. Group
dynamics and the general elements of a focus group
are reviewed. The role of the moderator and the significance of the moderator's style as the instrument
of the research are summarized. The logistics and
planning for an effective focus group are presented
as a checklist.

WHAT'S RESEARCH GOT TO DO WITH IT?

Historically, businesses have tried to determine customer expectations based on assumptions about customers' needs. Their perceptions were based on past experience, instinct, guesses, personal beliefs, and old reliable habits. Perceptions can be a valuable starting point in exploring customer expectations.

A number of reliable tools can be helpful in verifying customer expectations: surveys, interviews, brainstorming sessions, analysis of customer complaints, and focus groups.

A focus group involves hiring a moderator to gather qualitative data about a product, service, or concept. The process lasts about two hours, during which the moderator asks questions of a group of eight to twelve specifically selected participants. These participants do not know one another prior to meeting in the group, but they do share similar characteristics (subscribe to the same magazine, all became parents within the last year, eat out once a week, etc.).

Focus groups are often conducted in a special facility that has a one-way glass, behind which the sponsor's representatives observe the process. Sessions are tape recorded to facilitate accurate recall of what was said. Sessions may also be videotaped. The moderator is trained to ask questions that stimulate group conversation and to create a climate that is nonthreatening and non-evaluative. Typically, the participants are paid or given a gift for their time.

Qualitative Research

To understand focus groups, it is important to understand the purpose of qualitative research and how it compares to quantitative research.

Qualitative research addresses the structure of attitudes and motivations rather than their frequency and distribution. The underlying goal is to explore in depth the feelings and beliefs people hold and to learn how these feelings shape overt behavior (Goldman & McDonald, 1987).

The goal of qualitative research is to understand as much as possible about a given issue or group without having a preordained framework for the information. It is inductive analysis, an alternative to explaining the world through preordained structures.

Taylor and Bogdan (1984) list the following characteristics of qualitative methods:

- Qualitative research is inductive. Concepts, insights, and understanding are developed from patterns in the data, rather than by assessing preconceived models, hypotheses, or theories.
- The researcher looks at settings and people holistically; people, settings, or groups are viewed as wholes rather than as variables.
- Qualitative researchers are sensitive to their effects on the people they study.
- Qualitative researchers try to understand information from the people's own frames of reference.
- The qualitative researcher suspends, or sets aside, his or her own beliefs, perspectives, and predispositions.
- For the qualitative researcher, all perspectives are valuable.
- Qualitative methods are humanistic.
- Qualitative researchers emphasize validity in their research.

Qualitative research methods such as focus groups are descriptive, subjective, exploratory, and approximate. *Quantitative* research methods such as surveys or questionnaires are diagnostic, objective, definitive, and precise. At times you may wish to use a combination of both methods. Figure 1 compares qualitative research to quantitative research. This article is focused on the qualitative method.

Strategic Intent: Deciding Whether To Research

Market research is a wise investment for an organization attempting to make decisions that are customer- or market-focused. Selling a product or an approach because it is what the supplier decided to make ("You can have any color Model-T you want as long as it's black") is a way of the past.

One of the most important decisions a company can make is whether to conduct customer research, and if so, what kind of research: qualitative, quantitative, or both. Strategic intent is critical. One must consider the following[1]:

- Will the cost of doing the research exceed the value of the information obtained?
- Is there enough time to do the research?
- Is the proposed research capable of providing the information needed?
- Will the results of the research be believed and acted on?

---

[1]Adapted from information developed by RIVA, Inc., Chevy Chase, Maryland.

	Qualitative	Quantitative
Purpose	Describe	Predict
Form	No predetermined categories of analysis	Standardized measures, predetermined response categories
Sample/Result	Small group of people; large amount of in-depth explanatory data	Large numbers of people; limited number of questions; broad, generalizable results
Optimal Result	Greater understanding of individual differences, patterns	Greater understanding of group similarities, patterns
Possible Negatives	Overly complicated thinking, making the issues murkier than they are; failing to guide action	Reductionist thinking, making the issues less important than they are; failing to guide action
Scientific Paradigm	Rooted in phenomenological inquiry—naturalistic, inductive	Rooted in logical positivism—hypothetical, deductive
Outcome	Longer, more detailed, variable in content	Succinct, parsimonious, easily aggregated for analysis
Process	Illustrative explanation; responses can be interpreted	Numerical aggregation; responses can be aggregated
Approach	Supposedly subjective	Supposedly objective
Description/ Analysis	Interpretive—how and why	Statistical—what and how many
Sampling	Convenience	Random, quota, structured
Analytical Strength	Face validity	Statistical reliability
Methods	*The Researcher Is the Instrument* (Patton, 1990), e.g., interviewing variability	Careful development of the measurement instrument, e.g., standardization of interviewing, survey responses

Figure 1. Comparison of Qualitative to Quantitative Research

If the research is being conducted simply for the sake of appearances, it is not worth doing.

Abuses of Focus Groups

The use of the focus group has become very popular. Many organizations have used it as "the" solution to their information needs. Although the focus group is an excellent research method, it frequently is used inappropriately, in situations in which another method would be more appropriate. Some of these abuses include:

- Using focus groups as inexpensive alternatives to quantitative research.

- Using focus groups to produce data that they cannot accurately generate, such as estimated sales volume.

- Implementing more focus groups than necessary to achieve the research objective.

- Taking the focus-group technique to an extreme.

- Taking the focus-group technique too seriously.

- Assuming that the focus group will make "the" decision for you.

Group Dynamics and Focus Groups

Ernst Dichter used focus groups to perform the first qualitative research studies for Ivory Soap in the 1930s. He was a contemporary of Freud's and began his work by using group-therapy techniques that were popular in Europe at the time. Dichter began to note the dynamics of the group process and used these dynamics to guide marketing decision makers in U.S. product manufacturing companies.

Although some would argue that the effect of a group discussion would be to inhibit people's honesty, it is probably not likely to do so in a group of strangers. In fact, group dynamics may help to uncover certain issues, for a variety of reasons, such as the following:

- Members of groups respond to and interact with one another, stimulating more ideas and achieving a wider range of insights.

- Members often find the experience enjoyable so they "warm up" and contribute, even after shaky starts.

- Random comments can set off a chain reaction of other people's comments.

- A feeling of safety in the enclosed, peer environment can lead to more candid responses and a feeling of strength drawn from the group.

- Because people are not required to answer every question, answers—when given—are given willingly and meaningfully.

- The group can take on a unique identity or personality that can give the research a unique quality or perspective.

Traditional Elements of Focus Groups

Several traditional elements associated with focus groups follow:

- The focus-group session lasts from ninety minutes to two hours.

- A single moderator presides.

- The format is semi-structured: Certain questions are planned; a general flow or "logic" is established for the issues to be discussed; and time is allowed for follow-up or exploration of unexpected areas.

- Twelve to fourteen participants are recruited in order to ensure that eight to ten participants (respondents) show up.

- The participants have some features (for example, demographics, product use, experiences, life events) in common.

- The respondents do not know one another prior to the session.

- The respondents may or may not know the general subject to be discussed and know little else about the purpose of the session in advance.

- The respondents receive compensation (usually money) for their participation.

- The group meets at a facility with features intended to maximize the comfort, ease of recording, and observation of the group during the interview. This may include one-way glass for the observers.

- The participants are seated around a conference table.

- The interview has a focus—a product, service, idea, or experience.

Flow of a Focus Group

Although many variations are seen, certain elements are common to most focus groups. Often referred to as the "flow" of the session, the elements include an introduction, rapport building, in-depth investigation, and closure.

Introduction
Moderator/respondent
introductions. Respondents
are given ground rules.

Closure
Determination of overall group
attitudes toward specific issues.
Accurate summary of opinions.
Room for clarification by
respondents. Appeal for any
additional information.
Acknowledgments.

Rapport Building
Low anxiety/easy-to-answer
general questions. Moderator
forms a picture of the group
dynamic. Respondents learn
group norms and expectations.

In-Depth Investigation
Transition from general to
more focused questions.
Discussion follows a logical
pattern to allow in-depth and
specific questions and answers.

Figure 2. The Focus-Group Flow

Introduction. The moderator opens with an introduction of the topic in general. Focus-group participants may never know the specific organization for which the data is being gathered. At this point the moderator may tell the participants something as general as, "You have all been chosen because of your interest in gardening." The moderator also facilitates an introduction of all of the participants and provides his or her own credentials. To introduce the process, the moderator provides a set of ground rules and ensures that there is understanding and agreement of the ground rules among all participants.

Rapport Building. The moderator begins with easy-to-answer questions. They may further define the focus group topic such as, "Where do you purchase most of your gardening supplies and tools: nurseries, discount stores, hardware stores, or mail order?" These questions are not threatening and continue to shift to more specific topics such as, "What do you like most about purchasing garden supplies from a catalog?" During this time the moderator is forming a picture of the group, for example, who speaks readily and who may need a bit of encouragement; who answers questions in great detail and who may need to be prodded for more detail. In addition, the participants are also learning the group norms and expectations, which will increase their comfort level with the experience. Some moderators use a flip chart to help participants maintain focus.

In-Depth Investigation. As the transition to more focused questions continues, the moderator may provide products and request the participants to evaluate them. For example, the moderator may show two rakes and ask the participants to evaluate them for sturdiness, comfort in use, or quality of workmanship. The moderator may also ask participants to test some products. In another setting the moderator may ask participants to review concept statements, evaluate advertising copy, provide opinions about ads or commercials, listen to radio spots, or complete a photo sort. The moderator leads a discussion with predetermined questions that obtain the participants' reactions. If the moderator has managed the group dynamics well, participants will feel comfortable responding, even though the questions may seem more anxiety provoking.

Closure. An initial or "false" close may be used to allow the moderator time to gather final questions from the client observers behind the one-way glass. In this case the moderator may call a short break and leave the respondents for a few minutes. Then the moderator reconvenes the group, asks any final questions, and provides a summary statement. The statement may summarize the group's attitudes or opinions toward specific issues. This also allows an opportunity for clarification. The moderator thanks the participants for their time and input and reminds them of any compensation or gifts, which are often provided as participants leave the session.

Developing Questions

The success of the focus group is dependent on the questions asked. The difference between an answer and a solution is often found in the question itself. The questions are the stimulus for the respondents. Three primary rules apply to asking questions in focus groups:

1. Ask short questions that ask for long answers to gain as much as possible from the participants and to keep people with you.

2. Avoid asking double-barreled questions; people will not know which one to answer.

3. Avoid asking "why" questions. "What" questions prompt more multi-dimensional responses, taking participants' thoughts in many directions. Depending on the purpose of the focus group, the moderator will also need to know when to reign in the responses and add structure to the discussion.

Questions must be formulated to address the issues and needs of the client. The moderator must ensure that the client has provided specific and complete information in order to develop questions that quickly get at the client's issues. The moderator will list the questions in a guide prior to the session. In addition to the questions, this guide should include anything that will help the moderator facilitate the focus group efficiently and effectively, such as times and milestones. A list of probes could also be useful when the responses are not as broad or as deep as expected.

Questions should start general and become more specific. They must be developed around the one singular purpose of the focus group, whether it is product information, customer needs, or future predictions. Maintaining a narrow focus is critical because the session is limited in time. A two-hour focus group session may have five to eight questions with one or two potential probes for each. The same list of questions should be used if more than one focus group is conducted for the same client.

Ground Rules

Focus-group participants must be given the ground rules up front in a clear and concise way. This is the responsibility of the moderator. Some sample ground rules follow:

- The session will last two hours and be audiotaped or videotaped.
- Participants are asked to speak clearly and one at a time.
- Observers will be watching behind one-way glass.
- The moderator wants to hear from all participants.
- The discussion is open; commenting on or building on one another's remarks is fine.
- Participants will be remunerated for giving their time and input.
- There are no "wrong" answers.
- No smoking is allowed.

Preparing for a Focus-Group Session

Preparation for a focus-group session includes three areas: the facility, the session guide, and the moderator's mind-set.

The Facility. The facility contact person is a key part of the project. As soon as the facility has been selected, contact this person to work out the details. Refreshments generally are served, so determine whether you or the facility contact person will be responsible for the selection and delivery of refreshments. If you are not familiar with the facility, visit it in person prior to the event.

The Session Guide. Write a detailed plan for the session that includes every question you might use, preferably with times allotted to each section. Include any materials, equipment, and interventions you plan to use, such as flip charts, sample materials, etc.

The Moderator's Mind-Set. The worst thing a moderator can do is to pre-judge a group or assume that a particular group will be like all the others. Respect the respondents. Keep in mind that the respondents will do you a tremendous favor by showing up! Ask yourself how willing you would be to sit in a room full of strangers and talk.

Remember that every single respondent has the ability to generate essential data and represents hundreds, if not thousands, of customers who are not in the room. Each respondent is a potential gold mine of information. Use the checklist in Figure 3 to help you prepare.

The Moderator

There is no one right style for moderators. Some moderators are soft-spoken, unobtrusive people with gentle, calming manners. Others are rapid-fire, voluble types who exude energy. Some have a casual appearance, others adopt a formal look. Some can adapt their styles, appearances, and speech to fit more closely with the styles of different focus groups.

So long as a person's moderating skills are good, his or her personal style will have little effect on his or her success in conducting a group. However, during the opening minutes of a group, the moderator will be the major point of focus for the participants as they "check out" the person.

During the focus-group session, the moderator has to maintain a healthy ego. It takes a lot of guts to walk into a room full of strangers and put

(Allow a minimum of eight weeks from initial plan to implementation.)

Planning and Organizing the Focus Group

- Establish the research objectives _____
- Determine the budget _____
- Select and retain a moderator _____
- Decide on operational details _____
  - Number of groups _____
  - Location of groups and geography _____
  - Time of groups _____
  - Video/audio taping _____
- Brief the moderator _____
- Develop a screening mechanism _____
- Develop the moderator guide _____
- Select a facility _____
- Order refreshments for the participants _____

Preparing To Conduct the Focus Group

- Set up refreshments/food for the participants _____
- Manage/adjust for noise level _____
- Provide name tags for the participants _____
- Advise the facility of extra participants or late arrivals _____
- Ensure that the room is set up properly _____
  - Visibility _____
  - Easel/flip-chart placement _____
  - Video/audio set up _____
  - Writing supplies _____
  - Temperature _____
- Meet with the moderator for a briefing _____
- Coordinate communication between the moderator and any assigned observers _____

Delivering the Findings

- Conduct a post-group discussion with moderator and observers _____
  - Review the process _____
  - Review content issues _____
- Prepare the final report _____
- Arrange to present and deliver the final report _____
- Deliver the results to the research owner _____

Figure 3. Focus-Group Checklist

them at ease to talk while someone observes. At the same time, the moderator must be ego-free in the process of facilitating conversation and gathering data, not offering his or her own opinions.

It is essential that the moderator remain neutral and not allow personal value judgments to enter into the process. A moderator's perceptions, attitudes, opinions, or beliefs may bias the group, so the moderator must remain neutral. The moderator must be a model of objectivity, open-mindedness, and genuine interest in the respondents' points of view. Some tips for facilitating focus groups are given in Figure 4.

---

1. Encourage the expression of different opinions.

2. Discourage attempts to put down or forcibly change the opinions of others (encourage unconditional positive regard between respondents, too).

3. Turn to or respond to group members on the basis of their nonverbal communication as well as their remarks.

4. Use neutral, open-ended questions as much as possible.

5. Aim questions to the respondents' levels, terms, and ways of thinking about the subject and experience.

6. Reward productive responses through attention, acknowledgment, and follow-up questions.

7. Interrupt nonproductive responses nonverbally or verbally, e.g.:

   • look away

   • hold up your hand

   • restate or rephrase the original question

   • say you're going to interrupt and why

8. Keep your questions short and answerable, one question at a time, and give the respondents time to answer.

9. Use nonverbal communication to encourage the respondents to speak, e.g.:

   • eye contact

   • leaning forward with interest

   • open hand gestures

10. Balance your attention between process (how it's happening) and content (what's being said).

Figure 4. Ten Tips for Facilitating Focus-Group Discussions

Following the Focus-Group Session

After the focus-group session has ended, the moderator will evaluate the process for further learning by conducting a quick self-feedback session, asking some of the following questions:

- What did I do well? Good job!
- What could I have done better? Next time!
- Did I obtain answers to the critical questions?
- Did I facilitate discussion?
- Did I demonstrate active listening?
- What did I learn from this group?
- Did I achieve the purpose of the study?

If the session does not go well, a moderator must always look at the process. Were the right people in the room? Was the screening done correctly? Was recruitment monitored adequately? Was the purpose clear? Were the questions clear and answerable? Was rapport established and maintained? Was discussion facilitated without bias? Were appropriate probes used? Was the client briefed on the process of focus-group observations?

Following the session, the moderator will facilitate a post-group discussion with any observers who were behind the one-way glass. The discussion will review the process and the content issues. The moderator may use this discussion as the basis of the final written report. This discussion may also provide insight into client preferences for detail, emphasis, or wording of the report.

The moderator delivers the findings to the client in the form of a written report. Generally the moderator meets with the person who hired the moderator, the research owner. This meeting may also be used to discuss some of the highlights of the focus group session(s). If this is the case, other individuals may also be present for the discussion, for example, an advertising manager if the purpose was to evaluate ad effectiveness, or a training director if the purpose was to determine training needs.

The written report is the final deliverable and the last step in the focus-group process. The moderator seldom becomes involved beyond this point.

Remember, in the case of focus groups, "bad news is good data." The data is invaluable. The purpose of focus groups is not to persuade respondents to like the product or service. It is to find out what the respondents think and feel.

References and Further Resources

Goldman, A.E., & McDonald, S.S. (1987). *The group depth interview: Principles and practice.* Englewood Cliffs, NJ: Prentice Hall.

Greenbaum, T.L. (1993). *Handbook for focus group research.* Lexington, MA: D.C. Heath.

Krueger, R.A. (1988). *Focus groups: A practical guide for applied research.* Thousand Oaks, CA: Sage.

Morgan, D.L. (1988). *Focus groups as qualitative research.* Thousand Oaks, CA: Sage.

Patton, M.Q. (1990). *Qualitative evaluation and research methods* (2nd ed.). Thousand Oaks, CA: Sage.

Pope, J.L. (1993). *Practical marketing research.* New York: American Management Association.

RIVA, Inc. Market research and training services. Chevy Chase, MD. (301-652-3632)

Taylor, S.J., & Bogdan, R. (1984). *Introduction to qualitative research methods: The search for meaning* (2nd ed.). New York: John Wiley.

Templeton, J.F. (1994). *The focus group* (rev. ed.). Burr Ridge, IL: Irwin Professional.

Pamela J. Schmidt is a twenty-five year veteran of marketing, training, and organization development. Qualitative research methods have been an intricate part of her work, facilitating groups in corporate reengineering, customer service, diversity issues, employee benefits, financial services, fulfillment services, health care, religious education, technical training, total quality management, and technology utilization. Ms. Schmidt has a master's degree in human resource development. She is vice president of membership and program development for the American Society for Training & Development in Alexandria, Virginia.

HOW TO GENERATE REAL-TIME DATA FOR DESIGNING EFFECTIVE INTERVENTIONS

Robert Merritt and Richard Whelan

Abstract: Systematically collecting real-time information in an organization is an effective way to create a
readily accessible database for any subsequent interventions to address organizational issues. The data-
collection tool can then be used later to measure the
impact of the intervention.

This article describes a process of collecting data,
using it to create and conduct a survey, analyzing the
survey results and diagnosing the issues, designing
and conducting an intervention, and measuring the
impact of the intervention.

INTRODUCTION

Assessment of OD interventions is based, in part, on the belief that "what is real is what has effects" (Lewin, 1936). Pike (1990) notes that people do not argue with their own data. The process described in this article can help you find ways to assist organizations in resolving business problems using their own data. This can be accomplished by using the following steps:

1. *Collect data* about problems from a representative sample within the client organization (and from customers and/or stakeholders, where appropriate).

2. Use the data collected to *create a survey* to be administered to a larger sample within the client organization (and to customers and/or stakeholders, where appropriate).

3. Analyze the survey results and *develop a diagnosis* of the issue(s) to be addressed by the intervention.

4. Design and *conduct the intervention.*

5. *Measure the impact* of the intervention, using the same survey, as a way to assess changes in the organization.

The time required to design and implement this technique will vary with the organization and the issues to be addressed. Experience shows, however, that the time needed for the process can be relatively short.

PROCEDURE FOR GATHERING THE DATA

The procedure used to gather real-time data for designing effective interventions can be broken into an eleven-step process, as follows:

Step 1: Decide to Use Focus Groups

Use focus groups to obtain information from those individuals involved with, or impacted by, the presenting problem(s). Look at the presenting problem(s) as being part of a larger system or process. In this way, you can identify the range of individuals both inside and outside the organization from whom data will be gathered.

Step 2: Determine Focus Group Members

All relevant levels of the client organization should be represented in the data-collection process. It often is useful to include external customers and other relevant stakeholders because they can offer unique, fresh, and important perspectives on the issue(s) in question.

Step 3: Develop an Interview Guide

The next step is to develop the questions that will be used when conducting the focus groups. The purpose of each question is to elicit the information you need to diagnose the issues confronting your client accurately. You may want to use different questions for various parts of the client organization and/or for the customers and/or stakeholders.

Design the specific questions based on the nature of the issue confronting the client organization and the audience to whom you are speaking. Some sample questions are given below:

- "Who is involved with this issue?"
- "What is their role in or contribution to. . . ?"
- "What impact does this issue have on. . . ?"
- "What are the costs to or impact on the organization/customers/suppliers of. . .?"
- "What factors seem to contribute to the issue?"
- "What causes do you see for. . . ?"

Step 4: Conduct the Focus Groups

The next step is to gather the data you need using the interview guide you have designed. Some useful guidelines for conducting focus groups follow:

- Limit the size of each group to eight to ten people.
- Follow the interview guide you developed and record the answers on a flip chart or an electronic white board.

- Ask follow-up questions for clarification only; do not allow debates to develop.

- Plan each focus-group session to last sixty to ninety minutes, depending on the size of the group.

Step 5: Analyze the Data

After using the interview guide to collect data from the participants, it is necessary to perform a simple analysis of the data following the focus-group sessions.

Assume that you have collected the following six pieces of information:

- Supervisors do not follow the same rules as everyone else.
- There seems to be no agreement on the direction in which we are moving.
- Expectations of teams are not consistent among first-line supervisors.
- Employees are treated differently for the same rule infractions.
- Different bosses have different goals for their employees.
- Directions for teams are not consistent across supervisors.

First, *group common issues together*. For example, cluster the following four items, which are all related to inconsistencies among supervisors:

- Directions for teams are not consistent across supervisors.
- Expectations of teams are not consistent among first-line supervisors.
- Supervisors do not follow the same rules as everyone else.
- Employees are treated differently for the same rule infractions.

In this case, a second grouping would consist of the two items related to organizational direction:

- Different bosses have different goals for their employees.
- There seems to be no agreement on the direction in which we are moving.

Do not omit any of the data when creating the groups.

Next, *label each group* of statements to give definition to your diagnosis. This process of grouping information is similar to creating an affinity diagram after a brainstorming session. For example, you could label the first group of issues "Supervisory Skills" and the second group "Strategic Directions."

Step 6: Design the Survey

Using all the items generated in the focus groups, design a survey to explore topics and determine the frequency of occurrence. For example, you could ask, "To what extent do supervisors give consistent directions?" or "To what extent do supervisors follow the same rules as employees?" Design clear statements based on the information you have gathered. This allows you to quantify the results quickly based on the respondents' rating of the items.

Finally, review the entire set of statements. Edit those that are too long, eliminate redundancies, check for clarity, etc. Your goal is to develop questions that will generate sufficient information to describe accurately and adequately existing problem(s). You may find it useful to field test your survey with a sample of respondents to ensure its effectiveness and ease of use. It is important to include your client in this process.

Step 7: Select a Rating Scale

After you have determined the items for your survey, develop a usable rating scale to quantify the responses you receive. Such a scale also helps in standardizing the evaluations of the survey respondents. A seven-point scale provides a sufficient range of choices for the respondents without creating too much data to analyze effectively. The following is an example of such a scale:

"To what extent do supervisors give consistent directions?"

1	2	3	4	5	6	7
not at all			to some extent		to a great extent	

Step 8: Determine the Respondent Sample

The individuals you select to complete your survey should include all members of the target organization or work group with whom you are consulting. It is important to obtain information from all the individuals who are involved with, or impacted by, the presenting problem(s), including customers and stakeholders. They can offer useful perspectives on the issue(s) in question. Do what is necessary to ensure that all relevant levels of the organization are represented in the survey pool. This will be a larger population than the focus groups, but it may include some of the same individuals.

Step 9: Analyze the Results

The analysis of your survey results can be as simple or as complex as you choose. It is best to create a database of the survey results using a spreadsheet or survey software (see, for example, Jones & Bearley, 1989). Regardless of the analytical method you choose, the following are some general guidelines:

- Sort the surveys by respondent group (position, level in the organization, internal versus external customer, etc.).
- Review the data from all the respondents.
- Compare the data from each group to the whole surveyed population and to other groups.
- Determine what issues are shared across respondent groups and which are not.

Step 10: Complete the Diagnosis and Recommend an Intervention

The diagnosis of the issue(s) comes from the analysis you have performed. The issues you identify may be different from those originally described by the client. After all the information has been systematically collected from all the relevant parties and correctly analyzed, present your findings to the client and decide what to do next.

How you address this will depend on your initial client contact. Did the client draw conclusions about what the issues were and, if so, does your data concur? If not, do you have data that will convince your client otherwise? Does your data support the intervention requested by your client, or does the data suggest a different intervention? Did the data uncover new issues? If so, how do they fit with the client's priorities. You and the client must answer each of these questions before you design an intervention.

Step 11: Measure the Impact

After you have implemented or completed the intervention agreed on by you and the client, use the original survey to measure the impact of the intervention. It is also desirable to use the same respondent pool in order to conduct a reliable post-intervention evaluation. You can then compare the information with the pre-intervention data to determine the degree and direction of change as a result of the intervention.

Summary

Using clients' perceptions of the challenges they are facing is an effective way to enroll them in the change process. Generating real-time data about those perceptions allows you to move the client through the change process to achieve higher levels of effectiveness. By collecting real-time data and using the respondents' own words, you can reduce resistance to change and develop appropriate interventions.

References

Jones, J.E., & Bearley, W.L. (1989). *Organizational universe survey system*. Valley Center, CA: Organizational Universe Systems.

Lewin, K. (1936). *Principles of topological psychology* (F. Heider & G.M. Heider, trans.). New York: McGraw-Hill.

Pike, R.W. (1990). *Creative training techniques handbook*. Minneapolis, MN: Lakewood.

Robert Merritt, Ph.D., is the director of Organization Effectiveness Resources. He has ten years' experience as a human resources consultant with a specialization in planned change projects, tailored learning opportunities, and process improvement efforts. He has worked with clients in a range of areas, including utilities, financial services, health care, specialty chemicals, corrections, and community service agencies. He has published articles in a number of books including 101 Great Games for Trainers *(Jossey-Bass/Pfeiffer),* The Team and Organization Development Sourcebook *(McGraw-Hill), and* The HR Handbook *(HRD Press).*

Richard Whelan is the founder and director of Associated Consultants for Training & Education. He designs, develops, and delivers educational training programs to be used in conventional classroom settings, as well as computer-based and distance learning formats, pertaining to human resource and mental health issues for organizations in both the public and private sectors. He has had training and educational designs published in a number of books.

CONTRIBUTORS

Kristin Arnold
Quality Process Consultants, Inc.
18 Jayne Lee Drive
Hampton, VA 23664-1545
  (757) 850-4879
  fax: (757) 851-4879
  e-mail: QPCINC@aol.com

Jeanne Baer
Creative Training Solutions
1649 South 21st Street
Lincoln, NE 68502-2809
  (800) 410-3178
  e-mail: jbaer@binary.net
  URL: www.ncf.carleton.ca/~bk751

Andy Beaulieu
President
Results for a Change
10713 Lady Slipper Terrace
North Bethesda, MD 20852
  (301) 231-0077
  e-mail: andy-beaulieu@erols.com

Patricia E. Boverie, Ph.D.
Associate Professor
Training and Learning Technologies
University of New Mexico
Albuquerque, NM 87131
  (505) 277-2408
  e-mail: pboverie@unm.edu

Marlene Caroselli, Ed.D.
Center for Professional Development
324 Latona Road, Suite 6B
Rochester, NY 14626-2714
  (716) 227-6512
  fax: (716) 227-6191
  e-mail: mccpd@aol.com

Michael Danahy
Quality Innovations, Inc.
440 Jupiter Lane
Juno Beach, Florida 33408
  (561) 624-8681
  fax: (561) 624-7276
  e-mail: quality@pb.quik.com

Robert A. Herring III, Ph.D.
Assistant Director
Division of Business and Economics
Winston-Salem State University
Winston-Salem, NC 27110
  (336) 750-2345
  fax: (336) 750-2335
  e-mail: HERRINGR@WSSU1.ADP.
WSSU.EDU

Darcy Hitchcock
AXIS Performance Advisors, Inc.
15910 NE 270th Street
Battle Ground, WA 98604
  (360) 687-3075
  e-mail: axisdh@e-z.net
  URL: www.e-z.net/~axisdh

Lynette A. Hurta
26975 East River Road
Grosse Ile, MI 48138
e-mail: imaqt@concentric.net

Homer H. Johnson, Ph.D.
Professor, Center for Organization
    Development
Loyola University Chicago
820 North Michigan Avenue
Chicago, IL 60611
(773) 508-3027
fax: (733) 508-8713

H.B. Karp, Ph.D.
Personal Growth Systems
4932 Barn Swallow Drive
Chesapeake, VA 23321
(757) 488-3536

R. Bruce McAfee, Ph.D.
Department of Management
Old Dominion University
Norfolk, VA 23529
(757) 683-3539
fax: (757) 683-5639
e-mail: RMcafee@odu.edu

Valerie Revelle Medina
Staffing Manager
Keane, Inc.
901 Warrenville Road, Suite 220
Lisle, IL 60532
(630) 852-5577

Robert Merritt, Ph.D.
Director
Organization Effectiveness Resources
28 St. George Terrace
Bear, DE 19701
(302) 324-0347

Nancy Vogel Mueller, M.B.A.
Opportunities for Transition
3668 Rivercrest Road
McFarland, WI 53558
(608) 838-3575

Valerie C. Nellen, M.S.
Program Coordinator, Workplace
    Initiatives
Department of Psychology
Virginia Commonwealth University
VCU Box 842018
Richmond, VA 23284-2018
(804) 225-3866
e-mail: psy4vcn@atlas.vcu.edu

Sophie Oberstein
President
Targeted Training Solutions
1555 Beechnut Circle
Maple Glen, PA 19002
(215) 619-7929
fax: (215) 619-7935
e-mail: Soberstein@aol.com

Pamela J. Schmidt
Vice President of Membership and
    Program Development
American Society for Training &
    Development
1640 King Street
Alexandria, VA 22313
(703) 683-8139
fax: (703) 683-7259
e-mail: pschmidt@astd.org

Gary Schuman, Ph.D.
CDL Consulting
400 East Pratt Street, Suite 829
Baltimore, MD 212002
(410) 576-8751
fax: (410) 544-3060

Captain Garland F. Skinner
USN(Ret) MSEE
Management and Leadership Trainer,
  Consultant and Speaker
1336 Carolyn Drive
Virginia Beach, VA 23451
  (757) 422-1813
  e-mail: garskinner@aol.com

Sander J. Smiles, M.S.O.D.
Fel-Pro, Inc.
7450 North McCormick Boulevard
Skokie, IL 60067-8105
  (847) 948-4123

Eugene Taurman
InterLinx Consulting
2316 West Lagoon Court
Mequon, WI 53092
  (414) 242-3345
  fax: (414) 242-0137
  e-mail: ilx@execpc.com
  URL: www.execpc.com~ilx

Lorraine L. Ukens, M.S.
Team–ing with Success
4302 Starview Court
Glen Arm, MD 21057-9745
  (410) 592-6050
  fax: (410) 592-8263
  e-mail: teaming@erols.com

Arthur B. VanGundy, Ph.D.
428 Laws Drive
Norman, OK 73072-3851
  (405) 447-1946
  fax: (405) 447-1960
  e-mail: avangundy@aol.com

Richard Whelan, M.A.
Associated Consultants for Training
  & Education
P.O. Box 5312
Deptford, NJ 08096
  (609) 227-4273
  fax: (609) 228-9036

Susan B. Wilkes, Ph.D.
Manager, Workplace Initiatives
Department of Psychology
Virginia Commonwealth University
VCU Box 842018
Richmond, VA 23284-2018
  (804) 828-1191
  e-mail: swilkes@saturn.vcu.edu

Marsha Willard, Ph.D.
AXIS Performance Advisors, Inc.
2515 NE 17th Avenue
Portland, OR 97212
  (503) 284-9132
  e-mail: axismw@e-z.net
  URL: www.e-z.net/~axisdh

Mary Jane Willis
2739 Kathryn SE
Albuquerque, NM 87106
  (505) 266-2374
  fax: (505) 255-0824
  e-mail: Willis2@aol.com

Joe Willmore
President
Willmore Consulting Group
5007 Mignonette Court
Annadale, VA 22003
  (703) 855-4634
  fax: (703) 323-5781
  e-mail: Willmore@juno.com

Janet Winchester-Silbaugh
51 Pinon Heights Road
Sandia Park, NM 87047
 (505) 286-2210
 fax: (505) 286-2211
 e-mail: silbaugh@ccvp.com

Joan H. Wrenn
Director of Staffing and Employee
 Development
Keane, Inc.
901 Warrenville Road, Suite 220
Lisle, IL 60532
 (630) 852-5577

Jossey-Bass/Pfeiffer Annual Questionnaire

Place an X in the appropriate column, using the following scale to rate each item:

1=Very Little   2=Minimally   3=Somewhat   4=Moderately   5=Completely

Content	1	2	3	4	5

To what extent:

Do you view the content as cutting edge? — — — — —

Is the list of content areas complete and all-inclusive? — — — — —

Is the level of activities appropriate for your needs? — — — — —

Your Comments:
(other topics you'd like to see, etc.)

_____

_____

_____

Format	1	2	3	4	5

To what extent:

Does the format allow you to locate general topics easily? — — — — —

Does the format allow you to locate a specific activity or article quickly? — — — — —

Is the writing tone and style appropriate for today's audience? — — — — —

Are you interested in having the *Reference Guide* to the *Annuals* online or on CD-ROM? — — — — —

Are you interested in having the *Annual* activities, questionnaires, and resources on-line or on CD-ROM? — — — — —

Your Comments:

_____

_____

_____

Why do you purchase the *Annual?*

_____

_____

_____

What topics would you like to have added? Who would you like to see as contributors to the *Annual?*

_____

_____

_____

What other suggestions do you have to improve the *Annual?*

_____

_____

_____

About You

How many years have you used the *Annual?* _____

What is your occupation/title? _____

Return to: The Annual
Jossey-Bass/Pfeiffer
350 Sansome Street
San Francisco, CA 94104-1342
Fax (415) 433-1711

CONTENTS OF THE COMPANION VOLUME, THE 1999 ANNUAL: VOLUME 1, TRAINING

---

*See Experiential Learning Activities Categories, p. 7, for an explanation of the numbering system.
**Topic is "cutting edge."